COGNITION
AND
AFFECT

Psychology Series

James E. Alcock, Ph.D., Series Editor

COGNITION

AND

AFFECT

A DEVELOPMENTAL PSYCHOLOGY OF THE INDIVIDUAL

LAURENCE R. SIMON Ph.D.

PROMETHEUS BOOKS

Buffalo, New York

This book is dedicated to
my wife Rochelle
and my children Warren, Melanie, and Robin.

Published 1986 by Prometheus Books
700 East Amherst Street, Buffalo, New York 14215

Library of Congress Cataloging-in-Publication Data

Simon, Laurence R., 1940-
    Cognition and affect.

    (Psychology series)
    Bibliography: p. and index.
    1. Developmental psychology—Philosophy. 2. Cognition.
3. Affect (Psychology) I. Title. II. Series: Psychology
series (Buffalo, N.Y.) [DNLM: 1. Affect. 2. Cognition.
3. Personality Development. BF311 S595c]
BF713.S55 1986   155   86-18659
ISBN 0-87975-340-4

Acknowledgments

There are many individuals at Flushing Hospital Mental Health Clinic and Kingsborough Community College who helped bring to life the theory presented in this book. Leon Goldstein, president of Kingsborough Community College, and his administration helped create an atmosphere that fosters insight and clarity of thought. John Scheffer, Dorlt Whiteman, Milton Kornrich, and Karen Marisak were among a number of clinical colleagues who listened to my obsessions and offered valuable insights in return.

I wish especially to thank my friend, colleague, and the chairperson of the Department of Behavioral Science, Philip Stander, whose support, encouragement, feedback, and critical evaluation I will always appreciate.

My handwriting is an atrocity, but against such formidable odds Ethel Rosenberg and Debbie Wesley performed the bulk of the typing—thank you both.

Finally, I wish to thank Steven L. Mitchell, my editor at Prometheus Books, for supporting publication of the work, for offering important criticisms, and for untangling the grammatical knots found on every page of the work.

Contents

1

The Science and Religion of Psychology

The human race appears to be in trouble. We have been in difficulty since climbing down from the trees, but our woes seem to grow steadily worse. In addition to the perennial problems involved with getting along, living with loved ones, satisfying individual needs, and finding some happiness and contentment in life, we have wars, crime, and a host of other catastrophes that we create for ourselves. Since the beginning of the century, we have added several new problems to the list: environmental pollution, overpopulation, and the threat of nuclear holocaust. We feel a personal uneasiness, a sense of being out of control, and we have little or no confidence that our leaders are handling the situation in a responsible manner. (Or worse, we feel they may be culpable for many of the problems that exist.)

Why are these "created miseries" growing in magnitude? Are we helpless to solve our own problems? Is there a way to stop the erosion of faith in ourselves and of hope in the future that ultimately threatens to become our most serious problem? I believe we can find positive solutions for our difficulties; the evidence lies all about us. For while we can kill and destroy, we can also love and create: families come into existence, thrive, and their members nurture one another; musicians play the glorious creations of composers; and writers and artists continue to develop new works. Yes, we are in a quagmire, but there may still be time to reverse this dangerous course.

We seek solutions that seem to elude us; but perhaps the answers lie in the methods used to solve the problems. I believe one focus of our attention must be the psychology that differentiates creators and destroyers, artists and thieves, lovers and haters. Why is it that, in seeking to solve our common problems, some of us develop a capacity to think meaningfully about others and to recognize that happiness lies in creativity, love, and cooperation? Why do others, in trying to solve life's problems, remain focused only on their own needs, seek to dominate others, and collect the useless? Why do some seek ways of living that rest upon ethical principles, while others behave parasitically and destructively?

All human beings seek to *explain, predict,* and *control* not only their own lives but also the environment and the universe around them. These same goals are those of science. Science is a human activity and is motivated by the same need as all human activity. It differs from other intellectual activities, not in its goals, but in the manner in which it seeks to explain, predict, and control. A scientist is an individual who has learned to develop a cognitive, affective orientation that is geared maximally to learn about and solve problems of life.

Scientists, and those capable of behaving scientifically, represent a small proportion of the general population. They are, however, not only capable of being very unscientific in many areas of their own lives, but they can also behave in unscientific ways in areas that once reflected a scientific attitude. True scientific inquiry is a potent but rare means for solving problems. It is my belief that if the general population could be helped to think scientifically, the problems that now threaten to overwhelm them would become manageable and malleable. In the following paragraphs, I define the qualities of scientific thinking and some of the reasons such thought is so rare. Finally, I describe some consequences of psychology's failure to think scientifically.

Thinking is one of our main tools of survival; the desire to learn is a motive that enhances our probability of surviving. Scientific thought is motivated by survival needs, but usually it is also motivated by a love of learning. To the scientific mind, the universe is filled with awe and wonder, and discovery is an act of joy. Here the scientist's love of learning and his respect for ideas has either developed or has existed from childhood. The latter distinction is important because it means that we must either find a way of developing a desire to learn in the general population or prevent its loss in the first place.

Scientific inquiry begins with an *empirical* attitude, which means that science learns through firsthand observations. The scientist's laboratory procedures, which so impress the nonscientist, are merely procedures that enhance observation. The discoveries of Kepler, Newton, Galileo, Darwin, Freud, Einstein, and Piaget did not take place in laboratories; each of these individuals merely reported what was there to be seen by any individual who cared to look. It is the ability to look at the world and see what is there that seems in large measure to differentiate the scientist from nonscientist.

Bertrand Russell (1948) points out that the scientist's mode of observation is objective. As far as possible, the observer sees what is there to be seen and not what he wishes to see. The struggle to see reality for what it is and not inject our own wish-fulfillment seems to be a most difficult task. Once an individual abandons the empirical attitude, the processes of science stop. As we will discover, authoritarian dogmatism easily replaces the scientific attitude.

Scientists are not content merely to observe; they also draw conclusions about their observations. These conclusions take the form of theories. "Theories," writes Sir Karl Popper (1961), "are nets to catch what we call 'the world'" (p. 59). Theories contain explanations of their facts and elements. A theory is made up of guesses and, however educated these guesses may be, they cannot be viewed as true. The scientist must adhere to objective procedures that allow a theory's "truth" or "falsity" to be tested. Science not only stops with wish-fulfillment, but also when conclusions are treated as if they were "true."

What are the procedures or rules for testing theories? I can do no better than quote Popper:

> From a new idea (theory), put up *tentatively and not yet justified in any way,* an anticipation, a hypothesis, a theoretical system or a conclusion are drawn by means of logical deduction. Conclusions are then compared with one another and with other relevant statements as to find what logical relations exist between them.
>
> We may if we like distinguish four different lines along which the testing of a theory could be carried out. First there is the logical comparison of the conclusions among themselves, by which the internal consistency of the system is tested. Secondly, there is the investigation of the logical form of the theory, with the objective of

determining whether it has the character of an empirical or scientific theory, or whether it is, for example, tautological. Thirdly, there is the comparison with other theories, chiefly with the aim of determining whether the theory would constitute a scientific advance should it survive our various tests. And finally, there is the testing of the theory by way of empirical applications of the conclusions which can be derived from it.

The purpose of this last test is to find out how far the new consequences of the theory—whatever may be new in what it asserts—stands up to the demands of practice, whether raised by purely scientific experiments, or by practical technological applications. With the help of other statements, previously accepted, certain singular statements—which we may call "predictions," are deduced from the theory, especially predictions that are easily testable or applicable. From among these statements, those are selected which are not derivable from the current theory, and more especially those which the current theory contradicts. Next we seek a decision as regards those (and other) derived statements by comparing them with the results of practical application and experiments. If this decision is positive, that is, if the singular conclusion turn out to be acceptable, or verified, then the theory has *for the time being* (italics mine) passed its test; *we have found no reason to discard it.* But if the decision is negative, or in other words, if the conclusions have been falsified, then this falsification also falsified the theory from which they were logically deduced.

It should be noticed *that a positive decision can only temporarily support the theory, for subsequent negative decisions may always overthrow it.* (pp. 32-33)

Theories, then, are comprised of universal statements that explain the relationships of the facts referred to. Science cannot negate or ignore facts merely because they do not fit in a theory. When facts do not fit a theory that theory must be changed to accommodate the facts, or discarded and a new one sought. In a very real sense, a good scientific theory is designed to lead to its own demise and replacement: a good theory is at best temporary because it leads to new observations, often in the specialized form of surveys and experiments (highly technical forms of observation). The process of observation, theory building, theory testing, and modification of the theory that leads to new observation, is endless. This process leads to an endless cycle of learning and intellectual growth.

Another important point about scientists and the manner in

which they learn is that they must live with doubt. Theories are temporarily verified and ultimately changed by the weight of other scientific discoveries. The scientist must resist investing his theories with pride, permanence, or with authoritarian dogmatism. The scientist must be able to say "I don't know" when confronted with facts and observations that are not encompassed by existing theoretical explanation. The admission of ignorance seems to be a necessary element in the capacity to learn, one which is not easy for human beings to accept.

Not knowing is painful, not only because our minds are organized to seek explanation, but because of the nature of the questions we ask. Why do I live? What happens when I die? Why do I die? What is the meaning and purpose in living? Why do bad things happen to good people? If we think scientifically about these questions, we realize that each must be answered with "I don't know" and "I may never find out."

Science is often in conflict with religion, for it is religion that provides us with the answers to the above questions. Religion, I believe, springs from exactly the same set of needs as science: to explain, to predict, and to control. Science separated from religion not because its roots differ but because of the manner in which scientific explanations are formed and utilized. Erich Fromm (1950) points out that many religions begin humanistically and inspire awe and wonder about the universe around us, but eventually they give way to authoritarian dogmatism. It is not religion that concerns us, but the authoritarian dogmatic mode of thinking. Dogmatic religions are all around us and their practitioners can even call themselves "scientists." When a scientist stops behaving according to the scientific method, he often becomes a practitioner of dogmatic faith.

Those who practice dogmatic thought create a theory that explains and predicts but then forgets that it is a theory. In their need to explain, these individuals take the truth of their explanation on faith. Doubt is banished and replaced by certainty. Popper (1961) calls such truth "a priorism" and Russell (1948) refers to it as "dogmatism." Such universal statements are not tested against reality by further observation, but are repeatedly verified.* Falsi-

---

* The universal statements comprising a scientific theory are so stated as to be testable. One manner of testing (see above) is for a hypothesis to be drawn from the

fication becomes impossible. Often such truths are presented as moralistic dicta with punishment meted out to nonbelievers and rewards are promised to believers.

Human history reveals an incredible list of wars and horrors created by competing dogmatic authoritarian believers. Arthur Koestler (1978) points out that the ease and proclivity with which human beings embrace dogmatism and then express hatred for nonbelievers may be the flaw that is humanity's ultimate undoing. It may well be that the next world war will be fought at the insistence of the "faithful" and the "true believer." Certainly once the human mind "knows" the "truth," the search for new knowledge and better explanations is stunted. Has any nation gone to war without God being on its side and revealing to it the "true" path?

It is my belief that the ease with which human beings create dogmatic wish-fulfillments to "solve" their problems is one of the

---

theory that predicts the behavior of previously unobserved or unknown phenomena. The hypothesis (educated guess) is stated in such a way as to allow for its own rejection and the acceptance of an alternative hypothesis if the prediction made does not come true. When a prediction does not come true, not only is the hypothesis falsified but the theory and the universal statements that comprise it are also in danger of falsification.

When a scientist states a hypothesis and makes observations that will verify or falsify it, he must describe the exact conditions of his observations. He knows that other scientists may seek to test his theory by replicating his observations. Moreover he knows that the scientific community will not accept verification unless the manner of his observations is open to scrutiny and his observations have been verified by a second, *independently made* set of data. We can see that even if a scientist does not wish to open his theory to the possibilities of falsification, the entire set of rules governing scientific evidence force him to do so. The procedures of science are designed to demand falsification and thus provide a vigorous test of a theory's usefulness.

In a religion or other endeavor that relies on faith and dogma, the rules of verification and falsification are quite different. The universal statements that comprise the dogma are derived from authorities whose wisdom cannot be challenged. The statements are not called theories or guesses, but are stated as absolute truth. Predictions are made about phenomena but are not stated as falsifiable hypotheses. When a prediction does not come true, neither the hypothesis nor the universal statements are in danger of falsification. Alternative hypotheses are never made that can explain failed predictions. Offending evidence that refutes the dogma is ignored or reinterpreted to support the dogma. Only those predictions that verify the dogma are accepted as further proof of the statement that gave rise to them. The dogma is thus verified over and over again, providing an ever growing bulwark against falsification.

foremost impediments to achieving real solutions. Scientific activity is easily replaced with dogmatism. If psychological theory could deal with the causes of dogmatism and in so doing shed light on why scientific thinking so easily fails to develop, then these theories could aid in the growth of the kind of thought that produces solutions. But psychology has added little to this important search. As a field it seems often to fall prey to the very dogmatism that should be its central focus. Why does this failure take place? The reasons, I believe, fall into two categories, those that are general and ubiquitous and those that are peculiar to psychology.

I have already pointed out that scientists, as human beings, can and do leave the scientific mode of thought for the safety and security of authoritarian dogmatic faith. When this happens, their theories are treated as unquestioned truth, empirical test ceases, and those who believe the theory insulate themselves from other scientists and believers of other theories. Hostility and suspicion of the "outsider" replaces curiosity and excitement for new ideas and observations. This stultification happens in all fields, but it seems to be the mark of much psychological endeavor.

Jan Erenwald (1966) describes the conservative atmosphere of the psychoanalytic theorists, but he could be describing many other groups as well: "Freud's impatience with slight deviations from the teaching is a matter of historic record. In some of his followers this impatience seems to have increased in inverse proportion with their stature as scientists. The same tendency can be discovered in protagonists of virtually all other schools. The result, up to recent years, has been a dearth of interdisciplinary discussion, or even communication. With the same clinical restraint with which they avoid attacking head on the delusions of their paranoid patients, they avoid disputing each other's basic suppositions. Occasional bricks dropped or dissenting voices raised at closed scientific meetings are apt to perplex speakers and throw audiences into an uproar" (p. 6).

I would like to turn now to some of the reasons given for why people in general, and psychological science in particular, seem to slip so easily into authoritarian dogmatism. The present discussion is limited because chapter 4 will deal extensively with the role of defense in the fixation of thinking and the establishment of dogmatism.

We become dogmatic when we cannot find answers or solutions to questions or problems that demand them. It is impossible to remain emotionally neutral about death, birth, or the meaning of life. We are in "pain" when we lose pride or esteem and have to rebuild our sense of self. Life creates anxiety, insecurity, shame and a host of negative emotional states that need reducing and reversing. Science has not and probably never will, provide answers to the questions we ask concerning issues that create pain in our lives. Science therefore fails to allow a level of explanation, prediction, or control that will permit human beings to feel safe, happy, and contented.

The best we can do in the face of the scientific limitation is to remain open-minded and in doubt about any ultimate questions and answers. Doubt is painful, as are unmet needs, and the tendency to answer questions with wish-fulfillment is ever present. We have a compelling need to hold on to our wish-fulfilling created truths with the firmness and certainty of dogmatic faith. In this psychological climate, the scientific attitude is fragile and easily swept away in the face of our human need to find explanations for our problems, both real and imagined.

We also become "true believers" because of our indoctrination into dogmatic systems of thought. As young children we see our parents as omnipotent and omnicient, and we accept their view of life as our own. Many of us are exposed to formal religious training. I agree with Fromm (1950) that the religion into which we are indoctrinated is likely to be authoritarian and broach few arguments as to its truth. By the time we can question ourselves, we already hold certain assumptions as "truth." An individual's whole personality can be shaken if his fundamental beliefs about life and the universe are seriously challenged by competing beliefs or even (as unlikely as it may be) by objective reality.

It has been said that necessity is the mother of invention. We may say, too, that necessity is the mother of attitude and belief. Jerome Kagan (1984) points out that we justify the necessities of our existence by turning them into moralities. Karen Horney (1950) offers a clear description of how we take our weaknesses and our responses to threat and become "proud" of such behavior and attitudes. We can take pride in and feel moral superiority being rich or poor, white or black, lonely or abused, a member of any country or region on earth, liberal or conservative, religious or atheistic. Most of us have been taught by our respective religions that we are the chosen and the beloved of God, that upon death only we will be rewarded with heaven. The assumptions and wish-fulfillments fundamental in our belief systems are endless. Once invested with moral pride they are fixed and immovable. Ideologies dripping with virtues fill our heads.

It is Fromm (1980) who describes how in each historical epoch and place there is a system of beliefs, however untested, that represents the "truth." Anyone challenging this truth is seen as "crazy" or "heretical." Progress in human thinking has been a battle in which those who espouse scientific thought seek to present their observations to the faithful and are often met with ridicule, scorn, or worse. From Gallileo and Darwin to Freud, excommunication and derision have met each set of new ideas. And so it continues.

Turning to psychology, we find the same struggles between those who advocate scientific open-mindedness and the advocates of dogmatic faith. But while psychology has many problems in common with other disciplines, there are other difficulties peculiar to the discipline. For example, at the core of all personality theories there are various untested assumptions concerning human nature (DeCaprio, 1974). We often pay attention to postulates that are based on empirical facts and clinical observations while tacitly accepting their underlying assumptions. The personal (both normal and pathological), cultural, religious, and antireligious biases of theorists usually determine the content of these assumptions, which are usually reflective of familial and cultural value systems as well as a variety of philosophical issues.

The assumptions that underlie the postulates of personality theories deal with the basic good or evil nature of humanity, the degree to which an individual is at the mercy of nature or his environment, the nature and number of instincts or inborn qualities, and the nature of sex differences and their etiologies. All theories implicitly possess a notion of normative or optimum human behavior, reflecting the theorist's personal moral view of how people "should" behave.

Psychologists are human beings who are often affected by the underlying value systems that influence their thinking and to which they are committed. Jean Piaget (1971) demands that a scientific theory transcend the particular culture of the theorist who creates it. Unless the scientist can do this, he has a blind spot and a predisposition to allow his ideas to pass from the scientific to the religious. Just how much a scientist can transcend his own culture is open to question. Can the psychologist transcend deeply held religious and moral beliefs that have guided his personal life? Can the scientist transcend the particular language system that he uses to create his theory? A language is clearly a social tool that is the product of a particular culture and shaped by the values of the culture. It is learned in the context of the values of the familial matrix at a time when the child experiences its greatest emotional dependence on its parents. It is clear that we are capable of broadening our outlook and reducing biases, but I doubt if they can ever be fully overcome.

The biases contained in psychological theory often arise from the religious and cultural training of the scientists themselves. These basic assumptions offer fully developed explanations for human behavior, and when they are deeply embedded in human consciousness, along with a prohibition against tampering, they become formidable structures that direct and channel the theory-building capacity of the scientist. However, the biases in psychology are often antireligious dogmatism as well.

When psychology developed scientific aspirations the conflict with itself as science and as religion sharpened. Some religious assumptions became basic to scientific theory without anyone ever questioning the process. However, many psychologists rebelled and the conflict increased its tempo. The concepts of Darwin and Freud still lay heavily in the digestive tracts of many churches. By the 1920s, with the behavorist revolution, psychology began to assert itself more boldly and psychologists reacted strongly to the structure presented by authoritarian religions. Many scientists, including analysts and behaviorists, rebelled and rejected any concepts related to religion (Boring, 1957).

We then come to an interesting paradox that deeply reflects itself in many theories of personality: the religion of many psychologists is antireligious! The personal antireligious, dogmatic beliefs of the psychologists operate like any other religion, and often demand that the wish-fulfillments that comprise it not be tampered with. Thus, *many psychologists approach humanity with a set of assumptions that demand that theories and methods of observation not deal with any area addressed by formal religion.*

It is one of the ultimate ironies of psychology that, when examining some of the underlying authoritarian, "ameaningful" (Koch, 1981) assumptions of modern theory, we see that the violations of human beings exist precisely because scientists have confused the content of contemporary religion with the methodologies of traditional authoritarian religion. These theories refuse to deal with any *issue* or *problem* that seems to lie within the province of religion. We rarely see in the index of any introductory psychology text "values," "meaning," "dignity," "freewill," or the human need for spirituality. Scientists and modern psychology have thrown the baby out with the bathwater and have impoverished their fields enormously. Apparently, the nature of these biases renders them invisible to most scientists and psychologists.

Where do we begin to overcome our blind spots? We can start with Isidor Chein's (1970) suggestion that psychology has violated its subject matter as revealed in the field's "image of man."

> What is disturbing, however, is that scientific psychology has produced so little that is relevant to the humanities. One cannot help feeling that a science, that "inter alia" is concerned with human behavior ought to reproduce much that is at least relevant. (p. 4)

The image of humanity expressed by the analyst is that of beings pushed by drives, irrational and sly. The behaviorist often paints a picture of a robot pulled mindlessly by environmental stimuli. Both theories see humanity as unable to choose or create in any manner central to its existence.

What can be psychology's response to Chein? First, we can deal with issues that are central to human functioning: cognition, emotion, values, dignity, meaning, love and hate, morality, scientific and creative activities, and the manner in which we replace science with authoritarian dogmatism. We must study why we fail to become scientists in the fullest sense of the word. Second, we can reduce the dogmatism that now exists by overcoming the moral pride that forces psychologists to take arrogant postures of refusing to deal with theories that are opposed to their own ideas. By examining existing theories we can see not only their limitations but also their strengths and the areas in which they agree.

Freud wisely demanded that psychoanalysts expose their thought processes to other analysts as part of their training. [The personal analysis of the trainee was designed to alert him or her in their personal wish fulfillments and fantasies that would prevent the analyst from scientifically and meaningfully understanding the patient.] Freud, however, never dealt with the manner in which culture acts as a transcendent force. (According to Fromm [1980], the most serious problems confronting psychoanalysis exist in part because Freud confused "bourgeois middle class" problems with universal ones.) The question as to who would correct the shared cultural wish-fulfillments of both analyst and analysand was never solved. Who, in the ultimate analysis, is to awaken us to these distortions in our thinking?

I do not believe that any of us are free from defensive wish-fulfilling distortions. As Freud is reported to have said to Stefan Zweig (1964), "Absolute truth is as impossible to obtain as absolute zero temperatures." We all, at one time or another, invest our ideas with pride and become authoritarian and dogmatic rather than scientific. How do we then proceed to create a theory that does justice to the human image; one that simultaneously explains, predicts, and controls human behavior and the problems described earlier, including the central problem of dogmatism itself?

Let me begin by not overstating my own case as I have accused other theorists of doing. I believe that each of the major psychological theories in evidence today has added insights to our understanding of the human person. In the chapters that follow I will discuss the ideas of psychoanalysis, behaviorism, and the humanistic-existential theories of personality. I will then present the basic concepts of Jean Piaget and Carroll Izard, whose work can help us form the synthesis that I believe is presently missing.

Finally, I will sketch a theory of personality that will utilize elements from all of the existing theories. The present theory seeks both to augment and to integrate the important contributions of a large number of existing theories. It is in no way an effort to supplant the great works now dominating the field of psychology. I will try to create a synthesis that dogmatism and pride have heretofore prevented, and I will simultaneously attempt to explain the very dogmatism and rigidity that is at the heart of so much human misery. By explaining how dogmatism creates problems, we will see how such thought hides its own nature and prevents us from seeing the causes of the very problems nonscientific thinking creates.

One final point: In the subsequent pages, I will suggest that scientific thinking represents and promotes maturity, what we call mental health. Dogmatism will be equated with immaturity and mental illness. The underlying psychological processes of the scientist and the average citizen, between the religious fanatic and the inmate in the mental hospital, between world leaders and beggars, are all similar and on a continuum with one another. The only difference between them is the number of people who share the same immature forms of thinking. Similarly, anyone who thinks scientifically becomes capable of solving problems with the clarity and effectiveness of the scientist.

2

Psychoanalysis

GENERAL CONSIDERATIONS

The word *psychoanalysis* refers both to a body of psychological theory and to a mode of psychotherapy. The original psychoanalytic theory is credited to Sigmund Freud whose ideas are a mandatory starting point for anyone interested in the study of human personality. Freudian theory is in reality a collection of overlapping ideas, no one of which was capable of explaining all the behavioral phenomena that interested Freud. He cast his theoretical net far and wide in an effort to explain individual behavior, culture, and their relationship to one another (1966, 1957, 1938, 1962, 1952).

Freud's theory has huge explanatory value, although it is not easy to apply experimental tests to his ideas. His work has attracted devoted followers who, like disciples of a holy man, fight to keep his essential ideas intact and operative. Psychoanalysis also has enemies who villify the theory and constantly seek to disparage its developer. A good deal of dogmatism and authoritarian "religion" has surrounded psychoanalysis since its inception, and one of the difficulties when dealing with psychoanalytic theory has been the "religious" fervor surrounding it.

Freud was one of human history's great geniuses: his writings changed the intellectual face of Western civilization. People see themselves differently because of psychoanalysis even if they do not study it directly. Art, literature, and the study of all subjects

21

reflect an awareness of basic psychoanalytic concepts: Freudian theory revolutionized child rearing; Freud's name became a household word, especially with respect to "Freudian slips" and dream analysis. Each year millions of people are treated by psychotherapists and counsellors, all of whom in one way or another have ideas that owe a debt to Freud.

Although brilliant, Freud was also a human being who suffered from equally human flaws. For all his genius, Freud's theories and observations were not without problems. He was as guilty of false moral pride as any other person who desired immortal greatness. His was a career limited by an inability to transcend childhood prejudices and cultural bias. Thus, Freud neither deserves to be deified nor vilified: it must be recognized that his theories are not only illuminated by profound insight but also obscured by limitations, errors, and biases. With this in mind, let us examine some of Freud's key concepts.

THE STRUCTURAL MODEL OF THE MIND

The most famous of Freud's models of the mind is his structural theory. All students who study basic psychology learn of the *id*, the *ego*, and the *superego*, which are shorthand concepts that refer to a series of interactive psychological processes. As these concepts are discussed it is important that they not to be reified as "things" or active entities. For example, one may say "the *id* wants" or "the *ego* feels," but one should also not expect to find portions of the brain allotted to them. Let me then examine the *id*, the *ego*, and the *superego* and suggest the manner of their interaction.

Id

The basic human motivational system is represented by the term *id*. The *id* is comprised of a basic inborn set of "drives," "wishes," "instincts," or "needs." These concepts are interchangeable within psychoanalytic theory. Of particular note is the sex drive, fully operational at birth, as are the other instincts. The sex drive is referred to as the *libido*. Human beings also have an aggressive drive, according to Freud. Sex and aggression are particularly important to the developing personality because their expression conflicts so noticeably with the needs and demands of parents and of society at large.

The *id* functions according to the "pleasure principle," as its instincts seek immediate gratification without regard to consequences: the *id* "wants what it wants when it wants it." Delayed gratification means pain and discomfort, which are to be avoided. Human needs are so constructed that their satisfaction is pleasurable; any delay causes increased discomfort and eventually pain. Basic physiological drives, such as hunger and thirst will cause death if not satisfied in a reasonably short period of time.

While the mind is under the sway of the *id* all cognitive activities—thinking, imaging, remembering, and others—are organized around drives or wishes and geared toward their satisfaction; logic and order, as the healthy adult understands them, do not exist. Drive-organized forms of thinking are known as "primary process" thought. Freud believed that children, the mentally ill, and dreaming adults all think and perceive according to primary process mechanisms. Cognition organized according to the primary process is therefore illogical, overemotional, easily confused, and overtly concerned with need satisfaction and the here and now.

If life were simple and all human needs were instantly met through the efforts of a nurturing environment, then the *id* would remain the basic mental component. Freud believed that a parent who immediately gratified a child's needs and predicted its every whim would produce a person eternally doomed to be an infant. Complete gratification was not only impossible but undesirable according to the psychoanalyst. Life is never and can never be made simple; people are continually confronted with social demands and environmental dangers. Deprivation is, in varying degrees, the individual's lot, and he must learn to deal with it. Unlimited physical dangers emerge as one tries to satisfy one's needs. There are diseases, plagues, famines, and all manner of ways in which one can die. Each human being must therefore learn the skills necessary to survive in the face of so much danger.

Moreover, there are many fellow humans and other organisms competing for a limited number of need-satisfying objects, such as food, land, money, attractive people, power, and so forth. Not only do human beings have to learn to survive as individuals but they must also learn to cooperate and survive in groups. The *id,* whose goal is immediate pleasure and the avoidance of all forms of displeasure, is not up to the demands of individual and group survival. The goal of survival falls to the second construct of the structural model, the *ego*.

Ego

The goal of the *id* is pleasure, the goal of the *ego* is survival. How does the *ego* ensure survival? It is comprised of those skills that permit individuals to evaluate, predict, run, throw, catch, lift up, kick, and much more. Learning is a function of the *ego*. The more skills one possesses, the stronger the *ego* becomes; the fewer skills one possesses, or the more disabilities one acquires, the weaker the *ego*.

When people are born their *ego*-skills exist in rudimentary fashion. The *ego* grows in part because of pressures and demands within the environment, but its conflict with the voracious demands of the *id* is another factor. As will be described, much of the *ego's* energy, its motivation so to speak, comes from the *id*. Freud saw personality development, in part, as a taming of the *id* and a transfer of its psychological energy to the *ego*. As the latter grows and strengthens, it simultaneously masters the expression of *id* needs and the demands of the environment.

As power transfers from *id* to *ego,* the pleasure principle gives way to the reality principle while primary process is superseded by secondary process logic. The reality principle describes the functioning of the *ego,* which must delay gratification of the *id* impulse until it can be safely undertaken. The *ego* must also control behavior by gauging the consequences of actions: danger is to be avoided as much as possible, while the safe routes to satisfaction are taken. The *ego* makes possible the self control so necessary to human survival.

Secondary process thought is marked by logic, reason, and good judgment. When one thinks in secondary process terms, problem-solving capabilities are engaged, e.g., choosing the safest and surest route to one's goals or evaluating and predicting the future to its most effective advantage. Much of the *ego's* strength and ability to follow the reality principle is due to a shift from drive-oriented to reality-oriented logical thinking. The mature adult *ego* is describable in secondary process items.

I often pose the following problem to students: A hungry individual has not had his basic needs met for some time. He is feeling deprived and his survival is threatened. He sees a well-dressed, attractive young lady walking in the street and he proceeds to follow her. He keeps well back and out of sight, following the woman into an apartment house. At the right moment he overtakes her, robs her of her money and jewelry, and then rapes her. In order not to be pointed out to the police, our perpetrator kills his victim. When asked what is in control of the man's behavior—*id* or *ego*—most students immediately choose the *id*.

The answer is the *ego*. All of the requirements of the reality principle have been met. The young man satisfies his needs but takes all precautions to insure his survival. Earlier, I suggested that *id*-dominance of personality makes survival and social life impossible. The *ego* makes survival possible but, according to Freud, people need a third force in their personalities to control the manner in which the *ego* acts to satisfy the *id*—the *superego*.

Superego

The above example begins to illuminate the need for the *superego*. If the students are asked why the *superego* is necessary, the answers usually involve the importance of being good, the wrongness in depriving another of their life, and the need of the victim to stay alive. However, from the Freudian perspective, none of these represents the reason for the *superego's* emergence.

The Freudian sees the *superego* as a necessary addition to the survival of the individual. The dead woman has a family that will seek retribution for her death; not killing her may therefore aid in the man's survival. On a deeper level, however, what is morally prohibited or admired are those behaviors that diminish or add to the survival of the group that enhances the survival of the individual. The growing child's loyalty and support of his family is a necessary ingredient in their continued efforts to support and nurture him. If any group that supports the survival of its members fails to maintain the necessary qualities for its integrity, then each member's survival is threatened.

The *superego* emerges as the result of a father's castration threats to his son. The youngster adopts his father's values only to avoid mutilation and death. Goodness is a necessary expedient that is housed in fear. Much to the chagrin of the many modern advocates of permissiveness who speak in Freud's name, he believed that fear was a necessary ingredient in moral development. Just as the pleasure needs of the *id* conflict with the survival needs of the *ego,* the self-interest of the individual generally conflicts with the needs of the group. The desires and wishes of each individual remain in conflict with his need to be moral, upright, and perfect.

Summary and Integration

The following outlines and summarizes the structure and goals of the *id,* the *ego,* and the *superego*

	Goals	Comprised of:	Functions According to:
Id	Pleasure and avoidance of displeasure	Physiological drives Libido sex drive Aggressive urges All other wishes, wants, desires, and instincts	Pleasure principle: immediate gratification of desire, no awareness of— or care for—consequences Primary process thinking
Ego	Survival	Intelligence, thought, mobility, logic, judgment, perception, memory, attention all skills	Reality principle: delay of gratification, assessment of consequences Self control Secondary process thinking
Super-ego	Perfection	Moral prohibitions Ego ideal	None stated

Dynamics of the *Id,* the *Ego,* the *Superego*

According to Freud's psychoanalytic view, human beings are always in conflict and never really at rest or in equilibrium. In the healthy adult the *ego* remains in control but is always threatened by the pressures put upon it by the *id,* the *superego* and the environment. When people are ill, tired, drunk, or exhausted, their *ego*-strengths weaken and their *id*-impulses can overwhelm them. If they are so overwhelmed, they may do and say infantile things and behave according to the pleasure principle. The morning after a party in which an individual's *ego* has been put to sleep with alcohol, his *superego* may have much to punish him for. He may have done and said much to alienate and hurt others, while embarrassing himself.

As an individual moves through life, he passes through periods in which the *ego* is not taxed, while at other times the *ego* can be overwhelmed by life's adversities: war, unemployment, family crisis, civil unrest, final exams, moving to a new location, job changes. No one can deal with all of life's difficulties. It is true, however, that the same situation might be an interesting challenge for an individual with great *ego* strength, but overwhelming for one who lacks such strength.

The *superego* is always clamoring for the *ego* to be perfect. Some individuals try to achieve impossible goals or experience guilt when they fail to deal with impossible adversity. There are those who are religious fanatics and others who are guilt ridden if they relax or enjoy any pleasure at all. Just as the *id* can overwhelm the *ego,* so, too, can the *superego.* Often individuals will deny that they have any *id* impulses or desires for pleasure in their attempt to meet the impossible demands of their *superego.*

Throughout life the relative balance of the *id,* the *ego,* and the *superego* constantly changes, as do the environmental demands being made on the *ego.* If the *id* can be reasonably satisfied, if the environment is a reasonable source of nurture, if the demands of the *superego* are reasonable, and if the individual's *ego* continues to gain strength, then a picture of mental health emerges, according to the Freudian view. In such a situation the *ego* copes with the environment while taking from it that which will satisfy the *id* in addition to meeting the demands of society and the standards set by family, friends, and culture. But what happens if the *ego* is unable to cope with the environment due to weakness and instability? What if the *ego* is threatened with *id* impulses that it cannot handle? The *ego* will utilize defenses rather than cope directly with the problem.

THE TOPOGRAPHIC MODEL OF THE MIND

Before human defense mechanisms can be fully understood, it is useful to introduce a second model of the mind. The first model we looked at was *structural*. We now turn to a model that stresses levels of *consciousness*. Freud described human consciousness as involving three levels:

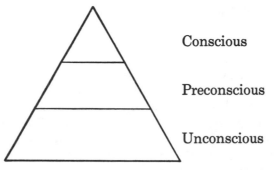

Conscious

Preconscious

Unconscious

At the top of the triangle we find focal awareness of some aspect of self or the environment. Consciousness is that of which we are aware: it is knowledge or perception that "we know that we know." Consciousness can often be verbalized. The *ego* controls consciousness through the attention mechanism; that to which our mind attends is in conscious experience. At any given moment there is very little in immediate focal awareness, compared to what there is to know or to be perceived. The reader is aware of the words she is reading, although she is capable of being made aware of thousands of other words not now in her consciousness.

Just outside or "below" conscious awareness is the information that can easily come into consciousness provided the *ego* attends to it. Such information is in the *preconscious*. If one is asked how much 2 + 2 is, or to imagine a living room or a library, to recall a birthday or to focus perception on one's feet in a pair of shoes, then one is being asked to select information from the preconscious. All that is known but not in the conscious mind at the moment and yet can easily be focused upon is in the preconscious. Similarly, any stimulus that could be perceived and given conscious representation if it were to be attended to is said to be in the preconscious.

One of Freud's most enduring discoveries involves the unconscious portion of the mind. Knowledge, desires, and memories are sometimes considered dangerous to the *ego,* which cannot rid itself of them. After all, what has happened has happened. If something terrible has been done in the past, if one's life has been threatened, or if a forbidden wish results in terrible consequences, there is little the *ego* can do but attempt to keep this awful information from coming to the conscious mind. Many childhood fears and desires are kept from consciousness by a barrier that the *ego* constructs and maintains. This barrier is known as the *ego mechanisms of defense,* about which more will follow in a moment. As long as the defense remains intact, the information kept behind the barrier cannot come into conscious experience.

Analysts often use the following metaphor to describe the levels of consciousness. One decends into a dark basement with a narrow-beamed flashlight. Wherever the beam shines is in consciousness. There are objects all over the basement placed easily within the focus of the beam. These represent preconsciousness. However, there are objects behind objects, objects buried or otherwise hidden. The beam of light cannot reach them. They are buried in the un-conscious.

That which is in the unconscious does not reluctantly remain hidden. Buried wishes and desires constantly press toward consciousness. When people are tired or the *ego* is otherwise weakened, unconscious material may gain conscious expression through behavior. People reveal unconscious fears and wishes through slips of the tongue, humorous remarks, or by losing things, all of which are referred to as "the psychopathology of everyday life" (Freud, 1966). Most significantly Freud believed that dreams, if analyzed, reveal the hidden messages of the unconscious (Freud, 1938).

Anxiety and the Mechanisms of Defense

All mechanisms of defense operate to deny and distort some aspect of reality that threatens to overwhelm the *ego*. The offending reality can exist in the environment or in the mind of the individual as a wish or a fantasy. The role of anxiety must be mentioned at this junction. Whenever the *ego* is threatened by internal sources, anxiety is experienced. Anxiety is an emotion that acts as a signal of impending danger to the continued functioning of the *ego*. The mechanisms of defense deny and distort reality in order to reduce what are considered to be intolerable levels of anxiety. The individual is aware of his anxiety but neither its cause or its removal. If anxiety is reduced, then either the *ego* found some way to cope with its source or has successfully defended against the source.

All defenses not only deny and distort reality in order to reduce anxiety, but they also operate on the unconscious level. Thus, the unconsious contains not only the ideas and emotions defended but mechanisms of defense as well. Once an individual denies and distorts reality, that reality is now considered true. Perceptions, thoughts, memories, and all cognitive processes are altered by the defenses—distortions that the individual is not aware of having created. His distorted reality is now a weak point, and if someone argues with him over the nature of his reality, further defensive distortions will be applied, thus compounding the weakness.

Psychological defense mechanisms often become long-lasting. Once a wish is buried in the unconscious, it remains preserved in its original form: e.g., infantile wishes or fears remain infantile. Since the unconscious wish or fear is constantly pressing the conscious mind for expression, the distortive defenses must remain in place. A permanent blind spot may result when dealing with some aspect of internal or external reality. Moreover, as time goes by, increasing amounts of material associated with the original wish can be buried in the unconscious mind while more defenses are created to keep it safely hidden from consciousness. More and more, the personality must expend energy denying and distorting reality rather than coping with it. The ego's growth deteriorates and a variety of pathological defense mechanisms can develop.

Repression is in a sense the master defense, playing a role in all other defense mechanisms, while maintaining the ability to exist on its own. In its simplest form, repression might best be defined as motivated forgetting: threatening ideas, thoughts, and images are "repressed" or expelled from the conscious mind and relegated to the unconscious. Most of us have experienced repression: often after awakening with a dream fully in consciousness, moments later it cannot be recalled.

Denial offers a simple way of avoiding threatening stimuli or thought. Children who are playing may deny signals from their bladder to urinate until they soil themselves. They are genuinely surprised when the accident occurs and will loudly exclaim, "but I didn't have to go."

Projection allows an individual to justify an unacceptable emotion and at the same time rid themselves of it by projecting the affect onto another. "I do not hate him—he hates me."

Sometimes an individual will become conscious of the opposite of what he actually feels, whereupon he is utilizing a *reaction formation.* A young mother resents her cranky newborn for burdening her with responsibilities. Her hatred for the baby creates intense guilt and anxiety. This defense mechanism emerges when she is suddenly overwhelmed with love for the infant and her conflicts are resolved. Analysts believe that one reason parents overprotect a child is reaction formation.

Having to resort to excuses, justifications and, "sour grapes" signals the defense mechanism known as *rationalization.* This is perhaps the most universal of all the defenses.

According to Freud, human personalities are heavily and inevitably shaped by defense mechanisms. *Identification* and *sublimation* represent two such character-shaping defenses. The former involves, for example, the child's introjection or "taking in" of parental beliefs and behavior patterns. The full name of the defense is "identification with the aggressor," which plays a key role in the resolution of the Oedipus Complex, the specifics of which are discussed below. When a boy fears his father's rage and subsequently develops a castration anxiety, he identifies with his father's prohibitions and values against incestuous and patricidal wishes and behavior. By becoming just like daddy, he is able to resolve his conflict and fears. "I do not have incestuous wishes and need not fear daddy, since I am just like him." Through the use of this defense mechanism, the boy's *superego* is developed along with his masculine identification.

Freud thus saw masculine character and *superego* as resulting from defensive processes: they are irrational in nature and ultimately reducible to sexual and aggressive drives. It is also clear that Freud saw fear as an indispensable element in motivating the development of one's conscience. While the father needs to be loving and available for identification, he must also be a feared figure to the son. This aspect of Freud's theory is overlooked by modern proponents of discipline, who justify extreme permissiveness in the name of psychoanalysis.

Sublimation is sometimes referred to as the "healthy" defense. To better understand sublimation it might be wise to differentiate it from another defense mechanism, *displacement.* A boy in the Oedipus Complex has patricidal wishes toward his father. He recognizes how formidable an opponent his daddy is and how dangerous it would be to express his aggression toward him. Instead, the son displaces his aggression onto his weaker little brother and behaves sadistically toward him. In displacement the original object of the drive is shifted to a new, safer object.

Sublimation involves an actual reworking of the drive itself into a new, socially acceptable motive. Instead of wanting to kill his father, the boy is infused with a desire to express himself in sports. He develops a healthy sense of competition or a desire to help others in some way rather than relating the murderous desire. The desire to kill can be sublimated, like the goal to become a surgeon. A voyeur can become a psychologist, his power need thereby sublimated to the desire to teach and to work with helpless young people. Freud believed that all art, science, and societal structures were sublimations of sexual and aggressive urges.

It is clear that Freud saw civilization as a defensive compromise (Freud, 1952). Similarly, the developing conscience that permitted life as a civilized individual was also based on the same compromise. Both civilization and conscience were based on fear, the necessary agony borne by each individual, who must constantly struggle to maintain the defensive lie that civilization and civilized achievements are the real goals sought. All individuals must defend against sexual and aggressive urges that are the true expressions of self-interest.

Since all civilization and conscience is based on defense, all attempts to find morality and meaning are neurotic. Religion, art, music, even the study of psychology itself are irrational and neurotic activities that can be instantly swept away if the defenses of identification and, more importantly, sublimation were to fail. At best all neurotic struggles to establish "human" activities and meaning are a thin veneer covering the real human nature—that of a pleasure-seeking, self-interested, and rapacious beast of prey.

The *ego* gets its motivating energy from the defense of sublimation, where it must constantly trick the *id* to give up a part of its motivating power for the sake of survival. Throughout the individual's life there is a constant struggle for the *ego* to maintain the defenses that permit it to borrow and desexualize energy, thereby carrying out its dual goal: maintaining a hold on reality while at the same time coping with it. When the *ego* cannot sustain its defenses, it too can be swept away by *id* desires. Then the manifestations of severe mental illness set in. The symptoms of neurosis are defensive compromises more severe than those created by just utilizing the *ego* mechanisms of repression or denial. And if the defenses fail altogether, then the individual can return to the infantile state of primary process thinking wherein the various psychoses are demonstrated.

The Economic Model

Freud was heavily influenced by the new sciences of physics and chemistry as they emerged in the nineteenth century. The physical sciences were based heavily on the concept of energy transformation. Matter cannot be created or destroyed, suggested the new physics; it can only be transformed into states of energy. Heat came from light or mechanical energy. Ice could melt thus shifting its molecular structure from a solid to a liquid. If heat continued to effect the water, the liquid could be transformed into a gas. Freud saw in the mechanics of his time a way of explaining human behavior.

Human motives are instincts based on a given quantum of energy. Each motive has a *source,* an *aim,* and an *object.* The *sources* of instincts are the physical tissues that become deficient in some way or another. Tissue needs (physical needs) give rise to hunger, thirst, sexuality, and other urges. The *aim* of the need represents the manner in which the individual seeks to satisfy the tissue deficiency: eating, drinking, and copulation as well as individual variations with respect to how to eat, drink, and copulate. The *object* represents that which will satisfy the need: a steak sandwich; a glass of cold beer; a breast, vagina, or penis; and so on.

When an individual invests energy in an object of desire, he is said to "cathect" that object. Instincts are describable as cathexes of energy. When the *ego* defends against an object, it must hold back the energy in some way. Defenses are made up of energy that acts as "anti-cathexes." Freud likened the defenses to outposts along a defensive perimeter in which small numbers of men hold off a larger oncoming army. When the *ego* defense successfully holds back a quantity of energy greater than itself, some of that energy becomes available for sublimations that are necessary for the survival and maintenance of civilization. When these outposts fail, mental illness is the result. An individual who must use more and more mental energy to hold back unacceptable impulses becomes increasingly crippled and unable to cope with reality.

The *libido,* or sex drive, represents a topic that needs special attention. The tissues that give rise to the sexual impulse or instinct are the erogenous zones. As we shall see, personality development depends upon the transition of various erogenous zones: e.g., mouth, anus, genitalia. Each zone gives rise to cathexes satisfied by different objects: The mouth may seek the breast, the male genitalia may seek the female genitalia. The mode of satisfaction, or aim, can also vary. Thus the infant may seek to suck on the breast or to bite and devour it. Freud saw the healthy personality as one in which each erogenous zone followed specific aims and objects, and not others. It is to his developmental theory that we now turn.

THE GENETIC THEORY

The first focused erogenous zone is the mouth. During the first two years of life the child is in the *oral stage* of development: its first sexual expressions are sucking, swallowing, biting, and spitting up, among others. The sexual impulses cathect the breast and whatever other object can satisfy the discharge of oral sexual energy. The breast is the natural object of choice and the one that most completely satisfies the oral libidinous needs. If the child cannot have the breast available, he will choose substitute objects such as his thumb, his feet, or an object in his crib. Freud felt that children must be breast fed if they are to develop normally. Other important issues include the timing of weaning, how long the child is given the breast to suck, the availability of milk in the mother's breast.

A vital psychological topic introduced by Freud concerned *fixation* and *repression*. If the mother deprives or overindulges her child's sexual appetites, a *fixation* or *partial fixation* of *libido* can occur. During the oral stage a decision to wean too early or too late will create fixation. Libidinal energies that should shift to the anal area remain at the oral erogenous zone. Deprivation creates unmet sexual needs, while overindulgence creates an unrealistic expectation of continued gratification. In each case, the individual will retain oral characteristics: nail biting, thumb sucking, drinking or eating too much, or even excessive talking.

If the child is fixated through overindulgence he might develop a passive, overly optimistic character fixation. If deprivation is the cause of the fixation, then angry, pessimistic, and demanding qualities of personality might emerge. The oral pessimist can develop a "biting" personality, attacking others verbally and utilizing a hostile sense of humor in order to hurt others. In any case, those who are orally fixated will retain characteristics of personality more appropriate to infancy than adulthood. Sexual difficulties will also emerge: sexual preference might focus on oral rather than genital satisfaction. The fixated individual might appear to develop normally but under stress the *ego* can regress to the oral stage or to any stage at which fixation occurs. Under duress the individual might then eat too much or too little, drink excessively, or manifest any number of symptoms.

Regression is also listed as a psychological defense mechanism. An overworked *ego* regresses to a time in life in which there were fewer pressures, a time when mother was present to gratify wishes and needs. The regression can be temporary, as when we stay home from work for a day and feed ourselves nurturing food, or it can be permanent, as in various mental illnesses.

During the years two through four, the anus is the primary sexual zone, placing the child in the *anal stage*. During this stage, toilet training becomes a focal point for the socializing parent. If the parent is overly strict (depriving), the child can react with rage or become passive and weak-willed. If parents are overly permissive, then indulgence will cause a delay in the development of willpower and self-expression. In the oral stage, fixations lead to personality styles metaphorically descriptive of taking in, or spitting out. During the anal stage, the personality types will reflect a "holding on" or a "letting go" characteristic. Issues related to sadism and anger also affect personality. Stinginess, over generosity, problems with time and money, all result from fixations at the anal stage.

The most important developmental issues occur during the *phallic stage*. It is during this stage that the genitalia become primary erogenous zones. Between the ages of three or four and six or seven years, children develop incestuous desires for their parents and siblings. Once developed, these universal conflicts lead to the development of the Oedipus Complex for boys and the Elektra Complex for girls. Let us trace each separately.

Once the boy develops sexual feelings for his mother, he is in conflict. He feels overwhelmed by the demands that his sexuality places on his *ego*. He recognizes that father is his chief rival for mother's affections, and patricidal wishes develop. Now he is full of conflict, creating nightmares and great anxiety. The father begins to respond to his child's incestuous demands (e.g., "You sleep in my bed and I'll sleep with mommy") as well as increased hostility and competitiveness. As this response unfolds, the little boy becomes fearful of father's wrath and develops a "castration anxiety."

The boy child resolves this dilemma by identifying with the aggressor, in this case the father. In one master stroke, the youngster makes significant gains in *superego* development: He introjects not only his father's prohibitions against incestuous behavior, but all paternal moral structures. Father is also the basis of the *ego ideal,* and thus the child's masculine identification is greatly increased. This phase of development comes to an end with a partial immobilization of the *libido* as the child enters the latency period. The latency period precedes adolescence and is marked by a decrease in sexual interest and activity. The boy decathects (or withdraws sexual interest in) his mother as a sexual object and is ready for adolescence. As the sex drive comes alive during the genital phase, the child is free to choose an appropriate sex object from outside of his family.

Clearly much can go wrong during the Oedipal phase. If the mother is overly seductive and the father absent, weak, or so tyrannical that he prevents identification, such an abnormal mother-father relationship makes Oedipal resolution more difficult, if not impossible. The child cannot possess his mother, so he may turn off his sex drive entirely. He may identify with mother and protect himself from the forbidden incestuous desires by developing a feminine identity. The child may become bound to mother and idealize her. According to Freudian theory, homosexuality results from a poor identification with a masculine figure and/or an overidentification with a feminine one. In any event, the result will be confused sexual identity, fixation at pregenital levels, and sexual problems in adulthood. Homosexuals* rail at Freud's theory because in it they are pregenitally fixated and thus have disturbed character structures. Freudian psychoanalysts assume that most sexual disturbances involve an unresolved Oedipus complex.

The Elektra Complex begins in similar fashion to the Oedipus Complex. The girl develops incestuous desires toward father and

---

* Homosexuality is presently described in the D.S.M. III, the psychiatric descriptions of mental illness, as an "alternative lifestyle." This classification avoids assuming that homosexuals are either immature or mentally ill or that psychoanalysis has an accurate theory of the genesis of homosexuality.

matricidal wishes. In this case, the girl cannot develop castration anxiety; she discovers she has already been castrated. Alas, the most prized of possessions has been denied her. Mother is seen as the culprit, and the girl is now in a quandry. She must identify with her mother but resents the latter for depriving her of a penis. According to Freud, she develops penis envy. The deprivation of a penis is proof of her biological inferiority vis-à-vis the male. To identify with mother, thus resolving her conflicts, means to accept biological inferiority.

Freud sees the female as inferior, both mentally and morally, in that she fails to develop a *superego* when she fails to identify with father. If the girl does not resolve her penis envy and accept her role as wife and mother, she will become castrating and competitive with men. She may enroll in college or go into business, thus competing with men on equal terms. Since she must always fail in her competitions, she is doomed to bitterness and anger. "Anatomy is destiny" in Freud's theory and, as such, many modern women rail against his idea as strongly as do homosexuals.

Following the resolution of the conflicts of the phallic stage, the child enters the *latency period*. The sex drive is withdrawn from the opposite sex and is focused in same sexed children. The latency period is often referred to as the homosexual phase. It is a time of consolidating gains made earlier and recovering from the traumas of infantile sexuality and the conflicts they produce. The latency period continues until the *libido* is again infused with sexual energy during the onset of puberty and adolescence.

Full sexual maturity is reached during the *genital stage*. A healthy individual who resolves the conflicts and traumas of childhood possesses a mature *ego* capable of balancing the demands of the *id,* the *superego,* and the environment. The mature individual is capable of "work, love, and play." Love includes sexual love, which is marked by the desire for a partner of the opposite sex (who is not a member of one's family) and the capacity to achieve mutual genital orgasm during intercourse.

A FINAL WORD

Freud's theory has had enormous impact on the thinking of Western humanity. The notion of the unconscious is probably his greatest contribution. The idea of defense mechanisms has had profound implications as well. For Freudians, the human animal is an irrational being, motivated by sexual and aggressive urges of which he is unaware. Human beings are directed almost entirely by motives of self-interest; other-directed behavior always has a self-directed aim. Art, music, and the entire edifice of civilization are but veneers covering the beast beneath.

Freud's theory is a highly pessimistic one. Existence in a civilization is an ordeal, albeit a necessary one. The basic natural tendency is for civilization to maintain itself only at an enormous loss to each and every individual. Toward the end of his life, Freud could see clearly that Hitler's rise to power would plunge the world into a new world war. His pessimism deepened as he revamped his view of the *id* one more time.

Freud's last view of humanity was his most pessimistic (Becker, 1973). The *libido* was recast as *Eros,* the life urge, while aggression was reconceptualized as *Thanatos,* the death urge. We are forever in a struggle, Freud believed, between the desire to grow and create and the desire to die and destroy. Society and culture reflect this titanic struggle. Given the continued reality and the ever-present threat of war in human history, it was clear to Freud that the human conquest of *Thanatos* was unachievable. What might Freud have said today if he could have seen a world armed with enough nuclear weapons to destroy itself hundreds of times over!

The Freudian vision of humanity and its relationship to society is most clearly revealed in William Golding's (1962) *Lord of the Flies.* A group of children crashland on a desert paradise as they are being evacuated from a civilization in the throes of a world conflagration. Even though their basic biological needs are met, we see an inexorable decline in civilized values as the boys regress toward savagery. Reason and conscience are swept aside as brutality and cannibalism reassert themselves. At the end of the book, Golding has his boys collected by human authority and brought back to civilization—a world at war. The vision of the Freudian is appalling in its hopeless view of how humanity will forever live. Freud believed that if we give up neurotic unhappiness it will be for a life of everyday misery.

3

Further Developments
in Psychoanalysis

GENERAL CONSIDERATIONS

In this chapter synopses of various supplemental and competing psychoanalytic theories will be presented. Ego Psychology and Object Relations Theory are "first cousins" and represent the modern outgrowths of Freud's theory. Both emphasize the structure and function of the *ego* rather than the dynamics associated with *id* needs. We will conclude with a brief exposition of the concepts of Alfred Adler and Karen Horney, both "rebel" analysts who are known as "social psychoanalysts."

Adler and Horney espouse similar theoretical positions, both of which have their roots in psychoanalysis, but their developments point in different directions. They are known as social analysts because basically they reject the biological emphasis of Freudian psychology. Adler developed concepts that place him as a link between analytic and humanistic existential theory. Horney's major concepts are very similar to those of the cognitive behaviorists.

EGO PSYCHOLOGY

Freud's psychoanalytic theory stressed the importance of *id* satisfactions, defense against *id* gratifications, and conflict between *id* drives as well as between the *id* and the *ego*. The *id* at birth was dominant while the *ego* was a poorly articulated aspect of personality. Freud's view of development has been termed the "viccisitudes of the id drives." Development of the *ego* is due to conflict, defense strategies, a capturing of *id* energy and transforming it into *ego* energy. Modern *ego* psychology shifts the emphasis from the struggle of the *ego* with the *id* to the struggles of *ego* with the environment, particularly the social environment.

HEINZ HARTMANN

There are many theorists who have contributed to the revision of the basic analytic views of mental structures. Heinz Hartmann (1939, 1958) and Erik Erikson (1969) are two major theorists credited with shifting the analytic view of personality from one dominated by *id* to one that conceptualizes the *ego* as the centrally important structure. Let us look at Hartmann first. Hartmann's famous monograph was *Ego Psychology and the Problem of Adaptation,* published first in 1939 and again in 1958. Hartmann disagrees with the more traditional Freudian view that the *ego* takes it's energy from the *id*. He posits a "primary autonomy of the ego" and a "conflict free ego sphere."

Hartmann suggests that the *ego* contains it's own motivations and energies from birth; it has "primary autonomy" from the *id*. Perception, memory, rudimentary intelligence, and so on, all exist from birth and are exercised not only for the sake of satisfying *id* motivations, but for their own sake as well. We see, hear, think, walk, read, and write not only to satisfy basic needs but because exercising these fundamental abilities is enjoyable and pleasurable simply because they exist. One can take a walk to release energy but also just for the sheer enjoyment of it. From the time we are born, exercise of our skills is intrinsically rewarding. Freud was once asked about which oral needs he might be sublimating by smoking his cigar. His response was "sometimes a cigar is just a good smoke." If Freud smoked to satisfy an oral need, then he smoked at the behest of the *id*. If he merely enjoyed smoking for its own sake, then he was satisfying an *ego* need.

We do not perceive, think, or act merely to satisfy needs, to act out defenses, or otherwise to express some conflict. When crossing a street, we can do so for no other reason than to get to the other side. This idea not only expresses the notion of primary autonomy, but also the presence of a "conflict free ego sphere." Any *ego* activity *can* become involved in a conflict. We can think for it's own sake or obsessively think in order to reduce conflict. Then again, we can defensively avoid thinking about something. Psychopathology, in Hartmann's view, is not merely the failure of defenses, but the intrusion of *id* needs into the conflict-free *ego* sphere. Such an intrusion threatens the primary autonomy of *ego* functions.

Just as an *ego* function can be coopted by conflict, defensiveness, or need, it can become independent of these as well. When an activity becomes independent of its *id* roots or involvements, then it has achieved "secondary autonomy" and joins the conflict-free *ego* sphere. A child may play the piano to avoid parental punishment and to seek approval. As time passes, the child may learn intrinsically to enjoy the piano and to play past the point at which parental wishes are involved. Any activity can begin as a defense or in order to satisfy an *id* need and eventually become autonomous of its original *id* or conflict motivation: e.g., fishermen do fish on their day off, and bus drivers do take the car for a Sunday drive.

ERIK ERIKSON

Erikson also stressed the role of the *ego* in development. But while Hartmann saw adaptation as the legitimate goal of the healthy *ego,* Erikson shifted its emphasis to the social environment of the developing personality. He created a theory of psychosocial stages instead of continuing to employ Freud's psychosexual stages. Erikson added three stages to Freud's five that described development in young adulthood, middle age, and old age. These eight psychosocial stages define the healthy as well as the unhealthy *ego* orientation.

Erikson postulated a specific epigenetic principle of development. This principle posits a fixed sequence in the emergence of the stages, where each has a crisis and a resolution describable in terms of social interactions. Unlike Freud, who would have described the conflict of the oral stage in terms of the *id* and its need for the breast, Erikson described the same phenomenon in terms of the infant's emotional interaction with the mother. Thus, his theory shifts the emphasis from the biological interaction of the *id* and the *ego* to the social interaction of *ego* and social other. The epigenetic crises is resolvable in either positive or negative terms. While each stage is describable in terms of its own epigenetic conflict and resolution, the current stage is clearly affected by the one preceding it and the mode of conflict resolution of the earlier stage. Development precedes more easily with positive rather than negative resolutions.

The particular conflict posited at each stage can occur at any of the other stages as well: for example, some individuals may struggle with issues in childhood that are more appropriate to adulthood, while some adults may continue to struggle with conflicts that have their root in childhood experiences. However, Erikson felt that normal development proceeded from stage to stage when *certain* conflicts "came due," so to speak, at the stage where they were most appropriate to do so.* Let us, then, examine each of the eight psychosocial stages and describe the positive and negative consequences of the conflict resolutions pertinent to each.

Stage One: Oral-Sensory Stage (Birth to Eighteen Months)

The epigenetic conflict involves feeding, mother-child interaction, and the emotional climate between parent and infant. If the mother is consistent, loving, and appropriately nurturing, the child chooses to *trust her*. However, if she lacks these qualities and is hostile, negative, inconsistent, and unavailable, the child will orient himself toward mistrust. The early resolution of *trust* versus *mistrust* becomes a paradigm for the child's perception of himself and others in his social world.

Stage Two: Muscular Anal Stage (Eighteen Months to Three Years)

Issues of discipline, toilet training, and socialization create the next conflict. The child seeks to break the dependency of infancy, express himself with newly found verbal skills, and exercise a growing repertoire of intellectual and motor skills. If the parents are accepting of these new skills and supportive of the child's moves toward independence, but firm in their setting of fair and appropriate limits,

---

* For example, an individual may struggle to establish autonomy at any point in the life span. However, autonomy becomes the central issue of the second stage, which occurs early in childhood.

the child resolves his conflict with an orientation of autonomy Excessive criticism, overprotection, disgust reactions, and harsh discipline will produce a sense of shame and doubt. *Shame and doubt* freeze the normal development of *autonomy*.

Stage Three: Locomotor-Genital Stage (Three to Six)

Issues of conflict at this stage include the Oepidus and Electra complexes, the continued search for independence, and increasingly complex interactions with peer groups and teachers. Autonomy is followed by an extension of the child's self expression in terms of making choices. Parental respect and guidance leads to a growing sense of initiative whereas parental outrage, indignance, and similar negative reactions lead to a child who is forever in guilt. *Guilt* is the emotional opposition of *initiative* or the making of one's own choices.

Stage Four: Latency (Six to Twelve or Thirteen)

Consolidation of sex roles and increased social contact, as well as greater demands from and responsibilities toward peers, school, and parents, set the stage for the struggle at this age. If the child takes responsibility for his new freedom and vistas, a sense of industry develops. If growing competence does not develop, then the child will come to have a sense of inferiority in those areas in which he feels himself to be inadequate: thus *industry* is undone by *inferiority*.

Stage Five: Adolesence

The struggle during adolesence involves continued separation from parents and the selection of vocational, social, and sexual directions. The adolescent who chooses directions that grow out of *ego* skills and complement interests and values begins to develop an identity. Failure to find one's self in the vocational and social world leads to a sense of role diffusion. *Identity* represents the positive outcome of adolescence; *role diffusion,* the negative.

Stage Six: Young Adulthood

The struggle during this stage involves moving beyond the dating patterns and social cliques of adolescent relationships. Issues related to marriage and the creation of a new family are the sources of new struggles. Successful resolution leads to *intimacy* while failure produces a deepening sense of *isolation.*

Stage Seven: Middle Adulthood

Existential crises become the focus of the epigenetic struggle during middle age. Having become increasingly aware of death, the individual seeks to establish patterns of meaningful and purposive behavior. Erikson feels that concerns for the next generation and the continuation of the species become manifest at this stage. Work must be meaningful, and children are looked upon as important to the adult's emotional well being. Success at this stage means a sense of *generative* power; failure symbolizes an awareness of *stagnation.*

Stage Eight: Late Adulthood

The individual must assess his life's accomplishments and come to grips with impending death. A successful life leads to the development of *ego integrity,* while a life viewed as empty and wasted leads to *despair.*

As individuals struggle with these eight stages of personality evolution, there is the opportunity, with successful resolution, for developing particular *ego* strengths. Erikson calls these strengths "basic virtues." Basic trust leads to *hope,* or a belief that needs can be satisfied and goals ultimately attained. Autonomy leads to the emergence of *will,* which involves the exercise of choices. The third stage (the genital stage) produces the virtue of *purpose,* which permits an individual to envision life goals. Industry fosters the *ego* strength of *competence.* Identity and adolescent struggle permits the emergence of *fidelity* leading to loyalty and honesty in human relationships. Intimacy fosters the virtue of *love* and allows the individual to care more deeply for others than for himself. Generative capacity will lead to the virtue of *caring,* while *ego identity* allows for the development of the all important *wisdom.*

OBJECT-RELATIONS THEORY

Closely related to ego psychology is the analytic variation known as *object relations* theory. An "English" school is advanced by Melanie

Klein (1948), D. W. Winnicott (1965), and Guntrip (1969). R. S. Spitz (1965), M. S. Mahler (1968), Edith Jacobsen (1964), James Masterson (1976) and Otto Kernberg (1967) are among the major American proponents of this theory. The object-relation theorists are concerned with the development of the *ego* as a consequence of the early social interaction, particularly with the mother. In the parlance of psychoanalysis, the important people "cathected" by the child are referred to as objects.

Various object-relation theorists suggest a series of stages whereby the child becomes aware of himself and his mother, becomes fused with her, and later separated from her. These theorists suggest that many important psychological disorders result from failures of *ego* development prior to the Oedipus Complex. The basic strengths of the *ego* are also the consequence of early development. While many theorists disagree as to the actual stages and when they occur, there are certain general agreements as to important events and their sequences.

During early infancy the child develops an intense dependence on mother that is known as *attachment* or *bonding*. The child introjects or internalizes an image of the mother that is inseparable from his/her image of him/herself. Not only is the infant dependent on its mother for need satisfaction, but it is psychologically at one with her as well. In various theories, the infant is "fused" "bonded," "in symbiosis" with, or "undifferentiated" from mother. During the stage of undifferentiation, the infant cannot distinguish the source of emotional reactions. The child will experience its mother's positive and negative feelings as if they were its own. That the mother feels positive toward the child and tends promptly to its basic needs is extremely important. Both unmet needs and anxiety or anger on the part of the mother will be experienced as negative feeling on the part of the infant toward itself.

As growth continues, the infant begins psychologically to separate from the mother. Mahler (1968) refers to this process as separation-individuation. The initial separation still involves partial fusions with the mother. Kernberg believes that initial individuation involves the separation of positive and negative feelings into two constellations, one good and the other bad. The self-mother fusion therefore contains two entities, one good and the other bad.

Continued development allows a separation of self from mother in which there is a good me and a bad me, a good mother and a bad mother. In the final phase, the child experences himself and his mother as completely separate entities, each possessing good and bad qualities. The early self-image and *ego* structure of the child develops from a fusion with, and later a separation from, the mother's *ego* and her perception of herself and her baby.

There are many potential problems in the above journey. If the infant's development is filled with pain from unmet needs, anxiety and anger from mother, then the final sense of self can be loaded with negative appraisals. Under such conditions, *ego* skills cannot develop properly. Negative emotions exist at preverbal levels producing a feeling of self-hatred and "badness" in an individual which is nameless and irrational. Clinically, we see individuals who hate and despise themselves even though they cannot say why they are deserving of such emotion.

The child may not fully separate from the mother and hence not develop *ego* skills that permit autonomy and independence. Individuals who remain symbiotically tied to another can remain helplessly dependent on the mother, or a mother substitute, for a lifetime. Another possibility is that the individual may be partially fused and partially separated from the mother. In this situation the person may perpetually vacillate between the fear of getting too close to others (fear of fusion) and the fear of becoming too distant (fear of nonexistence without the love object). Such individuals may live their lives swinging wildly from overly close and suffocating relationships, filled with jealousy and possessiveness, to bouts of utter isolation, withdrawal, emptiness, and depression.

An individual failing to fulfill the developmental demands of establishing good object relations may not develop a stable self-image or a stable view of others. He may hate himself one moment and love himself the next, hating and loving others in the same extreme manner. However, he may continue to experience others as if they were actually different people when hated or loved. Such is the consequence of not having achieved interpersonal object constancy. The phenomena of idealizing persons as perfect in one moment and hating them in perfect disillusionment the next is known in object-relation theory as "splitting" (Kernberg, 1967).

One of the consequences of internalizing the parent is the creation of the *superego*. Freud believed introjection (internalization) occurs as a result of the defense of identification utilized by a boy against the anxieties of the Oedipus Complex. Introjection of the parent is the analytic description of a process of internalization, which involves an individual making some aspect of the environment a part of his own psychological structure. How this process occurs is one of the most important puzzles to be solved by psychologists, most of whom agree, however, in one way or another, that children internalize the values and behaviors of their parents.

Many psychologists agree that conscience results, in part, when a child adopts, internalizes, or introjects parental values. The social behaviorists believe that the process is the result of imitation, or modelling. Such an explanation lacks the psychological status of introjection. Once a child internalizes parental values, he no longer imitates those of his parents but experiences them as his own. The values, attitudes, or images are not mother's or father's, but belong to the self: they become an integral part of the ego structure. Introjection allows the psychological description of a transition from "out-there" to "in-here," whereas imitation does not.

The object-relation theorists also describe a pathological condition in which the developing individual does not complete the internalization of parental values. The "pathological introject" exists when an individual retains an image of the "bad mother" and can neither rid himself of it nor integrate the feelings as his own. Such an individual behaves as if he carries the critical parent around in his own head. He experiences his conscience as a driving force that punishes and criticizes. It is hard to describe this special psychological state, although clinical psycholgists do become familiar with it.

Object-relation theorists will describe such individuals as possessing a "harsh punitive *superego*." Horney's theory, as we shall soon see, deals at length with individuals whose *superegos* drive them to perfection and tyrannize them with "shoulds" and "should nots." Often these individuals will behave childishly and impulsively, then later become self-punitive and self-hating. It is almost as if two people exist—a house divided against itself. On the one hand they are children; on the other adults, but seen from the perspective of a child.

Later, I will discuss the manner in which internalization of parental values adds to the development of conscience and values. The object-relation theorists make one aware that the process is more than simple imitation, and that fixations can occur leaving the individual with a primitive and poorly developed conscience. These theorists point to the fact that children do internalize parental behavior, and that this process is *multistaged* rather than continuous, smooth, and unseamed.

ALFRED ADLER

Adler's theories are left to us by student compilations of lectures and notes, and to a lesser degree by his own writings. He was not as systematic as Freud in organizing his ideas, recording and publishing them for posterity. Were it not for H. L. and R. R. Ansbacher (1956) and other disciples, a systematic recording of Adler's ideas might not have been accomplished. Adler referred to the conglomeration of his ideas as "Individual Psychology."

Inferiority and the Will to Power

Disagreeing with the Freudian notion of the *libido* as the basic human motivation, Adler felt that, as a result of the helplessness of infancy, each person develops an intolerable feeling of inferiority. Initially, Adler was concerned with handicapped individuals and their "organ inferiorities," though later he generalized the complex, making it a universal notion. The basic human need, he believed, is finding ways to overcome feelings of inferiority and the intolerable helplessness of infancy.

Adler saw human growth as motivated by a will to power, a desire for superiority or mastery. Like Freud, motivation is seen in essentially negative terms; growth is an escape mechanism, described by the behaviorists as "negative reinforcement" (see chapter 4). Though "power" and "superiority" were used alternately at various times in Adler's writings, they do not necessarily mean power or superiority over others, but are used in the general sense of growth, increased ability, or "*ego* strength."

Overcompensation

The healthy individual learns to compensate for early inferiority feelings and to maintain an equilibrium through continued growth of mastered skills. Children, however, are often made unnecessarily or unusually inferior during childhood: a youngster with a handicap, a boy who is short, or a physically ugly girl may well go through childhood feeling intensely and inescapably inferior. A child may have excellent potential but be told by parents and teachers that he is inadequate and does not live up to standards. Inferiority, Adler understood, was the same whether it was real or imagined.

Adler was critical of American education and culture for being overly competitive, a place where children are taught to set extremely high standards. When standards and goals are punitively unrealistic, people of extraordinary abilities feel perpetually inferior. A youngster who comes in second in a race may feel more inferior than one who comes in last and is glad to finish. When children experience intense inferiority feelings, they *overcompensate* in their attempts to maintain superiority. Such intense overcompensations form the basis for neurotic overstrivings for power, superiority, and mastery. In one way or another the neurotic seeks to dominate others and to punish them for their inferiorities while maintaining a self-image of invulnerable perfection. Men who feel deeply inferior seek to become superior in many aspects of life. They either become overly materialistic, athletically competitive, or bullies. Adler called such masculine overstriving the "masculine protest" and felt it explained male aversions to softness, gentleness, emotional expressiveness, and kindness.

Brotherly Feelings

Adler posited a genetic need to get along and to cooperate with other people. In this notion he included a whole range of humanistic needs for such things as love, affiliation, and cooperation. The need for others is basic to personality development and the survival of society; therefore, it must be satisfied. One of the basic individual conflicts involves the manner in which one compensates for inferiority, and, in feeling superior or masterful, satisfies one's need for love and cooperation.

The individual with neurotic needs to overcompensate satisfies his need for affiliation by dominating people rather than cooperating with them. Competition replaces shared effort as submission is defined as closeness and togetherness. Such individuals must forever employ "safeguarding techniques"—Adler's term for defense— to hide from themselves and to justify the truth of how they treat others.

Fictional Finalism

An important concept, and one similar to various existential ideas, is that of fictional finalism. Finalisms are life-goals that organize, focus, and give purpose and meaning to the life of an individual. Being good in some aspect of life, such as a profession or role, achieving some type of fame or fortune, writing a great novel, or whatever, are all fictional finalisms. Adler called these life-goals "fictional" because their value to the individual had to be taken on faith. Belief that one would be happy "if only . . ." cannot be tested against reality. Such finalisms are fictions for other reasons as well. Most often the goal of perfection, in being the best, is fictional in that it can never be realized and, in fact, is best not realized. The idea that we are happy when we reach our goals is also a fiction when compared to the fact that we are happiest when struggling to achieve goals.

Childhood Experiences and Birth Order

An individual's first memory was used in Adler's psychology in the way Freud used dreams. Through memory he believed one could interpret an individual's basic mood and perception of life. Adler was an analyst in his insistence that the first five years of life were the most formative for personality formation.

He also focused on birth order as a salient family phenomenon in the development of personality. The firstborn tended to be aggressive, success oriented, and in possession of much parental neuroticism. The youngest child, as "the baby" was gentle, laid back, and contented with life. The middle or "millstone" child was embittered, jealous, and unhappy—neither the favored firstborn nor the loved baby.

Lifestyle

The nature of an individual's fictional finalism, his early life experiences, the nature of childhood inferiority, and the manner and intensity with which he compensates for inferiority as he seeks superiority, determine individual lifestyle. Established in later childhood, it is Adler's equivalent to the concept of character type found in analytic and neo-analytic theories. Adler outlined various character types and lifestyles—some healthy, some destructive.

Adler began his professional career as a trained Freudian analyst. When he tampered with such basic Freudian concepts as the Oedipus Complex, he soon found himself outside the "gates" of the Freudian camp. His theories gained adherents and popularity when he came to the United States. Karen Horney also began her analytic career in Vienna with the Freudians, and she, too, rejected a number of key analytic issues including penis envy, the primacy of infantile sexuality as motivation, and others. Her theory bears a strong resemblance to Adler's, and together they are referred to as the Social-Analysts. It is to Horney's ideas I now turn.

KAREN HORNEY

Horney's theory is similar in both structure and dynamic to that of Adler. She posits the existence of a "basic anxiety" that is endemic to the existence of the infant, an anxiety she defines as "feeling alone and helpless in a hostile world" (Horney, 1950). Any or all of the three elements (loneliness, helplessness, or fear) may be present in an infant's experience of basic anxiety, depending upon the role played by his parents—most specifically his mother. Just as the infant cannot tolerate inferiority feelings, it must find some way to deal with basic anxiety.

In healthy development (merely alluded to in Horney's writings) the child is not subjected to an excess of basic anxiety, although the complete avoidance of such tension is generally impossible. Where anxiety is not overly strong, the child is able to develop along positive lines free from defensive involvements: its basic needs for *safety and satisfaction* are met by the environment—particularly the parent. When a child feels safe during childhood, normal intellectual and motor development take place.

Neurotic Needs and Trends

Often, however, the helpless infant is not attended to, or attention is given by parents who are incompetent to do so. The adults in a child's life may be overly critical, punitive, or in any number of ways inadequate, cruel, belittling, and so on. Under these circumstances the child's experience will be steeped in basic anxiety, the result being that the child is left to feel small, helpless, abandoned, fearful, enraged, or in any number of possible negative affective states. Under these conditions the growing child will develop defensive needs and styles for dealing with other people.

Horney's view of the child's defense mechanisms is that they are cast in terms of interpersonal strategies designed to minimize and avoid further experiences of basic anxiety. Initially, she suggested that the child will develop ten basic needs designed to protect against anxiety (1942). These neurotic needs are:

1. affection and approval,
2. a dominant partner in life,
3. narrow and constricted limits to life,
4. power,
5. exploitation,
6. prestige,
7. personal admiration,
8. personal achievement or ambition,
9. self-sufficiency and independence,
10. perfection and unassailability.

Later, Horney (1945) described three basic behavioral trends that encompass the original ten neurotic needs. Let us turn to them now.

Moving Toward People

Those who use this trend establish a submissive style of relating to others. It says in effect, "I will do whatever you say—as long as you do not reject me." The individual may experience him/herself as weak and helpless and take a posture that proclaims, "I cannot ever hurt you, I am too small and weak to do this." Often such individuals cannot assert themselves, show anger, or fight back. Fearful of rejection and anxiety, they give in, time and again, in the face of domineering others. Horney points out that individuals who consistently and frequently move toward people often seek out those who need to have power over others.

Moving Against People

The individual who moves against people seeks to dominate. By controlling others, he sees them as too helpless to hurt or reject him. Thus, he feels protected from whatever behavior patterns might have created the basic anxiety in his childhood. The moving-against individual is often a bullying or arrogant child, and an overbearing, unassailable adult. He is the boss who criticizes others but can accept no criticism in return. He may be a teacher or a parent who lashes out at human weakness while proclaiming himself as brilliant, all-knowing, or all-skillful. Such individuals often seek out persons who move toward others.

Moving Away from People

This individual becomes a hermit of sorts and has an isolated lifestyle. He may seek employment that permits the shunning of contact with others, fail to marry, or avoid close friendships. His behavior says to us, "I cannot be hurt through rejection if I reject first." In a 1960s Simon and Garfunkel song, the poet sings: "I have my books and my poetry to protect me. I am shielded in my armor. . . . I have no need of friendship 'cause friendship causes pain. . . . If I never loved, I never would have cried. . . . And a rock feels no pain. And an island never cries. . . ." Modern city life is a mecca for those who seek to live in anonymity.

Cognitive "Appeals" or Justifications

One of Horney's most brilliant contributions was her description of the way in which individuals who live according to neurotic trends tend to justify their behavior. How does one live a submissive or lonely life, or exist as a bully and avoid basic anxiety? Horney answers by describing how an individual interprets neurotic behavior—a weakness and a source of basic anxiety—as a source of pride. The submissive individual interprets his weakness as "goodness" and creates a self image of saintliness. The bully, on the other hand, appeals to the vision of being "masterly," while the loner thinks of himself as "independent." By convincing themselves of their goodness, masterfulness, or independence, these individuals feel psychically safe and satisfied. Horney brilliantly illustrates in *Neurosis and Human Growth* (1950) how people create self-images that are full of "neurotic pride."

The Real and Idealized Self

Horney's theory avoids talking about the *ego;* instead, she sees the "self" as the core agent in human personality development. (Her ideas are remarkably similar to Carl Rogers's descriptions, which will be discussed in chapter 5.) The real self is all that one is: emotional reactions, thought patterns, strengths, and weaknesses. An individual experiencing basic anxiety must be willing to admit to such feelings if he is to stay in touch with his real self. However, he who uses neurotic trends is creating a new self-image when "appeals" or justifications are utilized. In order not to be vulnerable, he thinks of himself as perfectly independent, perfectly masterful, or perfectly good. In his own eyes his self-image is beyond reproach, beyond weakness, beyond vulnerability of any kind. The more he invests in this perfect self-image the more idealized he appears to be, and the less in touch he is with his real self.

The Neurotic Paradox and the Devil's Pact

The less in touch an individual is with his real self, the less conscious he is of weaknesses, faults, and fears. Self-correction becomes difficult if not impossible. He is committed to perfection and neurotic pride. However, imperious and arrogant behavior, inability to accept criticism, bully tactics, submission, and rejection, only drives people away. The more defensively an individual behaves, the more the he creates the very anxiety with which he is attempting to cope, and as more anxiety is aroused. He becomes more and more committed to his idealized self-image. Horney refers to this creation of basic anxiety through the use of defense mechanisms as the "neurotic paradox," His increased embrace of the idealized self-image is called the devil's pact. (Horney uses the dramatic idea of a "devil's pact" to suggest that the illusory comfort achieved by embracing the idealized self is "Faustian" at best.)

Neurotic Pride and the Search for Glory

The more perfect an individual thinks himself to be, the prouder he becomes of his worst qualities. For example, the bully is proud of his ability to "manage people"; the submissive saint becomes proud of being a victim, since he experiences it as "goodness." Gentleness or assertiveness, in which the individual might justifiably take pride, is seen as a source of weakness to be avoided at all cost.

As the individual becomes committed to an idealized self, he forces himself to be stronger, better, and more independent. The idealized self is to be protected and buttressed at all cost. Demands for perfection can lead to the need for greatness or other exaggerated proofs of success, which, when pressed into the service of neurotic trends, often take the shape of what Horney calls the search for glory. Goodness, power, and aloneness must be pure, intense, and glorious.

Tyranny of the Shoulds and the Neurotic Claims

The reader may be aware that Horney's description of neuroses is similar to Freud's concept of the *superego* (conscience and *ego* ideal) and the object-relation theorists' notion of "pathological introject." The neurotic is really a fixated personality who sees the world as a child might if he were to look through the eyes of an adult. When adults lecture children, they often use the words *should* and *should not*. Neurotic individuals are tyrannized by shoulds and should nots: they should always be strong, independent, and/or good but should never be weak, angry, or get too close to people. Their behavior is driven by the perfection they demand of themselves: one should work hard, one should not relax too much, etc., etc., etc. Neurotics always suffer because they fail to live up to the impossible standards they have set for themselves. The world should be as they wish it to be, not as it is.

Not only do neurotics demand much of themselves that is unrealistic, but they make even more demands on others, which Horney labels as "neurotic claims." The neurotic states, "You should not be sick, weak, frightened—but perfect, like me." When waiting for a bus, he might insist that "the bus should be here." A husband who presents his wife with candy might be told, "You should have known I wanted flowers." Life with a "perfect" person is almost as difficult for the onlooker as it is for the perfect person to live with himself.

All of the psychoanalytic theories just examined have a number of features in common. All stress the importance of childhood experiences and the vulnerability of personality during the early phases of development. The analytic theorists, for all their differences, stress the effects of trauma in the creation of irrationality in human behavior, particularly as a result of the defense mechanisms that come into play when people are in psychological pain. Psychoanalysis has been brilliant in describing the dark, brooding qualities personality that control human behavior.

Psychoanalysis is known as one of the "three-forces" within personality theory. The remaining two forces, Behaviorism and Humanism-Existentialism will now be focused upon. In the past, each area has gone its separate way and has been a philosophical and empirical "enemy camp" of the others. Each area tends to stress very different aspects of behavior and each utilizes a very different semantic system to describe its area of interest. I will turn now to the Behaviorism of B. F. Skinner and follow with a description of its close relatives, Cognitive and Social Behaviorism.

4

Behavioristic Perspectives

GENERAL CONSIDERATIONS

An examination of Freudian theory reveals the heavy emphasis of biological influences on personality: *libido* and aggression, and later Eros and Thanatos, are inborn and produce inevitable conflicts as well as the concomitant need for defenses. Even Heinz Hartmann speaks of the inborn capacities of the *ego*. While the environment is important to the analyst, it is basically perceived as the source of objects necessary for the satisfaction of the inborn biological qualities. Hartmann describes an "average expectable environment" but, like Freud, his descriptions concern intrapsychic struggles pertaining to the gratification and the deprivation of internal needs. Psychoanalysis tends to be a fairly pessimistic theory that rests upon the inevitability of conflict, regression, and resentment toward societal demands.

Behaviorism, however, is virtually at the opposite end of the psychological spectrum with respect to its basic assumptions about humanity. It assigns a vastly different role to biological, intrapsychic, and environmental factors that shape personality. Behavioristic assumptions were formalized by John Watson in the 1920s, a man who had become impressed with Ivan Pavlov's work on the conditioning of dogs. Watson saw in stimulus/response conditioning a paradigm for the scientific study of human beings. His goals were to eliminate any vestiges of the "soul" or religious elements from psychology, to deal only with observable events, and to establish laboratory studies employing precise measurements (Watson, 1924).

The modern proponent of behaviorism is B. F. Skinner (1953, 1971), who looms as a giant in modern American psychology. Skinners goal was to eschew "mentalisms" from the study of human behavior. Like Watson, he tried to employ an "S-R" model to explain human functions. The "S" stood for observable stimulus event, i.e., environmental factors affecting behavior, and the "R" represented the individual's observable behavioral responses to those stimuli. All behavioral patterns were seen as the result of learning and interaction with the environment.

Skinner believed that focusing on internal states obscured the scientific and fruitful search for the real causes of behavior. All internal states could be described in terms of external, observable, and measurable operations: for example, we might say that an organism is hungry; Skinner and his advocates would suggest that the organism was six hours food deprived. By operationally defining internal states and placing behavior under the control of the observable environment, Skinner and the behaviorists hoped to explain all development, normal and abnormal, in terms of observable phenomena.

Skinner's theory is highly deterministic. We saw when studying Freud's views that he considers behavior to be largely determined by unconscious impulses and conflicts. These internal events occur in infancy but have been blocked from consciousness by defense mechanisms. The psychoanalysts feel, however, that if an individual develops insight into the unconscious determiners of his behavior, then he can exercise choice in determining the next set of reactions to his world. Skinner believed that individuals react to their environment but posits no mechanism that allows organisms to choose or evaluate. The individual is, therefore, completely at the mercy of the environment and at any given moment has no choice regarding how to act.

The behavioristic concepts allow for an optimistic view of behavioral change and the possibility of overcoming pathology. If we focus on the history of the individual, then pathology is created by improper conditioning or by a pathological environment. The lack of internal structure avoids Freud's *ego* damage, inadequate *superego,* and other concepts that make behavioral changes seem difficult. Therapy, for the behaviorist, implies recording the individual's reactions. If a bad environment produces pathology, then a good environment ought to foster health. One does not have to improve the person, only his surroundings.

The behaviorist believes that the conditioning history of each individual is unique. Unlike the Freudian who seeks generalized principles of intrapsychic functioning, the behaviorist seeks generalized principles describing the manner in which the environment can affect individuals. The behavioristic study of action focuses on the individual case. Since the behaviorist chooses to control the individual's environment, and since it would be both immoral and impractical to keep human subjects in laboratories, most of the significant principles of behavioral control have been worked out on animal subjects and later applied to human beings.

Freudians and the humanistic-existential school of psychology rail against behaviorism. The humanists balk at describing individuals as having no choice and at applying the results of animal studies to human behavior. Many psychologists, including modern behaviorists, admire the ingenuity with which Skinner and others observe and condition behavior but agree that the "S-R" model is too simple-minded to describe adequately the human personality and its development. Let us proceed, then, to examine the major concepts of conditioning.

RESPONDENT AND OPERANT CONDITIONING

Human personalities are composed of conditioned reactions. Two paradigms describe the conditioning of reactions; each paradigm is an aspect of the other and represents a special case of one mode of conditioning. *Respondent conditioning* is Skinner's term for classical conditioning represented by the work of Pavlov. Skinner defined a respondent as a response or behavior that is *elicited* by a *stimulus*. A respondent is automatic and unlearned. It involves responses of the smooth muscles (intestines, internal organs, and iris of the eye) and glands.

Respondent (classical) conditioning can be represented by the following model or paradigm.

1) An unconditioned respondent is defined as the unconditioned stimulus (US) eliciting (→) the unconditioned response (UR).

$$US \rightarrow UR$$

2) A neutral stimulus (one that does not in any way elicit the UR) is chosen to be a conditioned stimulus (CS)

3) The conditioning procedure is as follows: The CS is presented just prior to the US.

$$CS + US \rightarrow UR$$

This pairing is repeated until

4) The conditioned stimulus (CS) elicits a response similar to the unconditioned response (UR). The new response is called the conditioned response (CR).

$$CS \rightarrow CR$$

The elicitation of the CR by the CS defines the conditioned respondent.

Let me repeat the paradigm in its simplest form:

$$US \rightarrow UR$$
$$CS \text{ is selected}$$
$$CS + US \rightarrow UR$$
$$CS \rightarrow CR$$

The basis of learning in behaviorism is *association theory*. The animal learns to associate the CS (conditioned stimulus) with the US (unconditioned stimulus). The CS eventually anticipates the US, which mediates the CR (conditioned response). These internal events seem unavoidable even to the most ardent radical behaviorists. The descriptions given to these events are often made in neurological terms that suggest a system of internal wiring connecting the stimulus with the response.

A large class of unconditioned responses allows the behaviorist to use classical conditioning to explain a number of human personality traits. Many of our emotional responses are unconditioned responses. The child's affective responses to maternal pleasure, to loud noises, or to a host of stimuli are unlearned and automatic. Any number of visual, auditory, olfactory, or tactile stimuli can act as conditioned stimuli and elicit the affective response. When an infant is hugged and stroked by its mother, the affective pleasures with which the infant responds are automatic and unlearned. Eventually the sight, odor, and sound of its mother will elicit the pleasure responses. Later in life, the sight of his room, the smell of his food, or the color of the wallpaper, could elicit the pleasure response and become conditioned stimuli. We can also see how a negative affect can be elicited by an individual or a situation, and how the surrounding sensory elements act as conditioned stimuli.

The second paradigm describing learning involves *operant conditioning;*

$$R \rightarrow S$$

The operant paradigm is much simpler than the respondent conditioning model. *R* is used to symbolize a behavior that is *emitted* by the organism and has the goal of operating on or effecting some change in the environment. Note the word *emitted* in the last sentence. Unlike a respondent, which is a response elicited automatically or involuntarily by some stimulus, an operant is a voluntary behavior, emitted and under the control of the organism. Operant behaviors are carried out by the skeletal or striated muscles of the arms, legs, torso, and face. Examples of operant behaviors are: asking a question, opening a door, throwing a ball, tickling a child, eating food, scratching a mosquito bite, or any number of acts designed to accomplish or change something.

S represents the change in the environment produced by the operant act or behavior. To utilize the examples in the last paragraph, *S* might be getting an answer to the question, having a door opened through which one can walk, receiving a bouncing ball, hearing a laughing child, experiencing the reduction of hunger and feeling satiated, or experiencing less itching. The change in the environment (social or physical) produced as a consequence of the operant behavior may be what is defined by Skinner as a reinforcer. Reinforcers are those behaviorally produced consequences of an act that increase the probability of the operant behavior being repeated. The organism learns as the result of the consequences of its own behavior. Not all changes in the environment produced by an operant behavior are reinforcers. Some of the consequences may be punishment and thereby reduce the probability of the operant behavior. Some consequences will bear no relationship to the operant act and will neither increase nor decrease the frequency of the operant behavior. Let us first turn to that class of consequences called reinforcers.

REINFORCERS

A central concept of Skinnerian behaviorism is the reinforcer or *any consequence of an operant behavior that increases the probability of the operant being repeated.* Reinforcers increase a behavior's frequency. Special note should be taken that the reinforcer is defined in terms of its success in increasing a behavior and not in *a priori* logical terms. One would imagine that anything pleasing to an organism could be a reinforcer; however, the behaviorist does not deal with "that which pleases" an organism. It may well be that something pleasing can be predicted to be a reinforcer, but it is not called a reinforcer until it achieves its goal of actually reinforcing the behavior (Skinner, 1953).

Not all consequences of behavior are reinforcing: some are punishments that act potentially to decrease the repetition of some action. The nature of punishment will be examined below; however, I note that sometimes an individual chooses a consequence for a behavior that he believes is a punishment but that will act as a reinforcer. For example, a teacher chastises a student in the hope of stopping some behavior only to find the behavior increasing rather than decreasing infrequency. It may be that this particular child wants attention and negative attention is better than no attention at all. Thus, the teacher's disapproval is actually reinforcing rather than punishing the behavior in question.

Reinforcers can be categorized in a number of ways. *Primary reinforcers,* for instance, are things like foods, water, and sex—objects or situations that reinforce without the organism having to learn their reinforcing role. These reinforcers are identical to unconditioned stimuli, which act as the reinforcers in respondent conditioning. *Secondary reinforcers* are objects or situations that acquire reinforcement value through their association with the primary reinforcers. These reinforcers are precisely the same as conditioned stimuli in respondent conditioning. Money is a secondary reinforcer; it is useless in and of itself but of value when utilized to purchase necessary primary reinforcers such as food. Individuals all over the civilized world are reinforced with money for their work.

Any organism capable of operant behavior can be taught to utilize money. Behaviorists will utilize tokens as rewards once an organism has associated them with some desired primary reinforcer. In recent years, educators and therapists have established token economies with disturbed and other handicapped children: by making the receipt of a token contingent on the demonstrating desired behavior, operant conditioning has been utilized to make significant changes in many disturbed behavior patterns.

Reinforcers can be *positive* or *negative*. Postive reinforcers are stimuli that increase the probability of a response by following the response. Negative reinforcers, on the other hand, are unpleasant stimuli whose removal from a situation increases the probability of a response. Removing a shoe and casting free a pebble or taking an aspirin to reduce or terminate a headache would be examples of negatively reinforced behaviors.

The following diagram illustrates the positive and negative reinforcers.

Positive Reinforcement

Operant Behavior		Positive Reinforcer
R	→	S⁺

In the case of positive reinforcers, the efforts of the individual have the consequence of producing something that he seeks for its positive worth or pleasure. When a reinforcer causes pleasure, physical or psychological, it is positive. For example, positive reinforcers might be good tasting food, pleasurable sex, compliments, good grades, and the like.

Negative Reinforcement

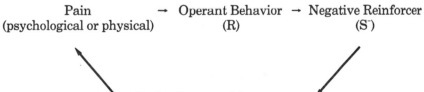

Pain	→	Operant Behavior	→	Negative Reinforcer
(psychological or physical)		(R)		(S⁻)

Reduction, avoidance, or
termination of pain

Operant conditioning with a negative reinforcer *begins* with some painful physical or psychological state. The behavior in this instance produces a lessening of the pain. The pain is negated, hence the term *negative reinforcer*. It is important to note that it is some discomfort that is reduced and not a behavior. The behavior that is successful in reducing, terminating, or avoiding the uncomfortable feeling or state is increased in frequency. (Hence we are dealing with a reinforcer.)

Behaviorists refer to the types of conditioning that utilize negative reinforcers as aversive conditioning. Avoidance conditioning (where an organism learns to avoid some pain, e.g., a child who studies to avoid an "F" grade, a worker who does his job to avoid being fired) and escape conditioning (where an organism escapes from existing pain) are both types of aversive conditioning.

A behavior can be both positively and negatively reinforced. Take, for example, an anxious teenager who drinks alcohol at a party. The drinking not only removes or reduces the anxiety (thus negatively reinforcing the activity) but elicits positive feelings as well (positively reinforcing the activity).

Schedules of Reinforcement

An important aspect of reinforcement involves its schedule. If an individual is reinforced each time an operant behavior is performed, then a *continuous* schedule of reinforcement is said to exist. It is rare that nature or people reinforce behavior on a continuous basis; for most behaviors reinforcement is *intermittent*. When an organism performs and must then wait a specified period of time for the reinforcer to occur, an *interval* schedule of reinforcement is in effect. When that organism is reinforced for a specified number of behaviors, then a *ratio* schedule is in force. Both interval and ratio schedules can be fixed or variable.

The following diagram illustrates the above and provides examples.

	Interval	*Ratio*
Fixed	salary paid on bi-weekly basis	piecework in a factory
Variable	rain for a farmer's crops	gambling, fishing

If we examine each cell in the diagram we see examples of various types of intermittent reinforcement. A worker who is paid every week or two is paid on an interval basis. Since he is paid every seven or fourteen days, the interval is fixed. He expects twenty-six or fifty-two equally spaced paychecks each year. A worker paid for piece-work gets his salary based on fixed, specific behavioral efforts. Such an individual is rewarded in a fixed ratio basis. For example, an individual may be paid for each pizza pie he bakes in a pizzeria. The more pizzas he makes the more money he earns.

Employers prefer to pay workers on a piecework basis. The individual so paid works very quickly in order to make as much money as possible. Unions try to establish an hourly or weekly wage for their members. Employees will now work up to the level of their fellow workers or at a level comfortable for them. In an interval basis the salary is no longer contingent on specific acts of productivity.

Variable interval reinforcements depend upon periods of time, but the intervals change. A farmer is rewarded with rain for his crops, but rain may arrive every day on one week and then not again for two weeks. Gambling or fishing represents a variable ratio schedule. The individual will not be rewarded unless he performs an action, but there is no way of predicting how many behaviors will be necessary to produce a consequence. One can win at a slot machine with the first drop of a coin or with the fiftieth.

B. F. Skinner believed that parents and teachers did much better using positive reinforcers and extinction to guide a child's behavior than by using punishment. It is true that punishing a child by hitting or yelling will stop a behavior rather immediately. But Skinner (1986) states that they lead to "three classical by-products of punishment: escape (truancy), counterattack (vandalism), and stubborn inaction" (p. 572). Why does punishment lead to immediate short-term gain and such severe long-term consequences?

In the long term, punishment does not teach the child the correct, desired behavior. Rewarding the child by using a positive reinforcer contingent on a carefully specified correct behavior teaches him what to do and why the behavior is correct. If a child is praised by a parent for cleaning his room (and if the parent demonstrates the proper techniques of cleaning), then the child knows exactly which behaviors are rewarded by parental approval. Punishing the child for not cleaning his room does not make clear what he has to do to avoid punishment or what he must do to be rewarded. The child is now free to decide what he must do to avoid the punishment, and may decide that cleaning his room is not it. *This brings us to an important realization concerning punishment.*

When a parent punishes a child it makes sense to demonstrate simultaneously what the child must do to be rewarded as well as to avoid the punishment. This not only gives the child a choice between the "wrong" behavior, which will be punished, and the "correct" behavior, which will be rewarded, but also guides the child's behavior once he begins to seek ways to avoid the punishment. Hence, parents and teachers discover that children often develop even worse behavioral patterns to avoid punishment and seek positive reinforcers not forthcoming from their adult punishers. For example, a child who is not rewarded by parents for cleaning his room may be rewarded by his peers with praise and approval for keeping his room even messier than it ever was before. Peer praise may be a more powerful reinforcer than parental punishment.

Self Reinforcement

Reinforcers can be set and applied to an organism's behavior by other individuals or by the environment. However, many behaviors result from actions on the organism's body that are reinforcing or by the organism's perception of the effect of its own behavior on the environment. If, for instance, a child is learning to hit a baseball, he may try many types of swings, different bats, stances, and the like. Finally, he comes upon a particular combination of bat, stance, and swing that allows for optimum success. The success can be seen as a self-created reinforcement and is likely to spawn repetition of that particular configuration of hitting the ball.

Personality can be seen as a set of behaviors resulting from both external and self-imposed reinforcements. Throughout an individual's life there may be conflicts between seeking the reinforcements of others on the one hand and achieving self-generated reinforcement on the other. The use of self-reinforcements can explain the development of normal and abnormal behavior patterns as well as the manner in which individuals successfully change their own behavior.

ADDITIONAL CONCEPTS OF IMPORTANCE

Stimulus Generalization

Once an organism has been conditioned to respond to a stimulus, there may be additional responses to stimuli similar to the originally conditioned configuration. Stimulus generalization involves the organism's confusion of one stimulus with another. A child conditioned to fear and avoid his second grade teacher might react similarly to any female teacher. Children conditioned to react with pleasure at the sight of mother will generalize their response to any female resembling mother. There is generally great difficulty predicting just which aspects of the stimulus configuration will generalize to other stimuli.

Stimulus Discrimination

If a child reacts with fear toward his second grade teacher and generalizes his response to other teachers, then he has confused aspects of the other teachers with his own. However, the child's fear response to the other teachers will not be as intense as to his own: to the degree that his fear response is less, the behaviorists assume he is able to discriminate differences between his teacher and the other teachers. Stimulus discrimination is therefore a reciprocal concept to stimulus generalization. The more generalization, the less discrimination; the more discrimination, the less generalization.

Extinction

Once conditioned, response to a stimulus is likely to disappear unless reinforced by additional associations with the primary reinforcer or unconditioned stimulus. If attacked by a dog, a child may show fear in the animal's presence, or in the presence of any dog (stimulus generalization). However, if the same child is brought repeatedly into contact with the same dog and no further attacks take place, then the fear reaction will diminish and eventually disappear.

Skinner believed that ignoring tantrums and other negative behavior in a child's (or any organism's) repertoire would eventually lead to extinction of that behavior. Extinction is more effective than punishment as a means of ridding an organism of a response because it deprives the child of a positive response rather than inflicting a negative one. In recent years, behavior therapists have created ingenious techniques to help patients rid themselves of unwanted behaviors through the use of extinction (Wolpe, 1982; Meichenbaum, 1977).

Spontaneous Recovery

After a conditioned response has been extinguished, it may, after a period of time, reappear. This phenomenon, known as "spontaneous recovery," has always raised problems for explanations of extinction. Behaviorists now suggest that extinction involves inhibition of the extinguished behavior rather than forgetting or removing the connections between stimulus and response. If the conditioned connections between stimulus and response were lost, spontaneous recovery would be impossible.

Once a spontaneously recovered response reappears it quickly becomes re-extinguished unless reinforced. The spontaneously recovered response is generally weaker than it was when first conditioned, and thus extinction can occur more quickly. Ex-smokers, ex-drinkers, and ex-drug addicts will often have spontaneously recovered desires to return to their addictions. However, these desires extinguish themselves more quickly and more easily than when these individuals first tried to deal with their habits.

Shaping

An important concept in Skinner's theory is known as "shaping." When an adult shapes the behavior of a child (or any organism) rewards are given for behavior that most closely approximates a desired response. Shaping is used when an organism lacks a particular response in its repertoire of behaviors. The shaper will continue to monitor each new set of responses by watching for behavior that is close to what is sought; such behavior will then be rewarded. Those behaviors that go unrewarded become extinguished while the reinforcers are applied to newly emerging responses that satisfy the desired criteria.

RESPONDENT AND OPERANT CONDITIONING:
VARIATIONS ON A COMMON THEME

Whenever an organism undergoes either respondent or operant conditioning, it generally goes through the other as well. A simple example will make this clear. If a rat is reinforced with food and thereby trained to press a bar, then each time the bar is pressed a pellet of food drops into the rat's dish. This is a simple case of operant conditioning using a primary, positive reinforcer.

Bar press   ⟶   Food
(operant behavior)   (positive, primary reinforcer)

Food, however, will lead to salivation, since primary reinforcers are identical to unconditioned stimuli.

Food   ⟶   Salivation
(US)   (UR)

The sight of the bar, which acts as a cue for the operant behavior, can also serve as a conditioned stimulus for the presence of food.

1) Sight of bar + Food → Salivation
     CS   →   US

2) Sight of bar → Salivation
     CS   →   CR

As the rat is pressing the bar (operant behavior) and being reinforced by the food, we see that classical conditioning is going on at the same time.

The following diagram outlines the respondent conditioning and operant conditioning going on simultaneously in the above example. It suggests that the two types of conditioning are related and, in fact, represent different elements in one overall process.

(1)	(2)	(3)	(4)
Sight of bar acts as cue for operant behavior of bar pressing	Bar pressing (operant behavior)	Acts as a positive reinforcer for bar press	
↓	←	↑	
Also acts as CS anticipating the food		→ Food →	Salivation UR
↓		↓	↓
CS		Acts as US eliciting salivation	Salivation CR

In column (1) we see that the bar acts simultaneously as a cue for bar pressing (column [2]) and as a CS for the food (column [3]) which elicits salivation (column [4]). The food (column [3]) is simultaneously a US for salivation (UR) and as a positive reinforcer for bar press (column [2]). Two types of conditioning go on simultaneously and are accomplished when the rat learns to press a bar for food and salivates at the sight of the bar.

CONDITIONING AND PERSONALITY

Using the above elements of behavior acquistion and loss, Skinner attempts to describe all human activity. Individual personalities are unique, complex bundles of responses to environmental stimuli, reinforcers, and the like. Fears and pleasures are generalized and extinguished; behaviors are reinforced, extinguished, and recovered spontaneously. Normal and abnormal behavior results from the proper and improper application of primary and secondary, positive and negative, reinforcers according to a variety of reinforcement schedules.

Skinner's view is both radical and visionary. He reshaped society according to a utopian ideal described in his book titled *Walden II* (1948). In this extremely influential volume, each individual would grow and live in a setting wherein the desired responses would be appropriately shaped by the physical environment and by the enlightened leaders of the communal village. Just how these enlightened leaders would emerge, or who would select the desired responses, and according to what value system, is not clarified.

What is clear is that Skinner sees such a utopian society as the only alternative to the chaotic civilization in which we presently live and in which our reinforcers are applied willy-nilly without regard for the effect they ultimately have.

COGNITIVE AND SOCIAL BEHAVIORISM

Skinner's behavioral theories have undergone substantial modification in recent years by a number of psychologists who might be called Stimulus-Organism-Response (S-O-R) theorists. Variables within the organism, such as cognition and affect, are seen as increasingly indispensible if behaviorism is to survive and not be bypassed by the main forces of psychology. While remaining true to the basic concepts of reinforcement and the primacy of the environment, S-O-R psychologists deal mainly with human subjects, both normal and pathological, and eschew simpler models that derive from the study of rats and pigeons.

Cognitive psychologists (as well as scientists of other theoretical persuasions) experience a dilemma in dealing with Skinner's ideas. For many scientists, avoiding all mention of internal psychological states and experimental variables is impossible. To simply operationalize all psychological states in objective terms violates the organism. Hunger must be defined in cognitive and affective terms and not merely in the number of hours for which food has been deprived. Other examples of problems created by maintaining a purely objective, quantifiable view of the organism are revealed if we examine the conditioning process.

If an individual is conditioned to blink at the sound of a buzzer, then it is clear, at least with human subjects, that the individual anticipates the buzzer. Anticipation is a cognitive variable, not a behavioral one, and for a number of cognitive behaviorists, it is a key concept. Another example can involve negative reinforcement defined as the removal of an unpleasant stimulus. A stimulus (out there) cannot be defined as unpleasant unless it arouses some physical or psychological pain (in here). What the subject seeks to remove is not only the stimulus, but the discomfort it causes. There ia no real way to avoid some subjective, affective variables in the description of behavioristic concepts.

In the pages that follow I will present a number of concepts developed by Albert Bandura (1977), Julian Rotter (1966, 1975), Aaron Beck (1978), and Donald Meichenbaum (1977), the leading advocates for modification of Skinnerian behaviorism. These concepts and modifications, taken together, represent what could be considered the return of subjectivity to American behaviorism, and what is called part of the cognitive revolution in modern psychology.

Modelling and Vicarious Learning

Albert Bandura (1977) has suggested that individuals learn not only when their behavior is reinforced but also when they watch the behavior of others. Bandura called this "observational learning." Throughout life, but especially in childhood, youngsters learn by watching and imitating adults and other figures called models. Bandura's research has shown that aggressive behavior can be increased if children watch behavior models act aggressively. The increase in aggression occurs whether the models are live, on television, or on a movie screen. His work suggests to Bandura that, in a complex media-dominated culture, children are exposed to many behavior models in addition to their immediate parents, family, and teachers. Many people feel that the wrong models are often available to children via the media, with serious consequences to society and the individual.

Numerous factors related to the characteristics of both the model and the observer tend to affect vicarious learning. Bandura (1977) has reported that children learn from live models more often than from cartoon figures. The model's age and sex relative to the learner are important, as are the factors of relative social status and prestige. Simple behaviors are more easily imitated than complex ones. Individuals who are low in self-esteem tend to be influenced by those with high self-esteem.

Bandura points out that factors which aid in the observers paying attention to the model increase the probability that the model's behavior will become the basis of the observer's behavior. A model with charisma, sex appeal, or glamor catches the attention of observers more often than behavioral models who lack these characteristics. The ability or willingness of the observer to pay attention to the model are affected by his state of arousal, his age, his sex, his cultural and family background, and a plethora of other variables.

Learning from models involves the critical variables of incentive and motivational processes. Individuals learn best when they believe that imitation carries with it some reinforcement value. Children, for example, will imitate parents in a desire to please them and receive both love and nurturing. Some people may choose to imitate those individuals whose behaviors are considered successful, especially when success is sought in a similar field of endeavor. Once again it is beyond the scope of our current discussion to address the hundreds of motivational variables that would make one individual an attractive behavior model to another.

Expectancy

One of the key concepts introduced by Julian Rotter and other cognitive behaviorists is that of expectancy, which refers to an individual's belief that if he or she behaves in a given way, in a given situation, a predictable reinforcement will follow. The individual learns to anticipate the reinforcers that follow from his behavior. The behavior then becomes affected by merely anticipating the reinforcer, affected to a degree sometimes surpassing the actual effect of the reinforcer itself. The cognitive theorist often studies human personality with the intent of discovering individual differences, normal and pathological, in the anticipation of reinforcement.

Rotter and others point out that an individual's expectancies are based on the history of his previous reinforcements. The individual expects from his future what he has known in his past. Similarly, the manner in which an individual generalizes his past will determine his predictions of the future. A child who is consistently given affection by his parents often grows up believing that people in general will continue to reward his behavior with positive emotional responses. The abused child will act in a similar though negative manner: he behaves toward others with an expectation of continued cruelty.

Rotter and other like-minded theorists also posit a broader range of motivations than do the Skinnerians, although the assumption is still made that all motives are learned. Rotter specifically suggests six categories of needs: recognition-status, protection-dependency, dominance, independence, love and affection, and physical comfort. The goals that an individual seeks and the manner with which expectancies are developed depend upon the particular arrangement of that individual's needs. The value of a goal is determined by the need it is intended to satisfy.

One of Rotter's enduring contributions to psychological theory and research involves the idea of *internal* versus *external* locus of control. Developed with E. Jerry Phares (1976), the "focus-of-control" concept expresses a cognitive relationship between the individual and the manner in which he seeks to reach his goals, or reinforcers. Persons with an internal focus of control believe that the reinforcers they seek are reachable through their own efforts, while individuals with an external focus of control tend to believe that if they realize their goals, it has more to do with luck, fate, the intervention of other people or God, and the like. Much research has been done on the many behavioral differences resulting from differing loci of control.

Clinical Cognitive Behaviorism

Aaron Beck (1967), Donald Meichenbaum (1977), Albert Ellis (1974), Frank Seligman (1975), Arnold Lazarus (1968) and others have extended the behaviorist position into the realm of psychopathology. Their central thesis is that mental illness involves pathological forms of reinforcement expectancies. Beck believes that depression results from an individual's view that the important reinforcers in life are beyond his control and are thus unobtainable. Seligman has called this concept "learned helplessness" (1975) and agrees with Beck that it is at the core of the hopeless attitude found in depressed patients. Whenever individuals feel overly responsible or too helpless in pursuing important need satisfaction, affective pathologies can result.

Meichenbaum, Ellis, and their behaviorist colleagues speak of the "irrational" views of the future found in anxious patients. Individuals who "catastrophize" their future, who perceive the future in gloomy, terrifying ways, without proof that such events will occur, are prone to anxiety, which can often lead to panic. Anticipatory anxiety, often based on past traumas, can make life miserable for an individual who becomes frozen in the present for fear of the future.

The more an individual anticipates that others will behave like behavior figures from his past, the less chance he has to find out how different they may be. By behaving toward the future as if it were a mirror of the past, the individual keeps reinforcing the cognitive assumptions that create difficulty for him. Not only does a self-confirming hypothesis create a vicious cycle, but the reinforcement values of the new persons are lost. When an individual seeks to escape from imaginary fears, the behavioral patterns involved in the escape are negatively reinforced. Many of these negative and positive cycles of reinforcement will be described later in chapter 7.

Cognitive-behavioral clinicians have developed ingenious techniques for reconditioning irrational thought mechanisms. Control of phobias, depressions, generalized anxiety, and obsessive-compulsive disorders is achieved by helping the patient reintergrate his relationship to important reinforcers. Even radical behaviorists and psychoanalysts find themselves utilizing cognitive-behavioral techniques in what is clearly a rapprochement in a very splintered field of endeavor.

SUMMARY

Cognitive and social behaviorism have been true revolutionaries with regard to traditional behaviorism. Perhaps this is most easily seen in Rotter's concept of the psychological situation. Rotter makes clear that a stimulus has no real meaning unless it has psychological status: Internal cognitive and affective variables, often reflecting an individual's entire psychological social history, establish the meaning of a stimulus. The uniqueness of the individual is found not only in his conditioning history but in the personal meaning that history has produced in his cognitive structures. Rotter's concept clearly borders on the phenomenological, a position that was at one time most distasteful to the behaviorist.

The behaviorist's embrace of cognition comes at the same moment in history when individuals in other fields are doing the same. Irving Bieber has written a description of *Cognitive Psychoanalysis* (1980) in which he disagrees with the notion that anxiety results from unconsciously repressed wishes. Instead, he suggests that irrational thought forms, which comprise the individual's consciousness and guide his view of the world, create anxiety. Bieber spends half an introductory chapter trying to defend the position that his theory is closer to Freud's than to Beck's. In my opinion he is only partially correct. The development of cognitive behaviorism and cognitive psychoanalysis offer a promising area of compromise between two historically hostile theories.

I will now turn to a description of "third force" psychologies representing the humanistic-existential schools of thought. The humanists are perhaps diametrically opposed to behaviorism, which stresses a deterministic view of behavior contingent upon environmental influences. As will be seen, the humanists interpret human beings as capable of choice, of transcending environmental influences, and of being motivated by internal, not external factors. Add to these fundamentally different viewpoints very disparate language systems used to describe behavior and one begins to understand the animosity between these schools.

5

Humanistic-Existential Perspectives

GENERAL CONSIDERATIONS

The humanistic school of personality theory is known as psychology's third force because the ideas developed here stand in critical opposition to behaviorism and psychoanalysis, psychology's first two forces. Humanists criticize their theoretical adversaries on a number of important points; for example, they oppose the view of basic human nature inherent in psychoanalysis and behaviorism. The humanists go further by trying to describe those qualities and aspects of human personality that are unique to human beings.

The humanistic criticisms of psychoanalysis are many and varied. The *ego* of the individual represents that which is healthy in a human being. In Freudian psychology it is a weak, miserable entity that gains strength through wily deceptions of the *id*. The *ego* seeks survival and all the while is harassed by an irrational *superego*. Humanists consider the Freudian view pessimistic and unrealistic. But most importantly, they claim human beings are not fully human if all they seek is their own survival; gratification and survival is totally congruent with animal behavior. Human beings are more than animals.

The objections to behaviorism are similar but often more strident than those lodged against psychoanalysis. Behaviorists utilize a model of humanity that is extrapolated from principles developed using rats and pigeons, a model that conceptualizes people as little more than complicated robots. The vast oversimplifications created by the behaviorists cannot visualize humanity as creative, capable of love, or able to behave in other ways that characterize a fully developed human being. Let us now turn to the basic concepts of the humanistic-existential school.

The ideas of four major theorists will be stressed: Erich Fromm, the rebel psychoanalyst who, along with Rollo May, is closer to humanism and existentialism than to psychoanalysis, and Abraham Maslow and Carl Rogers, two American born and educated psychologists who epitomize the humanistic movement. While differences exist between these theorists, they are matters of emphasis rather than substance. Taken together the humanist-existentialists form a consistent tapestry descriptive of humanity.

GROWTH AS A BASIC MOTIVE

All humanist-existentialists identify and focus upon a basic innate desire in each human being to grow and fulfill his human potential. They do not deny that human beings possess destructive capabilities and share basic needs in common with animals. Freud's "id" is not alien to the third force psychologists. It is just that as basic as the *id* is to the human motivational system so is the need to grow and develop one's potential. Both Rogers and Maslow refer to the development of full human potential as "self-actualization."

It is important to understand that, according to the humanists, the failure to self-actualize is not merely failure to fulfill potential but to demonstrate the most basic of human pathology. Later in this chapter I shall discuss the humanist's viewpoint on the etiology and consequences of fixation in human functioning. Failure to satisfy the basic need of growth is to the humanist as serious as the failure to satisfy any basic need such as hunger, sex, or even the need to survive. In healthy human beings the need to actualize can transcend the need to survive: to actualize is to be human, and to be human is to matter, to count, to feel, and to exist.

The Heirarchy of Needs

Maslow's (1968) most famous contribution to psychology is the heirarchy of needs, in which he describes the emergence of the need to self-actualize. Maslow considers the need to become human "instinctoid," thus emphasizing its innate characteristics. His theory suggests that in order to develop the specific human needs one must take for granted the satisfaction of the lower needs, those we share with other creatures. The following describes the entire need hierarchy:

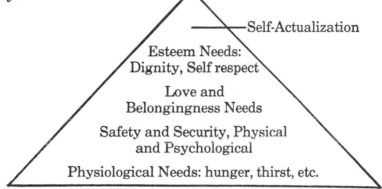

At the base of the pyramid are physiological needs such as hunger, thirst, sex, and others, which operate in much the same way as Freud described the functioning of the *id,* although Maslow feels that their full satisfaction is requisite for further psychological development. If the individual's environment does not provide complete need satisfaction, then the person becomes fixated and will remain concerned with satisfying basic needs. If, however, the individual can take need satisfaction for granted, then the innate needs are able to fulfill themselves and the next level of needs can emerge.

The second level of needs focuses on safety and security. Like the physiological needs, these demands for satisfaction are preemptive: unless and until each child feels safe and secure, both physically and psychologically, no further development takes place. But if the child is provided a loving, stable, nurturing physical and social environment, then the next level of needs—and with them psychological develpment—is encountered.

The third level of needs brings with it the craving for love and belongingness. These needs are significant because in them is found the first seeking out of others as people. At this juncture another important Maslowian concept can be introduced. The basic physiological needs, as well as the need for security, and the initial need for love are what he calls "deficit needs." Here the individual hungers for others to give him something, but there is no awareness that he should give to others or that they have needs too.

With the emergence of the need to be loved and to belong we see the earliest manifestation of the *meta-needs,* which are higher-order needs: the need to share with and recognize the existence of others. Meta-needs are uniquely human and, without their development, full human potential cannot occur. Such higher-order needs transcend those of the lower order but disappear in the face of unmet lower-order needs. In short, the higher-order needs have little meaning to an individual with an empty stomach.

The need for love represents a psychological turning point for the human being who is becoming truly human. Much has been written over the centuries about the importance of love to the human condition. In one of Erich Fromm's (1956) most powerful books, *The Art of Loving,* he differentiates between various types of love, including brotherly love, sexual love, mother-child love, and others. The healing and redemptive powers of love are described. One of Fromm's most important distinctions involves the difference between "narcissistic" and "productive" love.

Narcissistic love is deficit love; it is the love of the person for himself in the face of feelings of emptiness and having been loved too little. The infant's love is narcissitic: he demands and mother gives. Mother's love, on the other hand, is often productive love; here the needs of the other can transcend the needs of the self. It is precisely when an individual loves another that he finds himself becoming a genuine human being and begins to fulfill his human potential. Life can be its most meaningful in the act of love.

The next level of needs involves esteem, dignity, and respect. Once a developing human being experiences genuine esteem and dignity his psychological development transcends lower needs. Throughout history human beings have fought and died for their dignity and self worth, ignoring all of the lower needs and even the need for survival. Again, when people stand up for principles of human dignity they do what no animal can do, and they demonstrate their unique human qualities.

Maslow's final level describes the emergence of the need to self-actualize, or to become what Rogers calls the "fully functioning individual." Maslow believed that full self-actualization is impossible—no one can be fully developed. He believed that one would have to be at least fifty-five years old and have overcome a lifetime of struggles in order to demonstrate any self-actualized qualities; and less than one percent of humanity actually demonstrates them. In order to become actualized the individual had to satisfy those needs that are uniquely human.

Erich Fromm describes five such uniquely human needs, which he believed must be satisfied if we are to become full human beings:

The Need for Relatedness. Each individual must find a way to live with other human beings. Humanists cannot conceive of a healthy individual being a social isolate or living with hostile, destructive relationships. Mature, productive love is the flowering of the need for relatedness.

The Need for Transcendence. It is expressed in the human desires for dignity, purpose, meaning, privacy, creativity, and introspection. Each of these wishes demonstrates a difference between ourselves and the animals. While we cannot forget we are animals, we cannot be human unless we rise above the behavioral and psychological level of animals.

The Need for Rootedness. Each individual requires a knowledge of his cultural and historical roots. The child reveals a fascination when learning about his parents' background and history; he requires knowledge about their ethnic, religious, and nationalistic origins, as well as the folkways, morals, and customs of their immediate and more distant ancestors.

The Need for Identity. An individual must develop an awareness of who he or she is in more personal terms as well. Identity is sought in terms of social, vocational, sexual, religious, and leisure roles. The roles that "feel" correct and express the essential personality are sought, as well as behavioral patterns that help the individual achieve self-esteem, pride, and self-worth.

The Need for a Frame of Orientation and Devotion. People must develop a value system that allows them a vantage point from which they can evaluate the morality of their behavior and that of others. They must possess information to understand events in cultural and historical perpective, to comprehend themselves within a timeline in terms of past, present, and future. Each person needs to evaluate issues related to life, death, and the infinite.

THE ETIOLOGY AND CONSEQUENCES
OF FAILED DEVELOPMENT

Very few individuals become self-actualized or are fully functioning. There are a number of reasons suggested by the humanist-existential theorists for the fixation that prevents development.

Lack of Nurturing

Built into Maslow's need hierarchy is one of the main reasons for failed growth: the lack of a nurturing environment is a general cause of an individual's failure to satisfy one set of needs and move on to the next actualization level. An environment that will not satisfy a child's physical hunger or fails to permit a child to feel safe and secure is one that will produce a failure of development. A child who is concerned with hunger or fear will seek to develop skills and means the to reduce those affective states. Such a child will not be concerned with love, self-worth, dignity, or creativity. The humanists often cast society into a villainous role with respect to failures of growth.

The Phenomenal Self

Carl Rogers (1961) believed that, in order to grow, both the individual's family and the society have to provide "unconditional positive regard," otherwise fixations of development will occur. If a person is raised in an atmosphere of love and positive regard, if his essential individuality is acceptable to significant others, then the individual can accept his "real self." The real self contains weaknesses as well as strengths, negative emotions as well as positive ones.

Rogers points out that society often raises children under "conditions of worth." The child is told directly, or more likely indirectly, that he possesses qualities that are unacceptable for the continuance of love. The child may be told that he is not the right sex, not bright enough, not quick enough, not athletic or ingenious or talented enough, and so on. The youngster feels loved, yet his real self is unacceptable to those who love him. He wants and needs to live up to outside demands made upon him, but he cannot. As a result of this pressure and his efforts to deal with it, the child begins to distort his experienced self-image, his phenomenal self. In a healthy individual this phenomenal self will be congruent with the real self; but when a child defensively distorts his self-image to meet conditions of worth, the phenomenal self becomes more and more inconsistent with the real self. At the point at which the individual is no longer in contact with weaknesses, negative emotions, and the like, growth necessarily stops and movement toward the fully functioning person is halted.

Horney's self-theory is very similar to that of Rogers, whose phenomenal self is identical to Horney's idealized-self. The way they describe the dynamics of such an individual and the mechanism of his functioning are remarkably similar. In both instances they describe a person cut off from self-correcting criticisms, intimate relationships, new experiences, and all those situations of pain and pleasure that stimulate growth.

Escape from Freedom and Responsibility

Perhaps Erich Fromm's most significant contribution to psychology is his 1943 book, *Escape From Freedom*. In it he suggests that human beings are driven by contradictory desires: on the one hand is the desire to individuate and be free, on the other is the desire to be safe and to avoid responsibility. It is Fromm's contention that when individuals become part of a mass movement and seek a charismatic leader, such as the German people did with Nazism and Hitler during World War II, they do so as a defense against individuation and freedom.

Fromm believes that humanity is shaped by historical-social forces. During the Middle Ages, for example, each individual felt himself to be part of a divinely ordained structure, part of the whole of society, part of the universe itself. The Earth was the center of the universe with each living creature occupying a divinely created place and living out a predetermined role. Life and death had meaning and purpose. The pain of life had to be borne as there was no alternative to it; however, a reward waited at the end of life for those who suffered in this world.

As history progressed, as economic and educational growth took place, societies and philosophies changed. A significant result of this change was the development of individual consciousness. Each person could see himself as able to achieve more in life than society allotted to him. The individual's sense of worth increased and he was less willing to accept poverty, lack of opportunity, political helplessness and the like. Revolutions such as those in France and America overthrew not only kings but the philosophy of divine right as well.

However, each increase in consciousness and freedom carried with it a dark side: With increased individuality came decreased feelings of safety. Individuals could no longer feel the safety of God's power as manifested in the place He had created in the world for them. The divinely sanctioned king was no longer firmly and securely ensconsed at the head of society. Like a child who yearns for independence from his parents only to become frightened by his freedom, individuated humanity was to recoil in fear.

With increases in freedom come increases in responsibility: The cost of freedom is often very high, and increased conscious awareness instill feelings of alienation and loneliness never before experienced. An individual who suddenly has his own apartment not only has the freedom that it provides but the responsibilities for its maintenance and upkeep, as well as the loneliness that living on one's own entails. Societies of individuated people often become overwhelmed by responsibility, alienation, and loneliness; they seek the safety of the dictator—that supraordinary parent figure.

One of the most frightening aspects of individuation and freedom, one that individuals seek to escape from, is the awareness that purpose and meaning are not given at birth by higher authorities ·but must be developed and fostered. Fromm's writing reflects a theme found in all existential philosophy: There is no meaning to life except that which people bring to it. Often meaning can only be found in suffering and in accepting the terrible burdens of responsibility.

The Denial of Death, and Meaninglessness

Ernst Becker (1974) castigates Freud for seeing sex and its repression as the primary mental disturbance, which Becker believes is a representation of Freud's fear of, and failure to come to grips with, death. In the final analysis, it is death and nonbeing that the existentialist sees as the ultimate causes of defense. Fear of death ultimately causes fixation and failure to grow. For precisely this reason, it is death from which we wish to escape. At the core of existential philosophy is the notion that the need for security, power, perfection, and dictatorship is more a function of awareness of human finitude than it is fear of rejection, insecurity, isolation, loneliness, repressed sexuality, anxiety, and inferiority. From the moment an individual develops the conscious knowledge that he is going to die he seeks ways to defeat death. As with all irrational solutions, efforts to defend against this fact make life intolerable. The existential quagmire is the condition in which the individual's fear of death makes him fearful of life as well.

Hiding from life's dangers, suggests the existentialist, also means hiding from its opportunities. Joy comes to those who are willing to risk sadness. One allows love only if one risks rejection and ultimately the loss of the love object. If being hurt cannot be tolerated, then one cannot accept the kind ministrations of the other. People have no choice, suggests Rollo May; one must either live life to the fullest, with all the risks and pain inherent in that living, or exist in a meaningless, purposeless limbo. In the final analysis, all of humankind's protests and defenses against death will be for nought—in the end there is always the reality of death.

The denial of death often leads to the creation of religious fantasies that glorify death and deny the pleasure of living life, to psychic numbing (Lifton, 1979), and to constrictions of consciousness. In the final analysis, denying death means denying life, and leads to the most serious distortion in human behavior. In order to overcome the meaninglessness and alienation created when one tries to hide from human vulnerability, some people will engage in bizarre acts in order to feel something—anything. The sociopathic killer may perpetrate the most heinous crimes in order to be somebody.

Freud conceptualized anxiety as a signal that the *ego* was in imminent danger due to repressed and forbidden drives. The existentialists see anxiety as an indicator that we have not accepted the responsibilities of life and growth; they have chosen to diminish their human qualities and are hiding from the full range of experiences that life presents. Attacks of anxiety may find people attempting to flee from unavoidable suffering in life. They reject freedom, responsibility, creativity, and self-actualization. They are most anxious when they become nothing.

CHOICE AND COURAGE

Erich Fromm describes two kinds of freedom: freedom from and freedom to. "Freedom from" want, pain, and persecution is often what

individuals mean by *freedom*. The appeal of the dictator is sometimes viewed as a promise of freedom from hunger, inflation, social
instability, and the like. "Freedom to" involves choosing the responsibilities that engage life. One of the central concepts of humanistic-existential theorists is that people *do* have a choice at each
moment in life. The third force theorists oppose the determinism of
psychoanalysis and behaviorism. Even when life treats a person
unkindly he can choose how or whether to deal with and accept the
misfortune. Each of us is captain of his ship and master of his fate.

Choosing to grow, to accept responsibilities and burdens, and to
be fully human in the face of adversity requires courage. Existential
anxiety is created when an individual chooses to deny his responsibilities, which represents the failure of courage. Throughout existential writings one finds ideas concerning the courage to live, to grow,
to love, and to create (May, 1981). Existentialists have used the
concepts of choice and courage to resolve some of the thorniest problems confronting any student of psychology and philosophy. The
existentialist asks: How does one know if someone cannot or will not
do something? Existentialists feel that without choice people are not
human beings and for theorists to assume one cannot choose is to
create an image of humanity that is not human. How does one know
when an individual is capable of choosing? Why do some people
develop courage and others do not? Do sick people choose not to
develop courage? Where does courage come from? These are all
problems left unresolved by most existential theorists and, as such,
they create some serious problems for humanism-existentialism.

Perhaps the most serious problem the third force poses for many
psychologists and psychotherapists is the almost inescapable sense
that those with courage, those who self-actualize and become fully
functioning, are morally superior to those who do not. If, after all,
life is our own choice, then we chose our faults and lacks just as we
choose our benefits and advantages. Who but the morally deficient
would choose such narrow lives?

Behaviorism creates the extreme view that people are all victims
of their environment: the strong and the successful cannot take
pride in their achievements, and the weak need not bear the guilt of
their failures. Psychoanalysis makes the strong successful for irrational reasons while the sick and helpless are victims of their child-
hoods and unconscious impulses. Existentialism allows the strong to
feel pride in their accomplishments while the sick and the weak

must bear the guilt of existential cowardice. How is this quagmire to be resolved?

THE ENVIRONMENT

Psychoanalysts stress the family, particularly mother, as the environmental force most important to a child's development. Humanists, on the other hand, tend to stress the developmental role played by economic and political forces in society. The family is shaped by societal forces and in turn transmits these values to the child. It is the crucible of development reflecting the religious, political, and economic factors operating at a particular historical moment.

Fromm described character types that were similar to Freudian or Horneyan desciptions. Fromm's receptive, hoarding, and exploitative types paralleled Freud's oral, anal, and phallic personalities or Horney's tendencies to move toward, away from, or against people. However, Fromm's description of the marketing character type broke new ground in utilizing societal trends as formative aspects of personality. The marketing type thinks of himself, in response to the demands of others, like a shiny new pair of shoes to be sold in the marketplace. Fromm saw many individuals dress, groom, and act with a mind toward pleasing employers rather than satisfying their own aesthetic sense or principles.

Fromm believed that capitalism created various competitive stresses that twisted human development. A form of communal socialism ultimately had to replace capitalism if human beings were to develop into healthy individuals. The child would not be raised to love in a productive way so long as it was in a society that lacked justice and humane values.

The existentialists stressed the idea that each individual exists in three simultaneous worlds, all of which interact and thereby shape one another. The *eigenwelt* is the inner world of fantasy and self recognition. The *mitwelt* is the world of the family, close friends, and other social beings who are important to the individual. Finally, the *umvelt* is the outer social world made up of religious, political, and economic forces. None of these worlds can be ignored if one is to explain the individual personality.

Many existential writers describe the effects of war and the arms race on individual personality, something generally ignored

by theorists who focus on the family, mother, or intrapsychic factors. Lifton (1979), for example, describes the "psychic numbing"
that has invaded contemporary society as a result of the nuclear
arms race. Individuals feel powerless, defenseless, and unimportant
in the face of the arms build up. Moreover, the reality that human
history could end in a nuclear exchange has made individuals lose
faith in their own and in posterity's continuity. All of these consequences dehumanize the individual and create excessive anxiety.
In the absence of any real ability to cope, the individual becomes
numb, or psychically dead.

Existentialists point to the distortions in human expression that
are utilized to overcome psychic numbness. Individuals escape into
drugs, bizarre sexual and aggressive rituals, cult religions and even
suicide. Some people desparately buy all the materialistic items they
can in an attempt to feel human. In general the twentieth century
has seen a terrible loss of humanistic and traditional values as
nihilistic, live-for-the-moment philosophies arise in response to societal madness.

THE HEALTHY PERSONALITY

The humanistic-existentialist axis defines the healthy personality
in positive terms. Unlike the behaviorists, who define neither the
healthy nor the unhealthy personality, or the analysts for whom
health is survival and the absence of pathology, the humanists
clearly articulate the healthy personality. Fromm refers to the "productive orientation"; Maslow to the "self-actualized" individual; and
Rogers speaks of the "fully functioning personality." They each
draw from a general pool of characteristics in their descriptions. Let
us turn now to some of these characteristics:

1. *Efficient perception or acceptance of reality.* The
healthy individual perceives and accepts both positive and
negative aspects of the environment.

2. *Acceptance of oneself and others.* Positive and negative
characteristics in oneself or in others are not looked down upon
or idealized but noted as human and accepted as such.

3. *Spontaniety in expression of affect and naturalness of*

behavior. One is oneself with few airs or defenses in evidence. Carl Rogers believes that individuals get beyond social "masks."

4. *Problem orientation.* Self-involvement gives way to concern for others and to the problems that life presents. Such problems are approached wholeheartedly and joyfully.

5. *Autonomy and independence.* The healthy individual needs and wants others but can stand on his own feet when necessary.

6. *Need for privacy and detachment.* While each individual wants to be with others, the healthy individual enjoys and is comfortable with being alone at times.

7. *A freshness of appreciation.* The beauty and variety found in people, nature, art, and other expressive outlets are appreciated and that appreciation is retained. There is no arrogant or jaded quality in the healthy individual.

8. *The peak experience.* Maslow in particular utilized a concept similar to one found in eastern religions such as Zen Buddhism. To find oneself one must lose oneself. To live fully and experience the beauty of the world (as well as its ugliness) one must emerse oneself directly in the world. One must pay attention to the stimuli creating the beauty and not to the self as it experiences the stimuli. If an individual listens to a piece of music and is aware that he is listening then he cannot fully appreciate the music. In order to fully experience the pleasure of the music he must give up the consciousness of experiencing (lose his self or awareness of self) and experience the music directly. As he becomes emersed in the music (or whatever situation he finds himself in) he has a peak experience, and by finding the world he finds himself in the fullest sense of the word.

9. *Brotherly love or* gemeinschaftsgefuhl. Maslow borrowed this concept from Alfred Adler.

10. *Intimacy and productive love as the hallmark of interpersonal relationships.*

11. *A nonhostile sense of humor.* This involves the philosophical ability to laugh at life's absurdities but not at other

people. The healthy person laughs *with others,* not *at* them.

12. *Avoidance of conformity.* Fromm believed that the poorly developed personality uses "automation conformity" as a defense against freedom and negative affect. The healthy personality "transcends" culture, becoming part of it but not slavish, chauvinistic, or jingoistic.

13. *Integrity.* The healthy individual lives according to self-accepted values and principles.

I have now finished brief sketches of what I believe to be the main forces in personality theory today: psychoanalysis, behaviorism and humanism-existentialism. Each utilizes a language system different from the others. Each seems to deal with different aspects of human behavior as seen from a different perspective. Yet each is derived from descriptions of the same creature, the human being. I will now turn to a description of a number of other important, although more individualistic theories of personality and then discuss a number of factors that can be used to evaluate all of these differing conceptions of human behavior.

6

Additional Theories of Importance

GENERAL CONSIDERATIONS

Several more theories have played important roles in the general study of personality or in the clinical sphere, but they are not easily classified under the umbrella of psychoanalysis, behaviorism, or humanism. In this chapter we shall take a brief look at the work of George Kelly and Harry Stack Sullivan. Students of Sullivan may well object that their mentor was denied a place in our previous chapter on psychoanalysis. Sullivan considered his interpersonal theory of psychiatry to be psychoanalytic; however, his concepts—a collection of ideas rather than a systematic theory—fit well within the cognitive-behaviorist camp and relate as well to systemic theorists such as K. Lewin. Finally, we will briefly examine the role that biology plays in the development of personality.

GEORGE KELLY AND PERSONAL CONSTRUCTS

George Kelly (1951) calls his view of personality the theory of personal constructs, wherein he criticizes psychology for viewing psychologists in a different light than their human subjects. The scientific psychologist, he points out, seeks to explain and predict human behavior through observation and the development of theory. Theories are constructed to explain the relationships and to predict the performance of that which comprises the subject of the theory. All human beings experience wonder and make conclusions, just as scientists do. The central human activity is being scientific.

Kelly objected to seeing human beings described by psychologists "as pushed mindlessly by drives or pulled robot-like by external stimuli." Each person is motivated by a natural desire to know about his or her world and, in so doing, learn to explain and predict real events. The scientist is just an individual who has learned how to create more effective theories than the average citizen. Each individual develops a view of reality and observes the world through the "templates" or if you will, the "lenses" of his theoretical constructions.

If the human personality is made up of individual reality constructions, then it can be described by utilizing the same concepts that describe theories. Thus we find in Kelly's descriptions of human personality such concepts as *postulate* and *corollary,* words that are generally used in the description of scientific theories. Kelly believed that all human motivation, as well as normal and abnormal behavior, could be understood from the descriptions of a person's reality constructions. Let us examine Kelly's ideas concerning the nature of personal theories.

Constructive Alternativism

A basic idea in Kelly's theory is that an individual need not have a fixed view of reality; individual theories of reality are constantly open to revision as those who hold them age and undergo new experiences. In fact, an individual who is unable to revise his theories is often considered pathological. For most people, personality is comprised of a growing number of constantly revised constructs. He utilizes a fundamental postulate and eleven corollaries to describe the function, purpose, and individual differences in the person's construction or theory of reality.

> FUNDAMENTAL POSTULATE: A person's processes are psychologically channeled by the ways in which he anticipates events.

Here we find an idea very similar to the cognitive-behaviorists who focus on anticipation or prediction as the central issue of human personality.

Eleven Corollaries

These evolve from and build upon the fundamental postulate.

1. *Construction Corollary.* "A person anticipates events by construing their replication." This is the identical concept found in the work of the behaviorists: one predicts the future based on past experiences.

2. *Individuality Corollary.* "Persons differ from each other in their construction of events."

3. *Organization Corollary.* "Each person characteristically evolves, for his convenience in anticipating events, a construction system embracing ordinal relationships between constructs." Each individual's construct exists in a hierachy according to some value system.

4. *Dichotomy Corollary.* "A person's construction system is composed of a finite number of dichotomous constructs." Each idea or description of reality exists as part of a continuum bound by polar opposites. "High" makes no sense without "low," "light" requires the concept of "dark," "good" is compared to "bad," and so on with each concept.

5. *Choice Corollary.* "A person chooses for himself the alternative in a dichotomized construct through which he anticipates the greater possibility for extension and definition of his system." Each individual chooses the alternative he believes will work best. A basic choice described by Kelly was between "security" and "adventure."

6. *Range Corollary.* "A construct is convenient for the anticipation of a finite range of events only."

7. *Experience Corollary.* "A person's construction system varies as he successfully construes the replication of events." If events predict the future well, they are retained; if not, they must be revised.

8. *Modulation Corollary.* "The variation in a person's construction system is limited by the *permeability* of the constructs within whose range of convenience the variant exists."

This describes how open an individual's constructs are to his experiences.

9. *Fragmentation Corollary.* "A person may successfully employ a variety of incompatible construction subsystems."

10. *Commonality Corollary.* "To the extent that one person employs a construction of experience that is similar to a system employed by another, his psychological processes are similar to those of the other person."

11. *Sociality Corollary.* "To the extent that one person construes the construction processes of another, he may play a role in a social process involving the other person."

The latter two corollaries allow Kelly to extend his notions into the area of social relationships.

A final note on Kelly: Any individual at any given moment sees the world through his personal constructions of that world. His theory has been shaped by experiences of reality as he has construed it. Therefore, while a personal world view is in fact a theory, the individual utilizing that world view has no other way of seeing the world and therefore does not know about the theoretical nature of his viewpoint. Each human being has no choice but to experience the world in his own way, through his own lenses and *as the truth.* Doubting one's personal construction of the world leads to profound mental changes, great growth, or psychological breakdown and pathology.

HARRY STACK SULLIVAN

Interpersonal Psychiatry

Sullivan (1953) is as iconoclastic among psychoanalytic theorists as Kelly is among American psychologists. His basic theory is referred to as the interpersonal theory of psychiatry. Kelly believed that intrapsychic personality* was a myth. Instead, personality is a

---

* Freud's theory creates a view of personality as intrapsychic. The important mechanisms controlling behavior are contained "within" the individual. Behavior is

function of interpersonal relationships both in historical development and current functioning. Sullivan's idea is revolutionary in an analytic world dominated by concepts of intrapsychic relationships, a world that places him closer to Lewin (1938) and the field theorists than to Freud. It also makes Sullivan the spiritual father to those therapists, such as C. R. Whittaker (1976) and Salvador Minuchin (1974), who represent family therapy and the view that pathology reflects familial relationships and tensions rather than intrapsychic disequilibrium.

According to Sullivan, individuals only know one another as functions of their personality's impact. Personality is an open system (not closed as proposed by more traditional analysts) and constantly affected by interpersonal relationships. Thus, any time individuals interact they are helping to create the personality of others at the moment of interaction. Sullivan saw the therapist as a "participant-observer." Being an observer and at the same time objective and aloof is impossible since the very act of speaking to another person changes that other's personality. Sullivan's ideas are clearly related to the Heisenberg uncertainty principle* (Zukov, 1979), which states that the very act of trying to measure the speed and location of atomic particles changes their speed and location.

Were Sullivan to have remained true to his interpersonal principle, he would have not been able to ascribe a structure to personality. This would have placed him in the camp of the situationists of today, who believe that personality is a function of environmental effects on the individual. Sullivan does posit a dynamic sort of

---

largely determined by the interrelationships of *id, ego,* and *superego.* Moreover, the Freudian model creates an intrapsychic view of personality that is largely a closed system. The conflicts within the personality are established by biological forces and interactions with the environment occurring before the age of five. In the Freudian view, these infantile intrapsychic conflicts continue to exert a dominant role in behavior throughout a person's lifetime.

Sullivan not only conceived personality as continuously evolving but described it in terms of an individual's interactions with other people. Personality is thus created when an individual begins to interact with other and is a function of both interacting individuals. Personality is thus an open, interpersonal creation rather than a closed, intrapsychic mechanism.

* I can find no evidence that Sullivan's thinking was directly influenced by Heisenbergs, whose ideas created a revolution in physics. Both seem to be part of a general scientific awareness concerning the limits of objectivity in scientific observations. Physicists became aware that the personality and biology of the observer were very real factors in determining the data accumulated during an observation. The thing being observed changes *because* it is being obserbed. Both Heisenberg and

structure to personality. While he is clearly not a trait theorist,* his ideas are most closely allied with the interactionists (Mischel, 1979).

Dynamisms and Personifications

The closest Sullivan comes to creating a structure of personality is in the notions of "dynamisms" and "personifications." A dynamism is a "relatively enduring pattern of energy transformations, which recurrently characterize the organism in its duration as a living organism" (1953, p. 103). Translating Sullivan, one finds dynamism to be habits or stable patterns of behavior. The personality aspects of most concern to Sullivan would involve interpersonal dynamisms. Sullivan's descriptions of the development of these dynamisms are almost totally congruent with the behavioristic notions of positive and negative reinforcement. As a psychiatrist concerned more with

---

Sullivan were warning their respective fields that the evaluation of any observation would have to try and understand the effects of the observer on the observed.

*The terms *trait theory, situationism,* and *interactionism* arose in the last decade as a result debate concerning personality. Most traditional theories of personality see human functioning as determined by "traits," or qualities of the individual. Charles Morris (1982) defines a trait as a "dimension of personality within people" (p. 358). Freud viewed personality along traits of orality, anality, and the like. G. W. Allport and H. S. Odbert (1938) drew up a list of 17,953 English words for personal behavior traits. Their research began a long tradition in academic psychology to find a more limited list of basic traits that could describe all personalities. Digman (1977) suggests that a few key traits show up repeatedly in research: friendly versus hostile, active-gregarious versus passive-withdrawn, emotionally stable versus neurotic, self-monitored versus unorganized, and creative versus stereotyped.

Whether the traits describing personality are derived from dynamic theories (like that of Freud) or academic-statistical research (Allport and Digman), a number of problems are created by the use of traits. While these problems are discussed in greater detail in chapter 7, they relate to a view of personality as closed and self-contained. The environment is not seen as having a determining effect on personality once the trait has been formed. The radical behaviorism of B. F. Skinner led a number of psychologists to reject completely the idea of traits and to replace it with a view that sees personality as comprising reactions to the environmental situation in which the individual finds himself. Thus, personality is not determined by qualities of the individual but by qualities of the environment.

The attempts at resolving the trait-situation debate came from individuals such as Walter Mischel (1979), who argued that individual qualities of personality contribute to behavior to the degree that the individual has predilections, prejudices, and anticipations to interpret a situation in a certain way. However, the situation being interpreted contributes much to the final nature of the individual choices to behave. Personality can be conceived of as styles of interpreting real situations, and thus is in part intrapsychic or belongs to the individual and in part due to pressures of the environment.

pathology than health, Sullivan made more use of concepts reflective of negative than positive reinforcement. He describes human behavior as basically seeking interpersonal security while avoiding interpersonal tension. The infant responds to its mother by sensitivity to a "gradient of tension." The child moves closer to mother as long as her attitudes are positive and she satisfies the infant's needs. However, if she is tense, anxious, angry, or rejecting, the baby withdraws (into sleep if necessary) as an ultimate escape.

Sullivan described a "self system" made up of the reflected appraisals of others. How an individual sees himself is a function of how others see him. The self system is composed of defensive reactions in relation to the demands of other people. The self is designed to deal with those aspects of interpersonal relationships that create intolerable anxiety. Were society not irrational and were parents completely accepting and in tune with their children, the self system would not be necessary.

Sullivan believed that each individual has personification, an image of himself and others. Such personifications are rarely accurate, because they are the products of defenses as well as direct experience. Each individual has personifications of parents, teachers, policemen, and others, which often guide his behavior toward those individuals. On the one hand, personifications facilitate interactions, while on the other they prevent individuals from really getting to know themselves and others.

Sullivan coined the important term "malevolent transformation" to describe the flawed personification of self that develops if a child is continually rejected and made to feel bad about himself. A child who feels irredeemable, evil, or flawed may simply give up trying to please others or refrain from positive interaction with them. Clinically, psychologists often see patients who are unable to change their self-image and self-defeating patterns of behavior because they are convinced there is no use trying to do so.

Cognitive Processes

One of Sullivan's unique contributions is represented by an earlier version of the theory presented in this book. He believed that experience occurs in three modes: prototaxic, parataxic, and syntaxic. The prototaxic experience relates to the earliest months of life and is descriptively similar to the sensori-motor stage (see chapter 8).

The parataxic mode, identical to the preoperational stage, is dominant during childhood. The illogical nature of experiencing in the parataxic mode is the cause of many interpersonal problems. Experiencing in the syntaxic mode (operational thought) involves adult logic and problem-solving modes.

Development

Six stages of interpersonal development are described by Sullivan: infancy, childhood, the juvenile era, pre-adolescence, early adolescence, and late adolescence. As would be expected, each stage is described in terms of the effects of various interpersonal relationships on the developing individual. The early stages predictably involve interactions with mother and other family members. Sullivan stressed the developmental importance of friendships in later childhood: he believed that normal development involved positive interactions with playmates. Particularly important were the "chumships" of pre-adolescence, where for the first time an individual is free to choose to love a person who is not in his family. Sullivan believed that friends were capable of providing significant corrective experiences especially in cases where personality damage had occurred within the family.

CONSTITUTIONAL THEORIES

Some years ago, William Sheldon (1942) introduced the notion that personality was correlated with one's constitutionally determined physiques. Ectomorphs (thin, small-boned and fragile), Endomorphs (round, soft bodies and large abdomens), and Mesomorphs (sturdy body with strong bones and muscles) could be described in terms of various temperamentally determined traits. Cerebrotonia was characterized by restraint, intelligence, and self-consciousness; viscertonia by a love of food, people, and comfort; and somatotonia by love of physical adventure, risk, and vigorous activity. Skinny men were intellectual, fat men loved food, and well-built men enjoyed athletics because they were, in turn, skinny, fat, and well-built. Sheldon's theory is no longer well received but he did introduce to modern psychology the possible role that biological and constitutional factors play in personality development and function.

Most of the theories presented thus far, and those yet to be presented, are psychological in description: they describe social factors as the main determinants of personality. However, all of these theories must, in one way or another, come to grips with individual differences in personality that are biologically determined. While for the most part current theories do not discuss biological factors, they are implicitly assumed to play important roles in cognitive and affective aspects of human functioning. There is at present no one organized, biological theory of personality popular among psychologists, but there is a set of growing assumptions concerning the role played by constitution and biology.

Any personality theory must be cognizant of the fact that a massive amount of research is being generated on the role of the brain and nervous system in personality. Differences in the neural organization of left and right-handed people, between women and men, normal and pathological people, are continually changing the view of these personality differences. The role of brain injury in schizophrenia and of neurotransmittors in both schizophrenia and many forms of depression are causing many personality theories to be revised. In the future, work on hemispheric localization and organization, and of neuro-biochemistry will continue to develop and cause revisions in psychology's view of the psychological being, and any serious student of psychology will have to be familiar with these factors at some point in his career.

A second set of biological or constitutional factors have to do with infant states or temperament. Alexander Thomas, Stella Chess, and Herbert Birch (1968) were able to determine that infants were born with various reactive predispositions that become stable personality factors. Children could be described as "easy," "difficult," or "slow to warm up." Jerome Kagan (1984) presented evidence that perhaps ten percent of children are born "shy and retiring," while another ten percent are "bold and aggressive." Their early descriptions remain part of their personalities later in life. These factors are not only important in and of themselves but also as determinants of mother-infant interaction. A "difficult" child, easily upset, slow to adjust, strongly reactive to noises and lights tries a mother's patience much more than an "easy child," placid relaxed, slow to anger. The difficult child requires a more mature mother. Developmental psychologists now speak of the "fit" between mother and child and no longer immediately assume that a disturbed child or mother-child interaction is necessarily the fault of the mother and her disturbed personality.

Children who do not learn properly are more and more being labelled as "learning disabled" rather than "negativistic" or "disturbed." "Hyperkinetic" children, distractable and disoriented, have accidents rather than being "accident prone" children with deep-seated self hatred. Learning disabilities and hyperkinesis are viewed as functions of "minimal brain dysfunction" and "maturational lag" rather than social or intrapsychic dynamics.

While personality can be described in solely intrapsychic and interpersonal terms, it is important to note that each of us is are not a "ghost in a machine" but an organismic being in which body and mind are one. The form and function of the nervous system set rules on the form and function of psychological features of personality, which generate changes and determine the structure of the brain and nervous systems. It will probably be impossible to determine if the influence of physiology on behavior or behavior on physiology is the more primary. It will probably become increasingly difficult to determine whether the changes in behavior brought about by evolutionary changes is a greater determinant of personality than the changes in neurological structure brought about by behavior. I believe that as psychological theory becomes more mature behavior will be described by both the rules of psychology and physiology as well as the rules governing their interaction.

I have now completed brief descriptions of the major personality theories influencing the thinking of most psychologists. The differences between these theories often result from semantic disagreements as well as the tendency of different theorists to focus on varying aspects of behavior, observed in varying situations. I will now formally evaluate these theories according to several criteria that will permit an analysis of substantive-theoretical differences and those created by language, varying emphases, and the dogmatic overextension of ideas.

7

Criticisms

The plan of this chapter is to describe a number of issues central to a proper image of the human being. As each issue is discussed, it will be related to its general treatment in a number of important existing theories. In what follows, I employ the phrase "general treatment," which requires some explanation. Any theory has many adherents each of whom may differ from the others with respect to his or her specific understanding of that theory. Today's analysts and behaviorists will personally disagree with the image of humanity presented in the literature of their field. And since only a fraction of practicing psychologists actually publish their ideas, important information often does not see the light of day.

If we discussed with each psychologist just what his image of humanity was, we would probably discover that little actual consensus exists. Yet a consensus does emerge, particularly for students studying psychology; it appears as a set of assumptions inherent in each theory. This consensus emerges in undergraduate classes and in textbooks the contents of which are often homogenized replicas of one another. We learn of "schools of psychology" each of which thrusts forward a point of view that is collective, a view of psychology that tends to stand out in the minds of students. This general use of theory was discussed in chapters 2 through 6.

If we were to generalize the shortcomings of the human image in psychology, they would be the following:

a) Psychology has long been reductionistic. The traditional analyst often sees all higher human functions as derivative of sexuality. The behaviorist's paradigm of classical and operant conditioning are thought to permeate all human functioning. Association theory is often used to explain learning while drive-reduction theory will explain motivation.

b) Many theories of personality emerge from clincians who tend to be more concerned with abnormal than with normative behavior. Mental illness is defined more often than mental health.

c) Most existing theories have very important things to say but sometimes they overutilize their explanatory principles. Human beings do learn like pigeons, so to that degree what we learn about pigeons can be applied to human beings. But people also learn in ways that pigeons do not, and the theories that explain human learning cannot rely on pigeon studies. Sex is an important motive but not our only drive. Anxiety is an important emotion but psychologists often see it as our only motivation. Guilt, anger, shame, and a host of other reactions. are also emotions that lead to defensive behavior. Childhood, the analysts tell us, is the time when our personalities are shaped. While it is hard to argue with the evidence supporting the importance of childhood, all traumas do not take root in this epoch. Important events occur throughout life. It is difficult to predict behavior from one stage of human development to another (Kagan, 1984).

d) Overextension of otherwise useful concepts is often the "flip" side of a problem of narrow attention. As discussed in the first chapter, many theories will exclude from study whole areas of behavior that are central to human personality. Morality and values are rarely touched upon by traditional academic theories. Victor Frankl (1969) describes an ongoing discussion between Sigmund Freud and Ludwig Binswanger. The latter accused Freud of dealing only with the "basement" of personality, while Freud countered that his colleague described only the "attic" of personality. To continue the metaphor, personality requries both a basement and an attic.

I should like now to turn to six areas of personality in which the human image suffers most and to discuss each in terms of the problems outlined above. In the course of each critique, I will suggest a theoretical solution to the limitations described. Each proposed solution is drawn from existing theories in the literature or from theories whose viewpoints are narrow until complemented by a competing theory.

1. COGNITION AND INTELLECT

As described in chapter 1, humanity's clearest imprints are to be found in its scientifc and religious endeavors. Both are the result of intellectual and other cognitive processes. Psychology has not, for the most part adequately dealt with intellect in such a way as to explain the existence of science and religion as intellectually creative efforts. Our personality theories are often most anemic at just this point. George Kelly (1951) provides us with our starting point when he writes: "Yet curiously enough psychologists rarely credit the human subjects in their experiments (*or I might add patients in their offices)* with having *scientific aspirations.* It is as though the psychologist was saying to himself: I, being a psychologist and therefore a scientist, am performing the experiment in order to improve the prediction and control of certain human phenomena; but my subject, being merely a human organism, is obviously propelled by inexorable drives (or quantities of energy) welling up within him, or else he is in gluttonous pursuit of sustenance and shelter" (italics mine).

We can assume that all human beings seek to explain, predict, and control the important aspects of their lives as they understand them at each moment in time. We can also assume that the manner in which different individuals seek to solve their problems will vary from person to person. Some will be scientific and approach their physical, interpersonal, and intrapsychic worlds meaningfully; others will utilize inadequate intellectual modes to satisfy their needs. We can also ask whether or not the same individuals behave scientifically throughout the their lives. Just which developmental, biological, and emotional factors produce a "scientist" and which produce an "authoritarian dogmatist"? *But our starting point in describing personality must be with the individual's cognition and his mode of experiencing and processing information.*

Most modern psychologies have not done justice to human thought, its development, its pathology, and especially its creativity. Traditional psychoanalysis has described thought as resulting from conflict and deprivation. The individual's ego, the seat of thinking, is described in its dealings with the environment, its function in delaying impulse gratification and the creation of defenses. The defenses are described mostly in terms of outcomes, not intellectual processes.

Ego psychology gave greater prominence to the cognitive functions and placed them within "a conflict free *ego* sphere" (Hartmann, 1958). Cognition now belonged to an aspect of personality that no longer depended upon the *id* or neutralized sexual energy for its existence. The specific role of cognition and intelligence had not begun to be developed until very recently. Stanley Greenspan's (1979) and Irving Bieber's (1980) works have not yet had the effect they deserve on psychoanalytic theory of thought. Silvano Arieti writes: "Cognition is or has been, up to now, the Cinderella of psychoanalysis and psychiatry. No other field of the psyche has been so consistently neglected by clinicians and theoreticians alike. Isolated studies and manifestations of interest have not so far developed into a trend" (Arieti, 1980).

Rubin and Gertrude Blank (1974) present their theory of developmental *ego* psychology, which deals with the social interaction of the child and its effects on *ego* development. But the aspects of *ego* that are attended to still do not provide an adequate theory of learning or of intellectual development in its normal, nonpathological sense. The main thrust of *ego* psychology and object relations theory is a description of the interaction between mother and infant that leads to normal social growth.

Horney and Sullivan, two important defectors from the traditional analytic camp, came closer to explicating the role of cognition in human functioning. Horney's (1950) description of "neurotic pride" and its consequences is clearly a developmental cognitive concept; yet, her work still stresses and emphasizes abnormal development. She never faces, per se, the qualities of cognition that underlie neurotic defenses. Horney's work stresses neurosis and other deviant psychological forms while only offering a rough conceptual sketch of normalcy.

Bieber (1980), in a most important work, stresses the significance of the cognitive processes that become "irrational" through improper upbringing, inadequate resolution of conflict, and excessive anxiety. Pathology, he makes clear, must be seen in terms of rational and irrational thought mechanisms. While his work is a step forward in placing cognition in the center of human functioning, it still does not define what *rational* or *irrational* mean in cognitive terms. Moreover, he makes us aware of just how biased analysis is toward descriptions of the irrational or the pathological. Normalcy in psychoanalysis is still defined in negative terms as nonpathological. Normal cognition is that which is free from excessive conflict or anxiety. One is hard pressed to find a positive, normative description of human functioning. (with the important exception of Erik Erikson, but we will return to that seminal theorist in his descriptions of "generative man" [Erikson, Browning, 1968]).

If we turn to the human image as portrayed in American behaviorism, the picture turns bleak indeed. J. B. Watson and B. F. Skinner's insistence on dealing only with overt observables capable of operational definition precluded the direct study of thought, emotional experience, or other processes central to human personality. Sigmund Koch (1981), Isidor Chein (1972), and many others have written devastating rebuttals to the behaviorism of the Watson-Skinner axis, but these need not be repeated here. However, a few points in the present context of criticism are in order.

One of the behaviorists' signal achievements was to describe motivation in terms of external reinforcers. The behaviorist position forces us to focus correctly on the environment as one source of human behavior. However, by refusing to deal with the central processes of cognition, Skinner failed to attend to the most important of human reinforcers and modes of reinforcement. A pigeon is most strongly reinforced by food, a human being is most strongly reinforced by his emotional reaction, particularly those reactions created by his favorite, imaginative production or wish fulfillments.

Pigeons do not seek the meaning of their existence, human beings do. It is in connection with the search for meaning and purpose that humanity has used its most creative intellectual processes and has produced its most powerful set of reinforcers. Can anyone, after even a cursory study of history, fail to see that the most powerful human driving forces are found in those ideas, creatively invented, that *concern human salvation after death.* By reducing human beings to robots modeled after pigeons, Skinner is forced to ignore not only the results of human creativity but the very creative processes necessary to produce his own theory.

Much of the present theory includes the work of cognitive or social learning theorists such as Aaron Beck (1967), Donald Meichenbaum (1978), Julian Rotter (1966), Albert Bandura (1977), and Walter Mischel (1968, 1979). These theorists focus on the manner in which emotional reactions are created by an individual's mode of interpreting present and future events, as well as the consequences of the aroused emotions in cognitive activity. Thus, reinforcers are seen, in part, in a proper cognitive-affective perspective. Serious problems exist with these theories: their refusal to deal with normative man; a developmental psychology of cognition; and especially, a notion of ethics and morality to guide the technology of behavior control they have developed.

The humanistic and existential theorists, who have a more adequate and relevant view of humanity, rarely make explicit the mode of thought that differentiates those whose lives are determined by existential concerns and those who seek merely to survive by any means possible. What is lacking in most "third force" psychologies is a proper developmental model that deals effectively with cognition and intellect. Abraham Maslow's (1968) work points up these problems. His description of the development of the self-actualized individual lacks both an adequate theory of cognitive learning as well as explicit descriptions of the difference(s) between how the self-actualizer thinks and solves problems before and after his actualization.

In order to restore the human image to its proper perspective, we must look outside personality per se and turn to the work of Jean Piaget and other cognitive developmentalists. Integrating Piaget into personality theory is not easy. His developmental epistemology provides us with a central focus of cognition, but Piaget's work is an epistemological and not a psychological theory. Brian Rotman (1977) clearly shows us that Piaget never dealt adequately with the interpersonal and, more important, the cultural aspects of intellectual development. Rotman (1977) writes:

> Piaget's theory . . . is flawed as we have argued at precisely the point where the organism and the individual as a member of the social community have to be brought into contact. Piaget's paradigm of the individual is the isolated organism adaptively responding to its environment, his paradigm of structure is physiological self regulation

and his paradigm of the world is the physical environment . . . it refuses to accept the importance of the fact that individuals are immersed in a nonnatural world, in an environment of ideas, meanings,
intention and history, symbols, within a matrix of social influences
and cooperation.

Equally as important is the fact that Piaget never extensively discussed the crucial issue of the emotions and their relation to cognitive adaptation. For example, Seymour Lustman (1972) points out
that Piaget created a whole theory of moral development and never
really described the role of guilt and shame in moral behavior. With
these criticisms and problems in mind, let us turn to Piaget's con-
siderable contribution.

The strength of Piaget's theory is that he permits us an explicit,
empirical view of cognition as one of the central features of human
personality. His descriptions of cognition are based on simple observation and experimentation. Piaget sees intellect as our main
adaptational instrumentality. The instrumental cognition not only
permits adaptation but changes and develops as a function of
adaptation. Cognition develops from the interaction of innate bio-
evolutionary schema ("tendencies to behave") and objects in the
environment. If we look at cognition as the core function of the *ego,*
we see that Piaget provides us with a model that accepts these skills
as arising independently of conflict.

Piaget sees the interaction of the child's innate schema with the
physical world leading ultimately to a "construction" of reality.
Learning and maturation are both important concepts to consider
in the developing child and are expressed through the mutual processes (functional invariants) of assimilation and accommodation.
These ideas are infinitely more sophisticated and explanatory than
the concept of conditioning with its reliance on a simplistic theory
of learning based on association. As the child continues to interact
with his environment and under the tutelage of genetic factors,
cognitive skills change, and with it awareness of (and modes of
interpreting) reality.

Piaget allows us to see personality as a kind of functioning that
results from the constructed meaning a person has of a given situation. An individual's response to a situation cannot be determined
by merely describing the external stimuli, or in terms of describing
a history with that stimuli. History and stimulus situations converge

in terms of how each contributes to the individual's cognitive understanding of the situation. We thus develop a holistic view of the individual, whose bio-social-cultural background can be understood in light of his ability and mode of interpreting reality.

2. EMOTIONS AND MOTIVATION

What Piaget's theory is to intellectual development, Carroll Izard's (1977, 1979, 1984), Robert Pultchik's (1977, 1980), and R. B. Zajonc's (1980, 1984) work is to our understanding of the emotions. Both Izard and Pultchik's ideas represent attempts to place the emotions as concepts central to human functioning and motivation. Their work joins a growing body of evidence (e.g., Sylvan Tompkins [1962, 1967]) suggesting that our emotions are basic, bio-evolutionary reactions central to adaptation, survival, and interpersonal relationships. Each theory suggests that there are basic human emotions (Izard offers a list of ten; Pultchik, eight) existing as discrete bio-physiological-psychological experiences.

Izard (1977) calls his work a "differential theory of the emotions." Here the emotions are seen as one of six basic subsystems comprising the human personality; the other five systems being homeostatic, drive, perceptual, cognitive, and motor. "Each system has some degree of autonomy or independence but all are complexly interrelated." There are ten basic, discrete emotions that can combine with one another and with other systems to produce various motivational phenomena. Emotions are defined as "a complex process with neurophysiological, neuromuscular, and phenomenological aspects."

Izard and Pultchik see the emotions being shaped by evolutionary experiences. In this regard, their concepts are similar to Piaget's. All agree that the central concepts of personality are bio-evolutionary. Izard's (1977) excellent history and survey is concerned with the generally inadequate manner in which the emotions are treated by a variety of major theories. In the theory to be presented later, cognition is seen as a source of understanding of the meaning of a situation. Emotions can be understood in exactly the same way. When an individual enters a situation, his cognitive or perceptual evaluation of that situation produces an emotional reaction. On other occassions, an individual may enter the situation with an existing predisposition of emotional arousal that can influence the perceptual and cognitive appaisal of the situation. In each case, the total meaning of the situation cannot be seen as either exclusively cognitive or emotional but as a combination of the two. How the individual is motivated to behave in the situation is a function of the cognitive-emotional meaning the situation has for him.

Our motivation in any situation can therefore be seen as behavior resulting from our evaluation of the situation. Evaluations may primarily be conscious or they take place at less-than-conscious levels. Such a viewpoint of motivation allows us to recall Kelly's notion of the individual as "scientist." Scientists see after the meaning of things. We have expanded the mode in which an individual evaluates his world. Our problem (to be dealt with at greater length in chapter 8) is to expand Piaget's notion of constructed reality to include the emotions as part of our epistemology.

We can handle the drives in the same model. Drives act in a manner similar to that of the emotions; they change the meaning of a situation. With the arousal of a drive, certain objects necessary to the satisfaction of that drive are perceived, conceived, and experienced with a different meaning than before the drive or imbalance was aroused. Piaget (1981) refers to all the energizing aspects of personality, emotion and drives as "affect," a convention we have used in this book.

3. DEVELOPMENT

In order to restore a proper image of humanity, we require an understanding of the development of cognitive and emotional processes as well as their interrelationships. In order to be effective, a theory of development must articulate a concept of stages along with the principles by which the individual moves from stage to stage. Most modern theories err in one or both of two ways: they either have an inadequate (or nonexistent) theory of development or they fail to focus on the development of cognitive-emotional modes of experiencing meaning. Such theories focus primarily on social development or on the drives or other needs. For example, the existentialist view of personality, as represented in the work of Rollo May (1963, 1969, 1981), Victor Frankl (1962, 1968, 1969), Erich Fromm (1980), and Paul Tillich (1952) describes what might be called "the highest in man" (Browning, 1973). Each stresses the importance of including the highest as well as the lowest aspects of personality, so much in focus in psychoanalysis.

The existentialists criticize traditional psychoanalysis for dealing primarily with the "lowest" in humanity. If I continue with the metaphor used earlier in this chapter, personality can be likened to a "house" that has both a "basement" and an "attic." Freud and many followers become reductionistic when all human functions were seen as existing only as aspects of the "basement" or "ground floor." Freud declares, for example, that he "already found a place for religion by putting it under the category of the neurosis of mankind." Frankl correctly argues that not all religion is neurotic. Some of mankind's most creative achievements stem from religion and cannot be seen as neurotic.

The *ego* psychologists also deal basically with the basement functions of humanity. They affirm that the function of the *ego* is survival. Conscience, religion, and civilization itself are often perceived as the result of defense. While *ego* psychology will allow that civilization has its roots in the autonomy of the *ego,* civilization generally remains the result of sublimation, which is still a defense suggesting that all of humanity's achievements exist as experiences and compromises made in the name of survival, tension reduction, or conflict compromise.

It is clear that we need a view of the human being at his best; however, Frankl's theory lacks an adequate view of how such a human being develops. How does the human being begin life as the simple organism described by the analyst and become the fully developed organism described by the existentialist? When Frankl exhorts us to see our "will to meaning," how is this to be achieved? O. Hobart Mowrer (1964) writes, "whenever I read or hear Professor Tillich, the phrase that always goes through my mind is 'long on diagnosis, short on prescription'—just how do we come by this (existential) courage?" (p. 35)

Only if we build our notions of growth and development, can we understand why one individual becomes existentially courageous while others remain prepossessed by survival and act out childhood conflicts. Abraham Maslow (1968) does propose a theory to demonstrate such growth; he suggests that we are born dominated by lower-order needs (deficit needs) and, if these needs are satisfied, the higher-order needs emerge in a process that continues until the existential needs of "self-actualization" appear. We are born determined by such needs as hunger and thirst, and eventually we evolve until we feel forced to find dignity and meaning in life as well as the fulfillment of our human potential.

The weakness in Maslow's theory is that the role of intellect and culture are seriously askew. Intellect and cognition underly the existence of existential needs. Individuals can neither ask about the meaning of life nor fear their own deaths unless they have very sophisticated thought processes. Satisfaction of needs, the heart of Maslow's theory, reveals little about the growth of intellect and how individuals learn. In chapter 9, we will see how Maslow's theory becomes quite effective in explaining the relationship of the "low" and the "high" once we include the growth of cognition as the key factor in the movement from stage to stage.

Behaviorism requires just a cursory explanation in the present context. Behaviorism bases its notion of development on associationism and the accumulation of experiences. There is no developmental theory in behaviorism, which suggests that we change through the accumulation of experience and the effects of the situations through which we pass. Skinner does not focus on internal cognitive processes and thus does not trace their development.

The cognitive behaviorists (and analysts such as Bieber [1980] and Horney [1950], whose theories are quite similar to the cognitive behaviorists) do have a developmental notion of cognition but only an implicit one. Bieber describes "irrational" versus "rational" thinking, while Horney describes the processes involving "neurotic pride, tyranny of the shoulds," and so on, which are descriptive of primitive thinking. Meichenbaum (1974), Beck (1967), and others describe the type of thinking that produces loss of emotional control, and their descriptions are of "primitive" thought forms. However, none of these authors explicate the primitive forms of thought and their relationship to the normal thought processes of the child.

Psychoanalysis has a number of developmental notions of personality that in one way help restore a more complete image of humanity. Freud's genetic theory is based on the vicissitudes of the instincts. An individual develops as his libido moves from mouth to anus to genitalia. The human personality develops (or fails to develop) in relation to the mode and degree of sexual satisfaction. However, *Freud never made clear why intellectual progress was made when the individual shifted his mode of sexual expression.*

Freud (1967, 1966) did have important developmental concepts that are stressed in *ego* psychology. The *ego* operates either according to primary or secondary process thinking (see chapter 2). Secondary process, or logical, thinking develops as the individual moves from the pleasure principle to the reality principle. Logic exists as a necessary tool of survival, while more primitive modes of thought exist according to needs and impulses. All development ultimately rests on the base of instinctual development.

Higher-order thinking also occurs, according to analysts, because of the effects of sublimation, which is an *ego* defense designed to reduce anxiety, conflict, and so forth. However, the individual who sublimates must be intellectually different as a result of the growth required in sublimation. The development of intellect due to sublimation is implied but not made explicit. Freud does not propose a mechanism or process that explains the developmental shift from primary to secondary process.

One of Freud's important clinical contributions is the awareness that the adult is capable of using both primary and secondary process thinking. Once again, however, the lack of a transformational developmental principle expressing the relationship between primary and secondary process creates serious theoretical problems. Freud uses a topographic and energy model to explain the relationship. Secondary process thought marks conscious thought. Primary process thinking is "drive organized" and thus is the language of the unconscious. In Freud's model, the two types of thought can operate simultaneously, one in consciousness, directed by the *ego;* the other in the unconscious, organized by the *id.*

Freud's model can be thought of metaphorically as a mountain with a tunnel running under it. Out in the air, above ground, we find secondary process thinking. In the subterranean tunnel there is a different type of mental life going on. If there is a failure of the *ego* and of its defenses, a "fissure" appears. The pent-up energy of the drives emerges into consciousness, and with it primary process thinking. In a real sense there is no developmental relationship between primitive and advanced thought; they exist side by side.

Piaget's work, and that of modern cognitive theory, points to the fact that higher levels of thinking emerge from the reorganization of more primitive forms of thought. Primitive thinking does not have an independent life. That an individual can think in both primitive and mature terms requires an explanation that takes into account the principles that transform and reorganize primitive thinking, turning it into advanced thinking. The same principles are needed to explain how and why mature thought can be retransformed into its immature representation.

Emanuel Peterfreund (1980) has grappled with these same psychoanalytic issues, casting them in terms of information theory. Peterfreund suggests that when an individual is under stress, anxiety, or when strong drives affect the individual, the person is forced to evaluate information differently than when calm, non-anxious, or sated. Drives do not take over and direct the individual's behavior; rather, the decision-making process of the *ego* employs different rules of thinking when the individual is under internal or external pressure than when such pressure is not present. In chapters 9 and 10, a similar model will be suggested employing pre-operational and operational forms of thinking.

Ego psychology has added little to our knowledge of cognitive growth since emotional and social growth are their prime concerns. The work of James Masterson (1976), Margaret Mahler (1968), and Otto Kernberg (1967) deals primarily with the emotional and social development of the young child, later developmental phases not being fully described. Erik Erikson (1968) carries us through the entire life span but similarly stresses emotional and social development (in addition to libidinal development). He does not explicate the role of cognition in health or pathology. His concept of "generational man" is a most important one, but Erikson only implicitly describes the type of cognition that must underly the understanding inherent in such a character.

Perhaps the clearest and most complete developmental theory of cognition in clinical psychology belongs to Harry Stack Sullivan (1952). Sullivan describes cognition in terms of modes of experience or meaning. Moreover, his "prototaxic," "parataxic," and "syntaxic" modes are similar to Piaget's "sensorimotor," "pre-operational" and "operational" modes of thinking, although more sketchily described. Moreover, these different modes of thinking are assumed to exist purely as a function of age and development and not in accordance with libidinal or sexual energy distribution. As with Freud, Sullivan does not provide a psychological model that describes how and why thinking is transformed from stage to stage.

4. THE ENVIRONMENT

Many existing theories of personality are "trait" theories. That is, they describe an individual's behavior in terms of single or clusters of characteristics. Clusters of characteristics form typologies of one sort or another. Isidor Chein (1972), this author (Simon, 1981), Roy Schafer (1973), and others have discussed the serious problem arising from the use of trait or character descriptions. Let us turn now to a description of the problem in using trait concepts.

All that we ultimately know of an individual's personality is based on our observations of overt behavior, which we describe by using verbs. When we characterize an individual's behavior we are providing the verb that describes the behavior. Now, adverbs modify these verbs by further developing the description of the behavior. For example, an individual who behaves irrationally in some set of situations might be described adverbially by a clinician as acting "neurotic." The term *neurotic* is a trait word and represents, we would believe, a significant aspect of the individual's overall character.

However, to be consistent, we should not call an individual "neurotic"; instead, we should say "he has behaved neurotically." When we call the individual "neurotic," we have changed an adverb into an adjective. By doing so we are no longer describing behavior but are claiming to describe a central, inherent, quintessential characteristic of the individual. We now take this quality of the individual and use it to explain his behavior in a wide variety of situations. Our ignorance about the reason for the individual's irrational behavior in one situation becomes transformed into a statement of certain knowledge of why he *must* now behave irrationally in all situations. The situational qualities that may have led to the irrational behavior and the qualities of all subsequent situations are ignored. This linguistic mechanism creates a motivational system based solely on the presumed internal characteristics of the individual, and that individual is mistakenly identified as the main source of behavioral variation.

According to Walter Mischel (1979), experiments that depend on the replication of prediction based on trait performance have largely failed. He suggests that traits do not exist and that personality itself is a fiction. Mischel argues that our behavior is due basically to environmental and situational factors. His explanation falls within the social-behaviorist domain. D. J. Bem and A. Allen (1974) counter Mischel's interpretation by suggesting that the problems of replication are created by weak methodologies in which traits or personality characteristics are inadequately represented by experimental measures of the independent variable. Where personality variables are given adequate measurement, as in intelligence testing, replicability is less of an issue.

The argument over methodology still avoids confronting the main question: Is behavioral consistency a function of the individual or of similar situation? The problem is resolved in our definition of personality, which we must begin to define in an interactionist approach similar to that created by Piaget, who stresses a view of personality and motivation based on the individual interpretation of a given situation. This is a more satisfying approach because it takes into consideration both the individual and the environment in explaining variations and consistencies in behavior.

We behave in accordance with the manner in which we interpret our environment. Consistency across situations occurs because we often tend to interpret in consistent ways. But behavior also varies from one situation to another because no two situations are identical. To the degree to which our interpretations are autistic or inner determined our behavior is consistent and stereotyped across situations; to the degree to which our interpretations and perceptions are verdical (in conformance with reality), our behavior varies from situation to situation. It is important to note that our tendency to seek out situations that are consistent with past experience, or to make situations into replicas of the past, also accounts for much behavioral consistency.

In order to avoid the deficiencies and simplistics of the theories discussed, it is suggested that psychologists adopt a field theoretical approach to personality. Humans are constantly trying to adapt to some environment and to assimilate it in terms of past expectations, but are forced to accommodate present exigencies. The resulting constructed view of reality, as well as the immediate situation being interpreted, accounts for our moment to moment behavior. Decades ago, Paul Meehl (1969) pointed out that our ability to predict behavior from psychological tests was dependent not only upon how the person tested interpreted our tests but also upon what situation he would be in when the prediction took place. Our behavior is as much a function of what the situation brings to us as to what we bring to the situation.

The past is important, but no more important then the present in both normal and abnormal behavior. The work of W. Robert Beaver (1977), Carl Whittaker (1976), Jan Haley (1976), Salvador Minuchin (1974), and a host of others helps bring the individual's present social environment into focus and makes us aware that behavior is unintelligible unless understood in terms of its present social context. Past experiences do help to shape how a person interprets present realities but the fact that present realities help to shape moment to moment behavior cannot be ignored.

Erikson (1968) writes that identity* involves a nonstatic process: ". . . located in the core of the individual and yet also in the core of his communal culture. . . . The traditional psychoanalytic method cannot quite grasp identity because it has not developed terms to conceptualize the environment. Certain habits of psychoanalytic theorizing, habits of designating the environment as 'outer world' or 'object world' cannot take account of the environment as a pervasive actuality. The German ethologists introduced the word 'umvelt' to denote not merely an environment which surrounds you, but which is also in you" (p. 22).

Erikson is not only criticizing psychoanalysis for its failure to deal with the ever-present, shifting environment but also of the cultural and historical realities of that environment. "Men who share the concern of an ethnic group, who are contemporaries in a historical era or who compete in economic pursuits are also guided by common images of good or evil" (1968, p. 23). Erikson criticizes psychoanalysis, but what are we to say of behaviorism, which reduces the cultural environment to a "stimulus situation"? Seymour Sarason (1981) recently took clinical psychology to task for being "an asocial psychology."

Finally, if we conceptualize cognition and affect as having an adaptive function with regard to a social-physical environment, then any understanding of cognition and affect must begin with an evaluation of the demands for adaptation made by the environment. It is the specific adaptive demands of the environment that are interpreted, cognitively and emotionally, by the individual. If new forms of thinking evolve and replace older forms, it must, in part, be due

---

* Identity is a concept often used in psychoanalysis and described in intrapsychic terms. Erikson's comments concerning identity can apply in a more general way to the problems under discussion, i.e., describing the individual independent of his environment.

to newly evolving environments that demand new adaptive interpretations. When examining the nature of a thought or an affect, it behooves us to ask, what its usefulness in adaptation is to a given environment.

An example of the above is in order. A female student recently bemoaned the fact that there seem to be few men sensitive to the emotional needs of others, or themselves. Research does support her supposition that women are better at interpreting behavioral and physiognomic cues of emotion than are men. (Men are beginning to reveal cognitive-affective sensitivity as our culture makes demands on them to do so.) I suggested to my student that her anger, in part, comes from a misunderstanding of why men are insensitive in terms of the historical, evolutionary, and developmental contexts of masculine behavior. I further suggested that her awareness of male insensitivity and the demand that they be so also represents behavior that is historically very new.

Until recently men lived their lives as beasts of burden occasionally augmenting this role with that of soldiering. (In many parts of the world, and in our society, such role expectations have not changed.) What sense does emotional sensitivity make to an individual living like a beast of burden and struggling to survive? Could an individual continue to function if he were sensitive to his emotional pain? Women were responsible for their infants' emotional well-being and thus had to develop an emotional sensitivity. I doubt that in the historical context there were many women aware of being morally superior, superior by virtue of their sensitivity, or would have wanted a sensitive male unable to plow his field.

It is not that men and women consciously chose to be sensitive or insensitive. Both adapted to the demands of a physical, social, political, and economic environment. Both sexes were embedded in an environment that set the tasks of survival, which, in turn, demanded cognitive and emotional adaptation. In each generation there is a prevailing wisdom and morality that has its roots in the necessities of survival. As necessities change, so do cognitive-affective intelligences. Each generation's wisdom is the next generation's strength and folly. Each generation feels it is responsible for progress in human thinking and that it has cornered the wisdom market.

5. NORMATIVE AND ETHICAL HUMANITY

I have tried to demonstrate a number of failings in some important personality theories. I have suggested that these theories, including the behaviorist and the analytic camps, fail to develop fully aspects of intellectual functioning, motivation, emotional life, psychological development, the role of the environment, and the role of culture. I have further theorized that they focus too much on the individual, on early experiences, and on the intra-psychic. I have suggested that our central motivational system is cognitive, emotional, and is found in our interpreted meanings of the cultural situation in which we find ourselves.

I must now turn to the most serious failings of many theories. Psychology rarely provides an adequate, complete, and realistic normative view of humanity. It too often describes the worst in us, and rarely the best. Simultaneously, psychology generally fails to make explicit in its theories the place of values, ethics, and morality. The fact remains, however, that descriptions of the relationship between people or an individual's interaction with his society cannot be set forth without confronting, or making statements that contain, ethical and moral implications. This worst deficiency of psychology must be righted if we are to arrive at the proper and *empirically correct* image of humanity.

This section will be organized to deal with the following: 1) the failure of theory to provide an adequate description of humanity at its creative and actualized best (I believe that neither Freud nor Skinner can account for their own creative achievements on the basis of their own or the other's theory); 2) the failure of theorists to work from an adequate definition of the science of psychology; 3) the failure of most psychological theories to explicate the always present value system and the statement of ethics and morality implicit in any description of human personality; and 4) the devastating consequences of these inadequate, normative, and ethical concepts of personality, whether they appear implicitly or explicitly.

If it is argued that a balanced view of behavior must deal with interpersonal relationships and with a healthy role in culture, then ethics and morality cannot be avoided. The norms adopted by a society to guide the interaction of its members are expressed as morality and often codified as law. There is no way to separate a description of a healthy, loving relationship from one that describes an honest, ethically based relationship. A culture holds together only as long as its members agree to behave in a way that permits the society to continue functioning. Individuals flourish only in a moral society that respects the rights of individuals, who then reciprocate by respecting their neighbors and following laws designed to protect the common good.

As students of human behavior, psychologists cannot condemn the behavior of their subjects; to do so would preclude studying that which is in evidence. Science must be nonjudgmental and objective if it is to remain science. However, when science studies relationships that cannot be described without referring to ethics, then value judgments are inevitable. Science need not condemn in its manner of reporting, but it cannot shrink from making such judgments if it is to deal fairly with its subject matter. Yet many of our theories describe interpersonal, intracultural, and intercultural relationships and thereby refrain from making overt judgments. But judgments are made nonetheless, and often their implicitness proves more odious than if the judgments had been explicit.

In a brilliant and important work, Perry London (1964) suggests that most psychological theories define what is "healthy" in a different way than would the society. Sexual freedom, nonconformity, even resistance to the rules of society are descriptive of many statements of mental health. Can anyone deny that when a therapist helps a homosexual male accept his homosexuality and fulfill himself in that role, the therapist is making an ethical statement and a moral judgment? And can the therapist's moral position be anything but the polar opposite of the view taken by a fundamentalist preacher?

London suggests that we often play the role of "secular priests" when we function as psychotherapists. The very act of teaching may well represent a secular clerical function, as does the act of writing theories of personality that ultimately suggest how people *should* live. We have no way to suggest normative functioning other than with morally tinged "shoulds." Clearly, London suggests, science has not yet established "true" standards for human behavior, independent of cultural contexts and values. In fact, the idea of such an absolutist theory must seem silly in the face of this century's discoveries in sociology and cultural anthropology.

Not only do we render judgments about the general aspects of social relationships, but, as therapists and theorists, we take an active role in changing the nature of those relationships. Freud considered himself a morally neutral scientist, but can the effects of his theory concerning sexual gratification be seen as morally neutral when viewed by the members of the church dominated society in which he operated? How can the manner and mode of sexual fulfillment, given the nature of human relationships, ever be morally neutral? John Cuddihy (1974), in fact, suggests that one goal of Freud's theorizing was to wreak havoc with the inconsistent and hypocritical morals of the bourgeois Viennese society.

Let us further examine the so-called neutral morality of psychological science. Perhaps the most serious distortion of values occurs with the medical model that underlies nearly all clinical theories. We claim a scientific and neutral medical designation of deviant behavior. We call people "neurotic," "schizophrenic," and "character disordered," claiming that we are dealing with "sickness," while making implicit moral judgments and failing to take responsibility for them. Thomas Szasz (1967) and, more recently, Theodore Sarbin and James Mancuso (1971) demand to see proof that our patients are really "ill" or "sick." After reviewing 1,500 studies on schizophrenia, Sarbin and Mancuso could find no proof of a medical illness underlying the bizarre and deviant behavior of this "syndrome." They suggest that the medical model is an "incorrect paradigm" when describing schizophrenia. Indeed, we have the problem of an individual behaving strangely but no proof that he is ill. Therefore, the authors conclude that schizophrenia must be seen as a "moral judgment" and not a medical diagnosis.

If we turn to "neurosis" or, more importantly, "character disorder," we find little evidence and few arguments to suggest underlying organicity in these categories. We are speaking of "functional" or "learned" illnesses. Here again, we can only say that we are dealing with moral judgment and not scientifically established neutral concepts. Character disorders (individuals for example, who commit crimes without apparent guilt) clearly violate the morality of Western religious society, and these violations form the basis of diagnoses. Indeed, once a person with a so-called character disorder confesses his crimes and shows genuine remorse, his diagnosis is changed to "neurosis." The difference between the two diagnoses is usually the degree of guilt and anxiety experienced with respect to the moral transgressions.

I am not arguing that those whom we diagnose as schizophrenic or neurotic are not suffering from some type of disturbance. Often the implicit criteria we use to make a diagnosis is that the behavior of these individuals is destructive either to themselves or others. But if destruction of self or others is the basis of psychological or psychiatric diagnosis, then why are not war, racism, or religious fanaticism also diagnostic categories? The answer is that war, racism, and religion are seen by many as proof of society's moral superiority while schizophrenic or hysteria are not. Schizophrenia, even if it represents a genuine illness, is still a moral judgment when one considers that racism is not considered an illness at all.

Let us examine the specific normative and ethical positions of psychoanalysis. Analysts focus on the *ego* as the highest organ of expression. The *ego's* legitimate goal is survival. It must satisfy libidinous instincts and control the expression of aggressive impulses without arousing social ire and creating environmental dangers. Skills must be developed to deal with environmental dangers, and ways must be found to resist the demands of the irrational *superego*.

Freud sees art and religion as resulting from defense mechanisms and/or neuroses. Art emerges as we sublimate forbidden sexual and aggressive impulses to "higher" social aims. Morality springs from the *superego*, which is created when we identify with the aggressor parent who threatens us when we express sexual impulses. We have a moral sense *simply* because it aids in our personal survival. Religion exists as the social extension of our *superego*. It, too, is mere expediency in the *ego's* quest to survive. Freud sees any attempt to discover the "meaning" of life as neurotic: for Freud, normative happiness is a state of comfort brought about by need gratification and an absence of external threat.

Skinner (1971) suggests that it is time to move "Beyond Freedom and Dignity," into "Walden II." We must deal with these central human concepts "scientifically." Science would control the reinforcers that shape behavior, thus producing a utopia of happy people. "Dignity" is a matter of receiving such positive reinforcers as food and sex, while freedom is the individual effort to avoid negative reinforcers. The absurdity of Skinner's view of the struggle for meaning becomes clear when he admits that he would have a problem selecting those who would administer the utopian-producing reinforcement schedule. He seems not to see that his own theory would fail to be a guide for selecting those who could be trusted to condition the rest of us. Would he select the well fed or the least punished? He is forced to move beyond his own theory and toward real issues of freedom and dignity in order to find an individual into whose hand we would be entrusted. Skinner's theory is ultimately like Freud's in that they both conceive of humanity as content to survive and obtain biological satisfaction. But Freud sees us as animals while Skinner transforms us into robots. Neither model is adequate to describe the best that some of us become.

When "scientists" fail to state a positive ideal of healthy development, one that is realistically achievable by human beings, we create a vacuum, which has been filled in recent years by what might be called the "happiness school of psychology." On this view, the end product of human growth is ecstatic happiness. Shame, guilt, or any negative emotion is the enemy of happiness. Theorists of this persuasion join the happiness school of medicine, which has sought to banish death as the ultimate source of unhappiness.

Albert Ellis (1975) claims that the cognitive therapy he advances has as its goal the individual happiness of the patient. Cognitive behaviorism utilizes a behavioral technology (the same means to be created by Skinner) to reduce negative emotion and to teach us to avoid thought that creates unwanted anxiety and guilt. These theories implicitly assume that *all* guilt and anxiety *should* be reduced in much the same way that medical psychiatry negates "illnesses" with an increasingly sophisticated pharmacopoeia. However, neither cognitive behaviorists nor psychiatrists have a theory that permits differentiation between unhappineess that is genuine and, in fact, necessary to keep us human, and that which is genuinely irrational. *All* unhappiness is to be negated, while happiness is to be sought without wondering what brings it about. The idea that guilt might be based upon destructive behavior (not impulses, but deeds actually carried out) cannot be conceptualized by these theorists. They simply lack both the adequate normative description and an explication of morality.

Peter Marin (1981) poignantly describes the plight of Vietnam veterans suffering from "delayed stress syndrome," some of whom committed actual atrocities during war time and cannot forgive themselves. Not only have they failed to obtain forgiveness from their society, they cannot even convince their therapists to understand their plight. By describing this real and crushing guilt as "stress," the veterans are dehumanized and increasingly cut off from the society. In a society that denies the existence and reality of guilt and the need for expiation, the veterans can find no resolution to their problems.

Ellis (1974) would have us happily explaining that, "if I perform an action I must have wanted to and therefore since I am good my action must be good." We are extolled by a growing number of happiness experts that "I'm O.K. and You're O.K." Wayne Dyer (1976), whose success as a human being is so total, we are told by his publishers, that he has even been on national television, suggests that "guilt is a useless emotion." Dyer and those who share the happiness view have produced an atmosphere in which people feel guilty if they feel guilty and sad if they are sad. They could never show us, as Frankl does (1982), that some suffering is unavoidable and what enobles us is how we suffer.

Happiness theories misdirect us to the real causes of happiness, which will never come about by technologies and pharmacopoeia but by the quality and love in our interpersonal relationships. Real satisfaction comes from hard work and the achievement of real quality in our efforts and productions. The happiness school would rather tell us that hard work is "obsessive-compulsive behavior" and struggle is a producer of "neurotic unhappiness." Real joy results from following the golden rule no matter how simple this homile might seem. The wisdom of ancient Hebrew prophets, Christ, Buddha, Muhammed, and Confucius has not yet been surpassed by the modern prophets of the mall bookstore.

The moral consequences of accepting such simplistic views of psychology are staggering. They tell us that only we are important, that the other is not, which leads to what Christopher Lasch (1978) calls the "me" generation and what Rollo May (1981) describes as the "new narcissism." They tell us as well that if we express a need or emotion, it is automatically valid and equal to any other expression. Thus, the sounds of a computer programmed with random numbers and the notes written by Mozart are of equal value.

O. Hobart Mowrer (1964) suggests that within the Judeo-Christian morality humanity was held responsible for both good and evil behavior ("double responsibility"). With the coming of Protestantism and the doctrine of predestination, humanity was responsible only for good behavior; evil was a mark of one's predetermined place in hell ("single responsibility"). With the coming of Freud and the new therapies, mankind is responsible for neither good nor evil behavior ("double irresponsibility").

Modern psychology often deprives us of our responsibility by making our guilt and discomforts "neuroses." We are under the influence of infantile sexual impulses or the programming created by incorrect behavioral technologies. Moreover, by being unhappy, we are failing to live up to the standards of mental health and the need to be in a state of constant ecstasy. Since our responsibility is to ourselves, we must turn away from those who demand our suffering; and since we don't owe them anything anyway, this *should* be easy to do. Local doctors and psychiatrists will be eager to help, along with the liquor industry, to banish the blues and to correct the thinking that led us to ponder our human condition and feel grief.

One of the end results of the need to be happy is the trivialization of culture. We turn to clothes, automobiles, alcohol, and cocaine in a futile attempt to find the happiness that can only come from love, responsibility, and meaningful work. We turn away from the pain in the world, pretend it does not exist, and watch vacuous television shows that deaden our feelings. The sellers of soft drinks, airplane tickets, and hamburgers sing the praises of their products (designed for our unending happiness) with the pomp and ferver once reserved for praising God.

I do not wish to argue against games, play, or any activities that make life enjoyable. Cocktails with dinner can make dinner more pleasureable. I wish to avoid making my position one in opposition to fun, laughter, and happiness. However, the happiness school offers the extreme point of view that life itself is a joyful game and that pain is an avoidable commodity. Hamburgers are a wonderful food, but they are not important enough to sing about. When we refuse to see life's inevitable dark side we become trivialized and meaningless. We need fantasy, play, and all manner of escapist activity to add to life's pleasure, but we need these activities when the situation suggests that their indulgence is appropriate.

The theory I wish to propose holds that part of our motivational system consists of the basic emotions. Guilt and shame are two such emotions, along with joy, surprise, and other pleasant affects. Part of our humanness comes from the fact that we can feel guilt when we do wrong, and shame when we have let down those who are important to us. While these negative emotions can also be created by the irrational demands of others and by trying to live up to unrealistic standards, they exist as primary indicators of transgressions against a social order that is necessary for survival. Only a view that integrates a rational theory of morality can help us distinguish between irrational and rational guilt and shame.

6. THE IMAGE OF HUMANITY

Rollo May (1981) writes of a psychologist who published many papers and gained the acclaim of his colleagues; he now stands before St. Peter petitioning for entrance into heaven. His entreaty is denied because: "you are charged with *nimis simplicando* . . . you have spent your life making molehills out of mountains—that's what you're guilty of. When man was tragic, you made him trivial. When he was picaresque, you called him picayune. When he suffered passively, you described him as simpering; and when he drummed up enough courage to act, you called it stimulus and response. Man had passions and when you were pompous and lecturing to your class you called it 'the satisfaction of basic needs' . . . you made man over into the image of your childhood Erector Set and Sunday School maxim—both equally horrendous" (p. 3).

How can we rescue an image of humanity from such horrendous simplification by so much of our field? Can that image be rescued from existing concepts and yet retain a scientific methodology and mode of thinking as the process takes place? Can we find a way of disagreeing with Gregory Bateson, who believes that there is no science of psychology and that the whole discipline is a mistake to begin with? We can answer all of these questions in the affirmative and use existing concepts to achieve our ends.

I suggest that we focus on the roles played by the intellect and the emotions in our day-to-day lives. The intellect and the emotions interact; and with the development of the former over time, the interactions must inevitably change as well. The cognitive-affective interpretations of the eight-year-old are not those of a two-year-old— at least they need not be. Adult interpretations can be much different from the child's. Some emerge from childhood as mature, loving, caring, creative individuals, while others destroy themselves in a rage and in a state of fear.

Piaget enables us to catch a glimpse of intellectual development that is possible in any human being. Izard, Plutchik, and others describe not only the range of emotion of which we are capable but the interaction of cognition and emotion. The analysts reveal to us that our personalities may become fixated, regress, or fail to develop. I suggest that what becomes fixated is not our instinct but the manner in which we interpret our environment. If individuals are fixated, this focus is addressed to the meaning of the world.

Mature individuals learn and feel emotion in appropriate ways that lead to further learning and to the development of solutions to problems. They do not rely simply on intellect but also on their emotions to understand and interact with their world and those in it. Intellect combines with interest to produce individuals who are anxious and willing (and needing) to learn about the people and situations with which they interact. Finally, such people can be objective about themselves, tempering pride with insight about weaknesses as well as strengths. The individuals whose consciousness become directed toward the world by the emotions of interest cannot help but care about that world.

Fixated, "pathological" behavior, on the other hand, is the result of an interpretation of the world that is not appropriate for a person's age. Such individuals see the world egocentrically, believing that they are more important or more powerful than they actually are. They are unable to share, believing that only they deserve, suffer and need. Such individuals strive to be "perfect" in terms that only the child can conceive. They lack the flexibility provided by the kind of thinking that shows mature operations. Such people have exaggerated emotional responses to situations whose meaning they have misinterpreted. Their emotions are both inappropriate to the situation and poorly modulated and controlled. They see the world as divided between the "good" and the "bad" with themselves as the good. Their perceptions contain no shades of grey.

I suggest that pathologies are best understood as fixated modes of cognitive-emotional-interpersonal experience. The best and most mature among us can be understood as individuals whose modes of experiencing meaning are more fully developed. Such individuals behave in a "scientific" manner in all or most aspects of their lives. They observe, learn, enjoy learning, and keep an open mind when hypothesizing about themselves and others. Abnormal or pathological individuals think in narrow, fixed categories about a world they are convinced they understand and that has nothing more to teach them.

Sociology anthropology, social psychology, and communications theory all contain brilliant insights into how culture and society help shape our cognitive, emotional modes of interpretation as well as the bi-directional nature of the interaction between the individual and his society. The family therapists add insight into the role of marriage and family as the interfacing unit between the individual and the larger culture. By exploring their interaction, at a variety of ages and stages of development, we can formulate ideas as to why some individuals mature and others do not.

The existentialists and humanists describe the best that we can become. Erikson's concept of "generational man," developed so well by Browning (1973), is a proper model for the image of humanity that we seek, once we have recognized that the generational man interprets his world with a particularly mature mode of interpretative skills. How can we understand the particular mode of experience? Again, we find it in existing literature.

Sigmund Koch (1981) provides us with the desired model of maturity:

> On the other hand meaningful (scientific-mature) thinking involves a direct perception of unveiled, vivid relations that seem to strive from the quiddities, particularities of the objects of thought, the *problem situation* that forms the occasion of thought. *There is an organic determination of the form and substance of thought by the properties of the object and the terms of the problem.* In meaningful thinking, the mind caresses, flows joyously in, over and around the relational matrix defined by the problem, the object. There is a merging of person and object or problem. (p. 260, italics mine)

We see in Koch's quote the integration of person, situation, cognition, and emotion.

8

A Cognitive-Affective-Developmental-Interpersonal Theory of Personality: Preliminary Concepts

PIAGET'S COGNITIVE DEVELOPMENTAL THEORY

The theory being proposed in this book is based upon the notion that specific behavior results from the individual's interpretation of his/her environmental-cultural situation. The theory represents an eclecticism: interpretations are dependent upon the individual's cognitive-emotional mode of experience. In this chapter, I will begin by presenting some of the ideas concerning cognitive development as suggested by Piaget, followed by exposition on the theories of human emotion described by Izard (1978, 1979, 1984) and Plutchik (1977, 1980). In the final section, I will attempt to establish some tentative relationships between *cognition at various developmental stages* and the emotions.

Jerome Bruner (1966) points out that Piaget never developed a true psychological theory. His, was really a developmental epistemology. Piaget was concerned with the intellectual understanding of our world and the rules that governed intellectual organization. In effect, he investigated the capacity of the growing individual to understand the meaning of situations and events. In the organization of knowledge, Piaget sought the organization of the knower. He was concerned basically with intellectual knowing and not with emotional or drive-based meanings.

However, Piaget's epistemology provides a theory that permits us to create a psychology in which human interpretive modalities can play a central role. He understood that science, religion, philosophy, and art are all human creations or constructions, and as such they reflect the thought processes of the individuals who create them. By extending Piaget's ideas we can see that the mental organization of the scientist, the authoritarian religionist, and the delusions of the psychotic all come from the same wellspring and reflect the underlying unity of human understanding.

The psychotic and the scientist, while solving the same set of problems, are operating from different sets of reality constructions. The heart of Piaget's theory is that the infant lacks a constructed view of reality, but as he interacts with his environment, he begins to build or create a view of his world. It is this *constructed* view of reality that differentiates the psychotic and the scientist, the child and the adult. Few theorists spent as much time detailing the nature of the child's changing intellectual construction as did Piaget.

The following pages will contain only an outline of Piaget's theory, particularly those concepts necessary in the building of a personality theory. The reader who is interested in learning more about Piaget can turn to his own works (1952, 1954, 1973, 1975), those written with B. Inhelder, and a variety of excellent secondary sources. Special mention has to be made of John Flavell's (1968) most important work, which has much to do with the popularity that Piaget now enjoys in this country despite the very real difficulties in reading Piagetian translations.

The idea that the human being constructs a view of reality that is based both upon biologically inherited neurological capacities and environmental stimulation, falls between the position of the nativist and the empiricist. Piaget believed that at birth the child possesses basic schema, or tendencies to behave, and that these action tendencies lead to the development of thought after careful, long modification by environmental experiences.

Growth occurs, according to Piaget, as the result of two processes known as "functional invariants," so called because they describe the organism's functioning as long as it continues to interact with the environment. The two functional invariants are *adaptation,* which involves the organism's successful or unsuccessful attempts to master the environment, and *organization,* which describes the internal mental changes that occur as the organism adapts and develops new and complex cognitive and behavioral structures. Adaptation is comprised of two complementary processes: *assimilation* and *accommodation*. Adaptation is both of these processes, although each is individually describable in its own right. Just as a coin is indescribable without heads and tails, both heads and tails have their own properties and are indescribable without one another.

Let us examine the nature of assimilation and accommodation. The former involves the utilization of existing thoughts, schemes, or behavior patterns to solve new problems. The child actively attempts to make the world fit his conceptions of it or existing levels of skills. At birth the child possesses certain inborn behavioral patterns or schema. The utilization of these tendencies to behave represents the earliest attempts at assimilation. However, the environment constantly varies with respect to the demands it makes on the child, who is forced to change or modify behavioral and thought patterns to assimilate successfully the new stimuli or situation. In other words, the child not only accommodates in order to assimilate but accommodates *because* he assimilates.

Some examples are in order. Baby Warren tries to adapt to his environment; he applies the sucking schema with which he was born in order to assimilate the nipple and its milk. His schema is a generalized tendency to suck and his efforts with a real nipple are only partially successful. If Warren can accommodate his mouth to the actual nipple, he will successfully assimilate and hence adapt to the situation.

The dual processes of assimilation and accommodation continue as long as learning occurs. The growing child, as well as the adult, attempts to solve or assimilate problems by utilizing existing skills and behaviors. But each new situation requires use of particular skills not utilized before. Therefore, accommodations are continually made, with resulting changes taking place in existing skills.

Fantasy and dreaming are activities that emphasize assimilation. The real world is made to conform to our existing abilities. During periods of imitation and identification, accommodation predominates, as the individual extensively changes his behavior to match that of a model. Assimilation and accommodation can reach an equilibrium, but equilibria are always temporary in an individual learning to deal with an ever-changing environment.

Growth can be seen as becoming fixated when an individual is presented with an environment that no longer represents challenge. Boredom is the emotional result. Growth also stops when one is asked to accommodate a demand that is beyond the scope of one's understanding or behavioral repertoire. One central hypothesis of the present theory is that growth ceases when an individual cannot accommodate an environmental demand and henceforth assimilates into fantasy all similar environmental demands.

If development is normal, the growing individual will pass through four developmental epochs, in which the organization of skills and thought changes. The rules of thinking and perception are qualitatively different in each stage. Each new level represents a relearning of the achievements of the preceding stage but with new sets of rules. New stages represent qualitative and quantitative superiority over previous stages.

Piaget's theory describes in a very real sense the cognitive individuation of the child. At birth and through early childhood the youngster is embedded in his environment, which he sees as an extention of his feelings and thoughts. Moreover, the child is dominated by his perceptions of the field around him. Piaget describes how the growing child frees himself from the perceptual field by reducing his egocentric perceptions and developing a cognitive awareness of his surroundings and his relation to them. With the development of concrete and then formal operations, the youngster becomes capable of abstract ideas free of the content of the environment in which he lives.

The Sensorimotor Stage

The first developmental stage begins at birth and is complete by approximately age two. Piaget refers to this period as the Sensorimotor stage. At birth babies possess a number of reflexes or biologically-provided schema (action tendencies), which are purposive in that they involve motor behaviors designed to help infants survive. Babies, however, are not aware of the consequences of their behaviors in terms of survival, but, rather, in terms of the sensation produced by them. Throughout early development we see the child being rewarded to learn a host of skills without his awareness of the real function of his activities. The child's motivations to learn necessary skills is kept high without any external efforts to "teach" the youngster that which he needs to learn.

The earliest purposive behaviors under baby's control are the primary circular reactions: the awareness that sucking, rocking, grasping, and so on (the basic schema), produce pleasurable sensations. As a result, the schema are reinforced and thus repeated. Repetition plays a very important role for learning in Piaget's theory. In chapter 12, I shall suggest that primary circular reactions play an important role in the development of obsessions and compulsions, which are significant concepts in psychiatry.

The primary circular reactions reveal little means-ends differentiation, but this changes at about four months of age with the emergence of the secondary circular reactions. Melanie, at three months, discovers that her movements can make "interesting things happen." She repeats behaviors that cause her crib, her mobile, and her bumper to move. She makes sounds for their interesting qualities and not simply for the kinesthetic feedback they produce. The behaviors mastered during the secondary circular reactions are used to assimilate objects that are not a part of the body.

Throughout infancy, schemas are extended and coordinated as development continues. The looking schema is coordinated with the grasping schema as Melanie looks at the objects of her graspings and grasps what she sees. The sensory information about objects is received simultaneously through different modalities as she develops early object permanence.

There is constant shifting of means-ends relationships as today's ends become tomorrow's means. Robin will become interested in dropping objects from her crib or carriage. Before she becomes interested in the bottle's trajectory as it falls, she will be interested in her own hand as it closes and opens around the bottle. The hand is, at first, the object of the child's interest. As the hand and it's operation are assimilated, the child then becomes interested in the bottle after the hand is open. The hand has now become the means to a new end. The child becomes fascinated by the bottle dropping. This, too, will become a means when she learns that the falling bottle brings mommy who will retrieve the bottle.

We will see many instances in which initial learning begins with interest focused on the operation of the body and then extends to the object world. Adulthood offers many examples of this process. When Mark learns to drive a car, he will focus on the operation of his hands and legs as they interact with the vehicle's mechanisms.

As these are mastered, Mark will see the automobile as a means of transportation and no longer remain interested in it for itself.

By eight months, Warren has learned about his body and it's basic operations. He has discovered that acting on the body feels differently than acting on the rest of the world. He learns that he exists in a world of interacting objects that continue to exist even when he is not in sensory contact with them. The knowledge that objects exist independently of one's perception is known as object constancy. With object constancy, we see an improvement in memory and the initial internalization of thought. Warren begins to anticipate future events and begins to show planning or intentionality.

At about one year of age, Warren reveals tertiary circular reactions. He makes interesting things happen, but varies his movements upon a variety of objects to compare the resulting sensory events. For example, he will bang some pots, but vary his repetitions from loud to soft to loud again. He will bang on the pots with one instrument, then another. He will compare the sound produced by hitting a big pot with that of striking a little one.

Psychological infancy ends as Warren begins to internalize his schema to form the rudiments of thought. By eighteen months, he possesses mental representatives of actions and objects. He begins to draw his conceptualizations of objects, begins to show deferred imitation of the people and other important objects in his life. We see the emergence of imaginative play as well. Warren's early representation can be in terms of images or of movements. The child enters the preoperational phase of development as infancy draws to a close.

The Preoperational Stage

The preoperational period is a transitional phase between the sensorimotor period and the stage of concrete operations when true conceptualization and genuine logical operations will exist. In many ways description of the preoperational stage is difficult because one must deal not only with what does exist but also with what is not yet in existence. The youngster begins to utilize concepts, but these are preconcepts—they are not yet true conceptualizations. The preoperational period is subdivided into two main phases: the preconceptual subphase (two to five years) and the intuitive subphase (five to seven years).

Melanie, during the preconceptual phase, is still dominated by perceptual schema. She believes what she sees and lacks a conceptual framework to reinterpret what she perceives. Moreover, she tends to *center* her perception on only one element of an object in the perceptual field and cannot (until age five or so) de-center her perceptions to include more than one element. A famous Piaget experiment will demonstrate this phenomenon.

Melanie, age three, is asked to judge the size of two identical balls of clay. She correctly judges them to be the same. Then one of the balls is rolled out into a sausage shape. The child watches this procedure and is asked to make the same judgment again. She now states that the round ball is larger (or perhaps the sausage is larger) because it is higher (or longer). Melanie has centered her perception on one element of the clay (the height) and has made her judgment on that basis. Moreover, she lacks any mental operations such as the ability to reverse the sausage clay back into it's round shape to counter her perceptual domination.

The above experiment demonstrates the child's lack of *conservation of quantity*. It also helps demonstrate the reason that the child's thinking forms preconcepts rather than actual concepts. For example, if a child looks at an animal and is told that it is a "doggie," she then looks at a cat and calls it a "doggie." She has centered her perception on the fur, the tail, or perhaps the four leggedness shared by the animals. She deals with one common similarity and builds a class based upon her perceptual grasping of one common element.

In order to understand the concept "dog," the child would have to comprehend the variety of qualities that together make up a "dog," but also understand those qualities that are not "dog," but perhaps "cat." At ages three and four, the child simply cannot deal intellectually with that level of complexity. He will tell you that an "apple" and a "banana" are "not the same." However, if he cannot see a single perceptual similarity on which to center, he will be unable to go beyond that level of information.

The child's inability to form consistent classes of objects and concepts prevents the appearance of true logic. The earliest true logic appears as inductive reasoning where specific observations lead to a generalization. Children generalize from too little information. Their logic is therefore transductive. Thus, a child, putting on her mother's shoes, will say, "I am a mommy." She does not say "I am like a mommy." Her reasoning:

A mommy wears high heel shoes
I wear high heel shoes, therefore,
I am a mommy

The reason behind a delusion such as "I am Napoleon," is precisely an example of this transductive logic. The psychotic states that Napoleon is a man, I am a man, therefore, I am Napoleon.

A number of other qualities mark the thinking of the preoperational child. One of the most noticeable aspects of Robin's thought is her egocentrism, a concept that plays a central role in the Cognitive-Affective-Developmental-Interpersonal theory. Egocentrism is defined as the child's inability to see things from any other viewpoint than her/his own. Egocentrism means more than the inability to take another person's point of view, which of course the child cannot do. The young Robin assumes that when she is sad, everyone is sad; when she is happy, so is the rest of humanity.

The concept of egocentrism is not limited to the preoperational stage. It is a concept that can be applied to individuals of any age. The infant is the most egocentric when he closes his eyes and behaves as if the world no longer exists. One-year-old Mark, who covers his eyes and says to his mother "You can't see me," is being highly egocentric. We will see later that under strong affect even mature adults can become highly egocentric. In general, normal development means a reduction of egocentrism as an individual matures from stage to stage.

The child's thinking is highly animistic, which is in part due to the egocentrism. Anything that moves is seen as alive, as is anything that makes sounds. A one-year-old can be under a tree and laugh at the leaves as they move. Thunder is the "roar of a monster" while snow represents a "pillow fight between the angels." Normal egocentrism can be seen as the basis of the anthropomorphism that created the Greco-Roman Gods and perhaps is the structural basis of all religion.

Related to animistic thought is purposivism. Every event is related to a human purpose. Thus "the picnic was rained out just so I could not have a good time." Animism and purposivism are combined, as in the case of a child who cuts himself while playing with a sharp knife and then states, "The knife cut me because I was bad." Artificialism is the closely related concept that describes the child's idea that all natural features have human planning behind them. "This lake is the footprint of a giant" or "God is a man, men like blue, so that's why the sky is blue."

The child's egocentrism creates a very inadequate sense of causality. Melanie assumes that all events relate to her in some way: If her parents argue, for example, they do so because of her or about her, and it becomes her sole responsibility to stop these problems from continuing. David Elkind (1970) suggests that such children perceive any two continuous events as causally related. He calls this "phenomenalistic causality." This concept leads the child to believe that all negative occurrences she perceives are related to her in some causative manner.

A concept similar to purposivism and phenomenalistic causality is immanent justice. The child believes that if he does something wrong he will be punished; if he is punished he must have done something wrong. When bad or painful things happen to Melanie she lacks the ability to discern the true causes of the events and assumes that she is at fault. A child will assume guilt, and a concomitant need for punishment, for all manner of events that in reality have nothing to do with her. Parental conflict or divorce are often seen by the child as proof of her badness. The child can feel guilty even if the parents take pains to explain that the conflict or the divorce was unrelated to her in any way.

The Piagetian describes the play of the child as "imaginative" or "as if" play. Children three to seven years of age become intensely involved in both their play and in all fantasy activity. Dreams and fantasies may be remembered as real. Children can believe their thoughts to be real; that wishing for an event can cause it to occur. Childhood imagination when combined with fear can produce the well-known night terrors as well as friendly and frightening imaginary playmates. Selma Fraiberg (1968) has described these phenomena as creating a period of life known as "the magic years."

Magical omnipotence (thinking makes it so) is another characteristic of preoperational thinking. If Warren wishes for roller skates and his wishes are granted by his father, it is the wish that produced the skates, not his father's intention and ability to provide the toy. For many adults, God is an animistically created figure that assumes the physical characteristics of those who create him. For these individuals, prayer represents the same function as Warren's wish. God—a man in a literal place called heaven—will see and hear wishes (prayers) and grant desires.

Children of the preoperational stage do not yet possess a logic that leads them to order things from smallest to largest. Piaget called this ability to order objects and events according to some scale of values as "seriation." Moreover, children do not understand part-whole or fraction relationships: for example, Melanie breaks her cookie in half and exclaims, "Now I have two cookies." She also cannot understand how an object can belong to more than one category at a time. Thus Melanie can live in New York but not in the United States or in North America. Her aunt cannot simultaneously be her mother's sister, and her cousins cannot be the children of her mother's sister.

The ideas described above have other profound consequences. Something that is good cannot be bad. Moreover, that which is good cannot be good sometimes, or partially good and partially bad. Combine the concepts of egocentrism and imminent justice and we see that the child who feels herself to be good or bad tends to feel very good or very bad, and is somehow responsible for that goodness or badness.

The preoperational child has a limited concept of time. There is daytime, nighttime, mealtime, and sleeptime, but all of these "times" are in the here and now. Preoperational children have no real past and no future at all. A child in pain *is* always in pain, *was* always in pain, and *never will not be* in pain. Similarly, if the youngster feels good, that, too, is an eternal condition. When mommy is nice, she is always nice; when mommy is mean, she is always mean.

When we discuss the fixated preoperational thinking involved in defense mechanisms, we will see the cumulative effect of centering, egocentrism, magical omnipotence, animisms, literalisms, overgeneralizations, imminent justice, phenomenalistic causality, the lack of seriation, gradation, and time concepts on the self-images and social interactions of the fixated person.

Piaget and the orthodox Freudians intensely disagreed as to the nature of the phenomena we have been discussing. The traditional analyst sees the thinking of the young child as drive organized (Rapaport, 1951), while the Piagetian sees the same thinking as a normal transition to adult forms of thought. Stanley Greenspan (1979), in his attempt to relate psychoanalysis to Piaget's theory, clearly sees the egocentric thought organization of the young child in Piagetian terms, but he also describes those conditions under which thinking can be affected by the drives and the emotions. Piaget's notions are really quite comparable with much of *ego* psychology, which sees thinking as autonomous from the drives.

During the intuitive subphase of the preoperational period, Michael's ability to reason and solve problems improves, but his solutions are not based on logic. If we return to the clay experiment and ask a five-year-old which piece of clay, the ball or the sausage, is bigger, he is likely to say "They are both bigger." He has begun to decenter his perceptions, and further inquiry reveals that he sees one as bigger because it is taller, the other as bigger because it is wider. Thus, he is beginning to deal with more information, but cannot yet relate it to concepts such as volume or mass.

Concrete Operations

By the age of seven, the typical child has entered the stage of concrete operations. Michael possesses the ability to "behave" in purely mental terms. While he thinks best about the here, the now, and familiar objects, and is still, therefore, concrete in his thinking, he has become capable of true mental operations. He can add, subtract, multiply, and divide—all mental operations. He can form true concepts, as well as build up and break down classes. Inductive thought emerges and an adequate sense of time develops. He can understand part-whole and fractional relationships, and is capable of ordering a series of objects, an activity referred to as seriation in Piaget's theory.

Moreover, Michael's thinking follows certain rules in its organization, rules or principles based upon mathematical models that Piaget believed reflected the underlying organization of the thought patterns from which they were produced. Many of the terms used to describe thinking come from the rules that describe groups, groupings, and lattices. For our purposes, the discussion of concrete operation will remain nontechnical and basically descriptive.

One of the significant achievements of the concrete operational stage is that of conservation. Quantity, time, distance, and a variety of other attributes of the physical world become conserved. The experiment with the clay demonstrated the preoperational child's lack of quantity conservation. The same experiment with a seven-year-old demonstrates the achieving of conservation. Stacey is confronted with two identical balls of clay, watches one being rolled out into a sausage-shaped figure, and when asked to gauge their size she immediately answers that they are the same. Stacey's judgment is based upon her use of various internal abilities created by the relationships among her developed operations. She can utilize her ability to reverse mental operations. She watches the ball of clay being rolled out and can *reverse* the procedure in her mind. The operational child can use reversibility in many areas thus permitting great flexibility of thought. Stacey also understands that there is an *identity* element involved in making the judgment. An object (or number) to which nothing (or zero) has been added or taken away remains the same. Finally, she applies logic by implicitly realizing that "things equal to the same thing must be equal to each other."

The implications of conservation for personality development are enormous. The achieving of object constancy, or the object concept, at eight months means that the child can recognize objects as existing even when she is not in contact with them. Changing certain aspects of an object, such as it's shape, has changed the nature of the object. As we will see (and this is one of the significant contributions of object relations theory), the young child will react to an angry mother as if the latter were somehow different than when she was not angry. With conservation, the child has the ability to learn (this is not to say that she *will* learn) that an angry mother is *the same mother* who, a while ago, was not angry.

Formal Operations

If development progresses and Warren continues to encounter and assimilate problems of increasing difficulty, then, by the age of eleven, he reveals the presence of formal operations. Formal operations permit abstractions to exist. In other words, Warren can turn his thinking back on his own thought processes. He can think about thinking or be aware of his own awareness. He can be logical about logic. For the first time Warren can reflect about himself as an objective datum. In clinical terms, we would say that he has a capacity for *insight*. With these formal operations, Warren can ask himself, "Why did I say that?" or "Where is the error in my logic?" Not only can he be logical, he can correct his own lack of logic. The youngster not only utilizes inductive logic, but also creates hypotheses about future events utilizing *deductive logic*. The capacity to develop hypotheses is what Piaget calls "hypothetico-deductive thinking," and it is this type of thought that makes the scientific enterprise possible.

Warren as an adolescent is now able to formulate effective plans of actions as he deals with the probablistic nature of future events. He is capable of asking a series of questions beginning with "What if . . ." and answering them probablistically. In fact, the youngster's whole orientation begins to shift toward the future, which begins to count much more as an influence on his present behavior. He becomes concerned with his future and even involved with the rest of his life, including his own death. Later we will discuss the importance of an individual's emotional reactions to thoughts of death.

The youngster can now solve problems on a more sophisticated and complex level than was the case at earlier stages. In other words, he can combine various elements in an experiment utilizing every combination and permutation, having worked these out systemically in his mind before beginning work. He can think about the universe; the infinity of space, time, and distance; and begin to understand the relationships between these ideas.

Warren is now capable of understanding the nature of metaphor and allegory and what Lewis Carroll really meant in *Alice Through the Looking Glass* (a description of altered states of consciousness due to drugs and mental illness) or the meaning to be found in Jonathan Swift's *Gulliver's Travels* (a political satire critical of the pettiness of which kings are capable). Time concepts continue to improve allowing an appreciation of history and historical places. We see a further decrease in egocentrism, allowing the youngster to understand others sympathetically and empathetically. A real understanding of the abstract issues underlying religion and morality can emerge with the development of formal operations.

The child becomes capable of scientific activity with the emergence of formal operations. For example, Robin can now use inductive and deductive logic that permit generalizations and predictive hypotheses to be created. She can explore all of the permutations of combinations possible in the relationship of a series of variables. Such research can be carried out in any or all of the areas of an individual's life. The reader is referred to chapter 1 for a more detailed review of the scientific mode of thinking.

This description of Piaget's view of formal operations of the mind is thumbnail at best. As the developmental psychology of this volume unfolds, I will call upon his concepts, as well as others. However, the present description gives a flavor of the type of developmental concept necessary in any personality theory if it is to account for the rich complexity of human behavior. Utilizing Piaget's theory, and in particular the concepts described above, we can create a theory in which human creativity and thinking plays a central role.

IZARD'S DIFFERENTIAL EMOTIONS THEORY

As described earlier, Piaget does not deal effectively or extensively with emotions and their relationship with thinking, especially thought at different levels of development. Moreover, his theory lacks any real notion of motivation: learning and development are essentially seen as intrinsically motivated. There are few descriptions as to what determines the direction of individual interests in learning. By utilizing Carroll Izard's theory we can supplement Piaget's epistemology and turn the latter's theory into a true psychology that can become the basis of a psychology of personality.

Izard (1977, 1984) perceives the human personality as based upon six subsystems: "the homeostatic, drive, emotion, perceptual, cognitive, and motor systems." Motivation is provided by four types of phenomena: drives, emotions, affective-cognitive interactions, and affective-cognitive structures. The concepts of emotion are derived substantially from the work of Silvan Tomkins (1962, 1967). It is also clear that any system of personality can interact with the emotions; thus, drive arousal can lead to various emotional reactions, as can motor responses. Moreover, the relationship between an emotion and any other subsystem can be reciprocal. As we will see below, a thought can arouse an emotion, which in turn can arouse or affect another thought.

A key concept in Izard's theory is that thoughts, emotions, drives, and even motoric behavior can be linked by complex organizations of nearly infinite variety. A movement can arouse a thought, that arouses an emotion, that arouses another emotion, and so on. There is no end to the number of combinations and permutations of cognition, emotion, drives, percepts, and motor responses. Even internal homeostatic mechanisms can be involved, as when an individual feels a gas bubble, thinks it is a heart attack, and responds with panic emotions.

Emotions can be linked in "dyads" and "triads," according to Izard. Anxiety, shame, and guilt constitute one commonly linked triad with which clinicians often have to deal. Drives, such as sex, are often linked with a variety of emotions, such as love or joy. Psychology is only now dealing with the complex interaction of cognitive-drive-affective organizations that exist in all individuals, often without any conscious awareness on the part of the individual.

Izard assumes *ten basic discrete emotions,* which combine to comprise all emotional experience. "Differential emotions theory defines emotion as a complex process with neurophysiological, neuro-muscular and phenomenological aspects" (p. 48). There is in each emotion a "pattern of electrochemical activity in the nervous system, particularly in the cortex, the hypothalamus, the basal ganglia, the limbic system and the facial and trigeminal nerves" (p. 48). Unlike Stanley Schacter's (1977) theory, Izard sees a different physiological reaction and experience for each emotion. Involuntary functions such as glandular secretions and heart rate, as well as intestinal activity, are involved in the neurophysiological activity. "At the neuromuscular level emotion is primarily facial activity and facial patterning, and secondarily it is bodily (postural, gestural, visceral, glandular, and sometimes vocal) response. At the phenomenological level, emotion is essentially motivating experience and/or experience that has *immediate meaning and significance for the person"* (p. 49).

An element of each emotional response is unlearned. As infants, each of the ten basic inborn emotions are initally unmodified by learning. Only later is emotional expression modified by learning but we remain evolutionarily programmed to respond. Emotions are unconditioned responses, if we use the paradigm of classical conditioning. There exist, then, a number of stimuli or situations that can arouse an emotion in us without our first having contact with that particular stimulus in that particular context. Thus a loud noise can produce fear in a child without the child ever having heard the noise previously. Babies respond to a smiling face (and adults to a baby's smile) without learning taking place.

Emotional responses are learned, if at all, to the extent that they are aroused by specific situations or people with whom the child does not initially respond. Children are not ordinarily afraid of white rats or other small animals. However, if the white rat and the child come together at the time of a fear-producing loud noise, it may come to pass that the child might learn to fear the rat. While our emotions are not learned, there is the possibility that we can learn to respond emotionally to inappropriate cues or situations.

Izard suggests that there is a behavioral consequence of each emotion. Emotions are aroused by situations and demand behavior that presumably increases our survival. They call for us to approach or avoid, fight or flee, and so forth. Human beings, however, learn to override basic internal messages in a variety of areas: we eat when we are not hungry; engage in sex for money, power, and a hundred other reasons; we learn to fight when we desire to flee; and we laugh when we wish to cry. When under social pressures, human beings can become quite adept at ignoring the responses suggested to them by their emotions.

Some emotions seem to direct individuals to relate to their environment. Thus when afraid, it is natural to run and hide. However, other emotions seem to direct them toward social aims and goals. If emotions have survival value, then some emotions must exist that ensure group cohesiveness and solidarity. Twentieth-century psychologists often seem to forget that survival and intense emotional rewards come from our relations to other people. Shame and guilt seem to exist for the purpose of forcing us to relate to others in ways that run counter to other emotional reactions. Thus, the desire to run, hide, and abandon a fellow being can lead to guilt and shame strong enough to keep one individual at another's side despite fear.

Emotions have a social as well as a motivational role to play. We are social beings, and part of an emotional response is to tell those around us how they have affected us. Facial expressions and postural cues tell others that they have made us happy, sad, angry, or fearful. Humans can and do learn to inhibit the public expression of emotion and this often means immobilization of the face and other postural, gestural activity.

Emotional expression in one person is often the stimulus for emotional arousal in other people. The ease with which emotions are transmitted to and aroused in others lets us suggest that these emotions are unlearned responses. It may be that the principle class of unconditioned stimuli, where emotions are concerned, are the expressive gestures and sounds of another. Certainly, empathy and sympathy exist because of our ability to respond to the emotions of others.

Izard offers descriptions for "cognitive-affective interactions" and "cognitive-affective structures": the former refers to momentary or temporary linkages of thought and emotion, while the latter suggests more enduring linkages of idea and affect. We can think of a particular person, activity, or situation and always be filled with certain emotions. Such structures can exist as consistent motivations and can be powerful, permanent shapers of our behavior. Thus an object can arouse the same cognitive-affective structures in adulthood as when we were young children. We will then behave toward it as if we were still that child.

The "emotion" of interest warrants a special mention. We generally speak of interest as something we possess: "I have an interest in. . . ." We are really saying that the thing in which we are interested arouses interest in us for itself. "We feel an interest for or in . . ." is the proper descriptive sentence. This concept of interest is important for the *ego* psychologist who is always looking for nonsexual reasons to be positively interested in something. If the *ego* is our "organ" of survival, then interest is the *ego's* own motivation. Silvan Tomkins (1962) suggests there is no end of things for which we might learn to feel an interest. However, interest also provides a nonconflictual explanation for the infant's willingness to learn. Why does the infant become interested in one set of activities rather than another? We may answer by suggesting that the most necessary activities for survival may be the ones that initially arouse interest. We need not posit fear or sublimated sexuality as the reason for a child learning one thing or another, although such drives and emotions might also influence the child's involvements.

The following is Izard's list of our basic ten emotions:

1. Interest—excitement
2. Enjoyment—joy
3. Surprise—startle
4. Distress—anguish
5. Anger—rage
6. Distrust—revulsion
7. Contempt—scorn
8. Fear—terror
9. Shame/Shyness—humiliation
10. Guilt—remorse

It is beyond the scope of this section to discuss the emotions further, but after a discussion of the relationship of cognition and emotion, I will present a theory of how the various emotions shape our personality and form the basis of morality.

One final thought is in order. Freud (1905) considered the drives, particularly sex drives, to be our primary motivational system. Anxiety motivates defensive behavior if forbidden and repressed drives threaten either to break into consciousness or to be acted upon. The emotions were secondary to and dependent upon the bio-evolutionary drives for their existence. In the present context, we are considering the emotions to be the primary bio-evolutionary motivational system. Sex and the other drives exist side by side with the emotions and interact with them. Sexual arousal may be preceded or followed by a wide variety of emotions. Sex-love-joy is a common linkage in sexual expression. Sex can lead to anxiety, fear, shame, or guilt as well. An individual can be anxious but interpret the affect as sexual arousal seeking interactive tranquilization. Loneliness can motivate sexual desire as a means of achieving closeness and the cessation of loneliness. Sexual activity is rarely manifested by itself without being organized by and without provoking a wide range of motivating emotions.

If the emotions are as basic as sex, then we can consider them to be as much a part of Freud's *id* as the instinctual drives are. One of the most important contributions to psychoanalysis has been the description of the pleasure principle, the mode of operation utilized by the *id*. When dominated by the pleasure principle, an individual seeks pleasure and avoids pain in as immediate a fashion as possible without regard to reality or social consequences. The younger the child the more he is under the sway of the pleasure principle.

If we accept the emotions as part of the *id*, in fact its most important part, then the pleasure principle can be seen as a mode of emotional functioning. I believe this to be the case: that psychic pain is emotional pain, and our capacity to accept such pain is very limited. I suggest that our primary pleasures are emotional and that our need for pleasure is almost as intense as our inability to deal with pain. Furthermore, I am suggesting that throughout life there are psychic pains with which we cannot deal, and each new stage of growth contains such pain. The pleasure principle remains in operation throughout life. The difference between the healthy person and the unhealthy person is, in part, a function of which pain or pleasure dominates. When we are children, it is appropriate to fear abandonment; when we are adults we fear death. The adult psychotic fears both abandonment and death. However, neither the child nor the psychotic can tolerate the fear, and, as a result, both utilize defensive fantasy to solve their inescapable pain.

Moreover, if we consider the concept of "conflict-free *ego* sphere" (Hartmann, 1958), we can suggest that interest is at its base. As long as the emotion of interest survives as a response to various situations, the skills we refer to as *ego* skills will grow and thrive. When fear, shame, and guilt replace interest as our main motivation, then healthy *ego* motivation is lost. The "libidinization of the *ego*" is thus a question of the *ego* being disorganized by strong, negative emotion.

In our developmental theory, the word *affect* will be used to describe our motivational system. Affect, suggests Piaget (1981), represents any of the energizing systems of the personality, and includes the emotions and the drives. While our theory holds that the emotions constitute our primary motivational system, it in no way denies the importance of various drives and instincts that energize behavior.

SOME THEORETICAL LINKAGES
BETWEEN COGNITION AND EMOTION

We are now at the heart of the basis of our developmental theory. I have suggested that human behavior can be understood as being motivated by the cognitive and the affective meanings we find in each situation with which we interact. I have defined emotions in terms of differential emotions theory: i.e., emotions are reactions to situations; they tell us the meaning of a given situation and predispose us to behave in certain ways. Cognition also has its roots in bio-evolutionary development and seems to emerge in stages. The function of cognition is to evaluate the meaning of situations and to permit the individual to cope with these meanings.

What, then, is the relationship of cognition and affect (emotion in particular) and how can developmental aspects of cognition be described in that relationship? The assumption here is that both emotion and cognition are bio-evolutionary functions and thus are necessary for full functioning and human effectiveness. These processes operate in a bi-directional mutuality that can either be healthy and growth-producing or susceptible to going awry, thereby leading to fixation of the personality as well as intra- and interpersonal destructiveness.

The Importance of Both Cognition and Affect

The viewpoint just outlined is in opposition to historical tendencies that see the emotions as "base" or "animalistic" and the source of "bad manners." Similarly, it rejects the position that the emotions, by their very existence, produce pathology and that only reason and intellect should dominate the individual. "If only we could be rational" is the call of many individuals, decrying the lack of logic or rationality in our affective processes.

The theory here presented also rejects the view that intellect is representative of obsessive-compulsive pathology, and that only with the unbridled expression of our emotions can we be happy. In recent years, various anti-intellectual forces have crept into psychology, almost as a counter force to the "hardheaded" scientific view. These individuals suggest that thinking and logic are the mortal enemies of human happiness. (This argument is not new, but a repetition of the Apollonian-Dionysian, rational-romantic, and now left hemisphere-right hemisphere arguments occurring through the ages.) The thesis can be represented by Piaget. Philip Cowan (1981) writes that Piaget's position suggests that "affect and cognition are inseparable, they constitute two different aspects of every sensory-motor and symbolic act" (p. x). In one of his few statements on the relationship of cognition and affect, Piaget writes (1981): "Affective life, like intellectual life, is a continual adaptation, and the two are not only parallel, but interdependent, since feelings express the interest and value given to actions of which intelligence provides the structure" (p. 9).

Cognition Exists to Service the Emotions

Plutchik (1977) suggests that, when viewed as a developmental evolutionary set of processes, "cognition developed in order to predict the future" (p. 208).

> An organism must predict on the basis of limited information whether there is food, a mate, or danger in its environment. Depending on the

prediction made, the organism makes a decision to attack, run, play, or mate. From this point of view, the complex processes of sensory input, evaluation, symbolization, comparison with memory stores and the like—those processes we call cognitive—are in the service of emotions and biological needs. (p. 203)

Plutchik is placing cognition in the role of the psychoanalytic *ego* vis-à-vis an expanded concept of the *id*. In this case the *id* is primarily emotional rather than libidinal. Implicit in Plutchik's description are cognitions that are evaluatory and responsible for arousing emotions, as well as cognitions that are postemotional and have a function of carrying out the dictates or demands of the affective processes. Arnold Lazarus (1980) refers to the former cognitions as "primary appraisals" and the later as "secondary appraisals."

Primary Appraisals

Evaluation requires getting appropriate and adequate levels of information about a situation and correctly processing that information. Implicit in such a statement are assumptions about the health and integrity of the evaluating individual. Individuals deprived of perceptual modalities or suffering neurological handicaps will have increased difficulties in evaluating situations and possessing appropriate emotional reactions with which to respond. Any activities that interfere with perception and thought in addition to disability and disease, such as drugs or alcohol, will lead to incorrect evaluation and improper emotional arousal.

Evaluation requires social honesty, as much of our information about situations comes from those around us. When we cannot gain access to information or are given faulty information about situations or about other people our emotional reactions will be different than if we were provided with correct or truthful information. Parents who teach prejudice, and politicians, salesmen, and advertisers who lie for whatever reason, produce in us emotional reactions that would differ if the truth would be known. It would seem that the pathological effects of lying should be one of psychology's prime topics of interest.

One prevalent cause of irrational emotional reaction to a situation involves misinterpretation due to immaturity of the cognitive system. Children sometimes misinterpret situations simply because they *are* children. The preoperational thought of children forces a view of themselves as causative agencies in all manner of circumstances. Divorce or the death of a parent is often interpreted by children as being their fault, a state of affairs that causes irrational guilt and shame. In cases where children are needlessly punished they will blame themselves for the punishment. In chapter 10 we will explore at length the manner in which preoperational evaluation produces irrational emotional reactions.

In general, immature thought can lead to a whole range of incorrect interpretations of one's environment and therefore the arousal of motives inappropriate to the arousing situation. The emotions brought about by preoperational interpretations will be, at best, different than they would have been had mature, formal operations been used to assess the arousing situation. Throughout development our emotional reactions to the same situation keep changing as functions of the development of the cognitions comprising our primary appraisals.

Inappropriate evaluations can also be produced by preexisting emotional states or thoughts made immature by defenses and other secondary appraisals. When an individual enters a situation with intense emotional arousal resulting from incorrect expectations, evaluation of the actual situation can be quite different than if the negative expectation had not occurred. Julian Rotter (1966), Walter Mischel (1968), George Kelley (1951), and other cognitive psychologists have described this process in depth. (See chapter 4 above.)

Finally, a word about defenses in advance of their discussion in the next section: The distinction between primary and secondary appraisal is purely for a pedagogic purpose. Defenses can be seen as secondary appraisals or attempts at managing painfully aroused emotions. However, such defenses or forms of thinking can be the basis for the next set of primary evaluations in the never ending sequence of evaluation and emotion.

Secondary Appraisals

Emotions call for behavioral reactions toward the physical and living objects in our environment. Each situation demands accommodations to the peculiarities of the environment. If fear tells us to flee a situation, it makes a difference if the flight is in an open field, a crowded stadium, or a room on the tenth floor of an office building.

The emotion says flee, but the choices of how to flee must be based on appropriate cognitive appraisals.

The ability to delay gratification of affective needs, as well as the ability to survive, demands the control and modulation of affective expression. The analyst calls this the "reality principle" (Hartmann, 1958; Brenner 1955). Expressing rage to someone much bigger than oneself may not be in one's best interest. Smiling at a poker hand can cause one to lose money. Allowing emotions to rule while fleeing from a fire in a crowded room can result in death. The secondary appraisals are necessary for survival.

Once again, it is the maturity of an individual's thought that will, in part, define how that individual chooses to express (or not express) his affective arousals. Immature thought leads to inappropriate and poorly controlled affective expression. Egocentrism, a lack of conservation, or poorly defined and inconsistent logic make an individual appear frantic, out of control, and unable to assess reality. To the extent that reality is dealt with poorly one is less able both to meet emotional needs and to survive.

Secondary appraisals also define morality and civility. Social maturity can be defined in terms of emotional expression via secondary appraisals. Each society makes demands as to how secondary appraisals are to operate. Each culture teaches the individual how emotions are to be expressed socially or if such emotions are to be expressed at all. The study of society cannot avoid dealing with the myriad ways in which cultural expressions of emotions differ.

Often good manners and emotional needs clash significantly. Survival and civility can also come into conflict. The impossible psychological demands made upon individuals in Victorian society are classic. This era demanded not only that emotional expression be controlled, but that emotion be crushed entirely. The pathologies described by Freud in his clinical work were created when individuals had to develop secondary appraisals demanding that sexual needs and many emotional needs be entirely eliminated from conscious experience.

Defenses are secondary appraisals that either deny the existence of an emotion or lead to primary appraisals that prevent various emotions from being aroused. Whenever individuals are raised according to "conditions of worth" (Rogers, 1961) and must relegate emotions to the "not me" (Sullivan, 1953), secondary appraisals that deny and distort reality will come into existence. In chapter 9, it will be suggested that such secondary appraisals involve preoperational modes of thinking and are one of the chief reasons that thought can be fixated in relation to various social situations.

Affect Organizes Cognition

If cognition exists to service the emotions, then it owes its existence to the demands made by the emotions. I concur with Izard that emotions organize consciousness. The early analysts described how the drives organized cognition. In our developmental theory, emotion organizes thought as well as drives. Decisions are made primarily on the basis of emotion. Clinically, individuals who cannot "read" their emotions often become totally unable to decide on even the simplist course of action. An emotionless person would in fact not only be unable to function, but would also be inhuman.

We divide our world into the pleasant and the unpleasant, the approachable and the avoidable, from the moment of our birth because of emotional responses that we have to the objects around us. Could an infant decide to pay attention to this or that on the basis of cognitive evaluation alone? We pay attention to that which arouses interest or fear or that which satisfies hunger, and so forth. The hierachy of our values is based upon emotions and not simply upon intellect.

The very motivations for cognitive growth are emotional. Psychoanalysis has long held that conflict produces *ego* growth. While one cannot argue that deprivations, conflicts, and other negative emotional experiences motivate the growth of skills, our theory suggests that positive emotions stimulate growth too. The most rational of scientists follows his *interests* and becomes scientific in the pursuit of those interests, as well as other rewards perceived to be contingent on intellectual growth. Such rewards might be social approval or the economic security and status that being successful signifies. Cognitive discovery becomes exciting and emotionally rewarding simply because of the nature of the process.

Throughout childhood we learn because of positive emotional reinforcers built into our actions. Throughout infancy children engage in primary, secondary, and tertiary circular reactions because of the bodily pleasure and interesting consequences of such actions. They learn about the world because pleasure is built into the learning. During the preoperational phase children learn about social relationships and work out issues of morality while playing inherently enjoyable, imaginative, or "as if" games. "Cops and robbers" allows the child to understand good and evil while being motivated by fun rather than duty. Throughout life, learning and exploration can be powerfully motivated by interests and by the intrinsic rewards found in such activities.

Emotional Intensity

A common view exists that only cognitive decisions are correct and adaptive. This view is based on the idea that emotions are disruptive. While emotion can disrupt, most often this is not the case. Some time ago R. W. Leeper (1940) suggested that emotions become disruptive, in part, because we are taught to ignore the information contained within them. In many cases of conflict between emotion and cognition, it is the emotional appraisal of a situation that is correct while the cognitions, which may be defensive, are incorrect. In general, the more we try to deny the existence of an emotion the more easily the emotion becomes disruptive. Many individuals and cultural groups would do well to recognize that the conscious supression of behavioral affective expression has very different consequences then the suppression of the emotions from consciousness itself.

Psychologists have studied the conditions under which emotions become disruptive. Figures 1a, b, c express the "Yerkes-Dodson law."

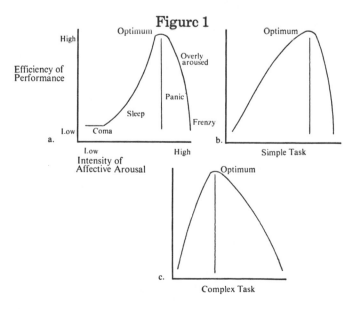

Figure 1

Figure 1a describes the well-known "inverted U" function. At very low levels of arousal, we find poor or little performance due to a lack of motivation and energy. As interests or other emotions (and drives) come into play, we find cognition becoming organized and beginning effectively to direct behavior. A point of arousal is reached at which individuals are at optimum enthusiasm or curiosity and capable of their most effective efforts. If arousal continues, then another point is reached at which secondary cognition becomes disorganized and begins to fail in its "executive function." Emotions take over and the individual functions according to the demands of the emotion without regard to the specific situation in which he is involved.

Figures 1b and 1c are also "inverted U" functions. They reveal that, as a task becomes more complex, the amount of arousal necessary for optimal performance and disorganization lessens. Conversely, the secondary appraisals required in complex situations must become more adequate as well. It is, therefore, easier for a trash collector to express anger on the job and still work effectively than it is for a physician performing open heart surgery. Moreover, as our society continues to increase in complexity, the demands for emotional controls and for more complex secondary appraisals will be made of every individual.

As society becomes more complex it demands greater cognitive development in order to manage living in that culture. Such societies foster increases in cognitive development through nurturing and education. As individuals become more complex and mature in their thought patterns, inventions, technical achievements, and scientific research also become more sophisticated. These changes have the effect of further stimulating social change. Ours is a society of increasing and monumental diversity, which requires very complex primary and secondary appraisals by each individual.

One can ask if a society can become so complex that all but a few of its individuals are able to grasp its intricacies. During the Middle Ages, nearly all members of society seemed to operate on preoperational thinking. Today, preoperational adults function in only marginal areas of society. Even those with formal operations have trouble comprehending the rules of the culture. Might it be that under the stimulation of computers, we will face the emergence of individuals with post-formal, operationally cognitive appraisal systems?

Cognition and Emotional Arousal

The prevailing view of our theory is that emotions are always dependent upon cognition for their arousal* (Lazarus, 1984). What is clear, however, is that different degrees and levels of cognition are necessary for emotional arousal in different situations. According to R. B. Zajonc (1980), "In interpersonal situations our cognitive transmissions are steeped in affect both in tone and voice (which can be understood even if information or content is obliterated)" (p. 155). Body language or kinesis has become an important field in recent years, attesting to the importance of emotional transmission in interpersonal relationships. In such situations perception (a cognitive process) is all that is necessary for emotional arousal. Thought seems unnecessary for arousal in this instance.

We seem to be born receptive to a host of cues that can arouse our emotion with little or very rapid cognitive processing. Izard (1977) suggests that facial cues and posture express emotion and that we are biologically vulnerable to such cues. Our expression of anger will arouse fear or anger in another thus motivating them to behave appropriately to us. A baby will respond to mother's smile, and vice versa, quite automatically. Konrad Lorenz (1980) believes that the child's tiny features, as well as its facial features, provide an innate and unlearned releaser of emotions leading to tender care of the infant.

As situations become more complex, however, the degree of cognitive evaluation necessary for appropriate emotional reactions in-

---

* Zajonc and others (Izard, 1977, 1984) feel that cognitions are not necessary for affective arousal. They argue that the emotions belong to an independent class of psychic events and that one need not think in order to feel. Lazarus (1984) and others have joined a lively debate as to whether or not cognition precedes emotional arousal. He argues that part of the controversy has to do with one's definition of *cognition*. Our theory suggests that cognition involves more than conscious thinking.

Perception is often defined as the meaningful recognition and organization of sensory stimuli. Therefore, perception is or involves a cognitive process even if the degree of cognition is slight or if we are not conscious of how we recognize objects or how we process information. I believe that a perceptual act is minimally needed for emotional arousal. Therefore, cognition precedes emotional arousal.

The argument is also continued by briefly reexamining the nature of emotions, which are aroused in response to specific situations. Their arousal is meant to motivate us and to increase our probability of surviving those situations. Emotions are adaptational responses to specific situations. Our behavior would be chaotic if emotions arose in some spontaneous fashion. Some cognitive or perceptual process must be present to evaluate each situation requiring an emotional response.

creases. Some may require extensive cognitive evaluation when, for example, we receive mixed or conflicting messages. Communication theorists such as Jan Haley (1976) and Gregory Bateson (1978) have provided ample evidence of the confusion and disorganization that takes place in a double-bind situation wherein one cannot properly evaluate the conflicting messages. Certainly extensive cognitive processing is required if we are emotionally to experience a book, a scientific problem, or some other situation in which cognition is required. Many people marvel at the degree of cognitive control necessary by astronauts, who live in a few cubic feet of a shuttle hundreds of miles from Earth.

Finally, we note that the evaluation of a situation need not be conscious. While American psychology was dominated by behaviorism most internal processes were held in disrepute. Only the clinicians, and analysts in particular, recognized that individuals could have their emotions aroused by cognitive processes that were outside of awareness. More recently, experimentalists such as A. Triemsman (1958) and D. F. Broadbent (1958) have individually proposed theories to deal with the phenomenon of perceptual monitoring of the environment that constantly seems to go on within each individual. The mother who wakes up at her child's first cry evinces an emotion-produced response when monitoring her baby; she responds even when asleep and without consciousness.

Cognition and Emotion: An Equilibrium

In many of the preceding paragraphs evidence was presented to suggest that emotions and cognition, while present in our every behavior, exist in a complex relationship with each other and with the social and physical environment. Optimum functioning is dependent on the cognitive appraisal and control abilities of the individual, the nature and intensity of the emotions, and the qualities of the situation in which the individual must function. Figure 2 summarizes some of these relationships. In the diagram, the individual is represented by the vertical axis while the qualities of the environment are represented on the horizontal axis.

Figure 2

I		
	Rested	Pleasant emotions II
	Satiated	Optimum arousal
	No negative	Straight—No drugs or alcohol
	anticipations	Formal operations, maturity,
		Homeostatic mechanism in
		reasonable equilibrium
	Optimum	
	performance	
Light	predicted	Dark
Safe	*Individual*	Threatening
Quiet		Noisy
Clean	Situation	Dirty

Unambiguous   Ambiguous
Simple   Complex
Honest   Dishonest

Poorest
performance
predicted

	Fatigued	High emotional arousal
	Intense drive arousal	High on drugs or alcohol
	Negative anticipation	Preoperational
		thinking—immaturity
		Serious imbalances in
III		homeostatic mechanisms **IV**

As we examine Figure 2 we see that a given level of functioning can be predicted in each of the four quadrants formed by the two axes. Quadrant I is created by situations (including people) that are well lighted, safe, non-threatening, clear, unambiguous, and honest, and interacted with by an individual who is rested, safe, optimally aroused, straight, mature, and using formal operations. Quadrant I represents that balance or equilibrium in which the individual's ability to function would be maximal.

Quadrant IV represents those conditions of situation and individual that would predict a poor balance of cognition and emotion, and one in which the individual would perform at his worst. The situation is dark, threatening, ambiguous, dishonest, and complex, while the individual dealing with the situation is fatigued, perhaps hungry, frightened, drunk, immature, and utilizing preoperationally organized thoughts. Quadrants II and III represent equilibria predicting levels of functioning of varying degrees of competence less than Quadrant I and more than Quadrant IV.

Maturation and Cognitive-Affective Development

One final dimension of the relation of emotion and cognition needs to be described. Piaget (1981) writes: "We shall be able to put intellectual structure and the level of affective development in parallel, stage by stage. Since structure does not exist without energetics (emotions and drives) and reciprocally since every new structure involves a new form of energetic regulation, a particular sort of cognitive structure will be found in concert with every new type of affective regulation" (p. 12). Piaget is suggesting that we are born with a set of primary emotional responses. The interaction of cognition and emotion leads to the emergence of a set of emotional reactions that changes with the development of cognition. In chapter 7, I suggested that Maslow's hierachy of needs is emotionally based. The emergence of the higher-order needs or emotions must involve the emergence of higher-order cognitive functions. As higher-order functions of cognition develop, not only are more complex emotional responses produced, but the motivational and expressive aspects of the emotional response change as well. Not only do secondary appraisals differ in their increased effectiveness with development, but new qualitative structures of emotion continuously emerge.

Jerome Kagan (1984) describes the emotional development of children in the first five years, in the middle years, and again in adolescence. During infancy we see "surprise to novelty," "distress to physical privation," "startle to the unexpected," and "relaxation to gratification." Because of the maturation of the cognitive function, especially retrieval memory and evaluation of the relations of the event to knowledge, we find "fear to the unfamiliar" and "anger to frustration" (p. 112). "Depression and sadness" await development in the second year, when there is a prolonged absence of the caretaker, because at this stage the child is capable of retrieving past schemata. In the second year there emerges "anxiety to possible task failure." By the age of four, a child has the ability to recognize that he could have behaved differently and thus "guilt" can emerge. Kagan feels that the emergence of shame and guilt early in life are necessary if the child is to become neither "too humble nor too aggressive, just civilized" (p. 173).

During his middle years, the child is able to use other people's perceptions as a standard of his own behavior and thus emotions such as "insecurity," "inferiority," "humility," "pride," and "confidence" begin to emerge. Formal operations permit one to evaluate whether or not an individual's behavior is consistent with beliefs, and thus emotional states such as "cognition dissonance" emerge. The reader is referred to Kagan's superb description of emotional development, but the point is made here that, as primary and secondary evaluations change as the individual constructs new and more complex views of his world, new emotions emerge.

As sensorimotor intelligence changes to the preoperational intelligence, so, too, it changes the emotional response from intra-individual feelings to interpersonal ones. Morality and idealism, Piaget makes clear, are emotional or affective reactions whose existence depends upon the "structuralization of affective experience." While our original pure emotional reactions can still occur, we expect that development will bring about the emergence of higher-order cognitive-emotional structures that play an important role in regulating the behavior of the individual.

These higher-order cognitive-emotional structures function as needs that change the meaning of the situation in which an individual functions. Their emergence creates a remarkable change in the meaningful way in which a person lives his life. Failure of the higher-order cognitive-emotional structures can be caused by the fixation of cognition at earlier stages. Such a failure of development has profound consequences for psychopathology and morality. These failures of development will be discussed in chapter 12.

The present discussion is not intended to be an exhaustive description of all of the relationships that can exist between emotion and cognition. Rather, it is an attempt to introduce a developmental view of the individual wherein emotion and cognition are seen as both necessary and appropriate to an empirically correct image of humanity.

SOME FINAL THOUGHTS ON THE
RELATIONSHIP OF COGNITION AND AFFECT

If it is true that more mature emotions must depend for their existence on the emergence of more mature forms of cognitive evaluation, and that each emotion is aroused in the context of a particular social situation, then it may also be true that the separation of cognition, affect, and the situation into discrete terms is a serious error. It may mean instead that Kagan (1984) is right when he suggests that there are an infinite number of emotional or "feeling states." It may be that terms such as *pride* and *guilt* are neither emotional nor cognitive but complex, unique experiences (for each individual) for which no adequate language exists.

I suggest that in the final analysis no thought is free of some affective experience and that affect organizes and motivates all thoughts. Neither the affect nor the thought to which it is inextricably bound is fully independent of the situation arousing it. Since no single arousing situation, nervous system, or history of an experiencing person is a complete duplicate of any other, then no emotion is the same as any other, even though we label them with the same word. If this is true, there is no reason to despair that organizing and classifying emotions mask as much of the nature of emotional experience as they illuminate. People still show similar reactions when feeling a given emotional experience and they display similarities of behavior guided by the aroused emotion. We must keep in mind that our theories are merely approximate descriptions of cognitive-affective development. We therefore have much to do before laws of such development can exist.

9

A Cognitive-Affective-Developmental-Interpersonal Theory of Personality

NEEDS, PROBLEMS, AND THEIR SOLUTIONS

Personality can be viewed from a perspective that conceptualizes the individual as a "scientist" (Kelly, 1951) trying to satisfy needs and solve problems that emerge from living. Some individuals utilize "meaningful" thought patterns to solve their problems, while others are quite maladaptive in their attempts at problem solving. In this chapter we shall explore some of the reasons given to explain why some individuals develop meaningful coping patterns while others fail in their attempts.

Before discussing the differences between "scientific" and "unscientific" behavior, the nature of problems and needs must be examined. Problems and needs are the cognitive-affective representations of adaptation. It is in the act of solving problems and satisfying needs that we adapt, grow, and develop our personalities. Needs and problems motivate assimilations and accommodations. The successful resolution of problems and the satisfaction of needs represents successful adaptation. The lack of success in these endeavors leads to the fixation of personality and the development of pathology.

Problems can be defined as interactions with the environment requiring accommodations by the individual. Needs arise from within the organism and require assimilations from the environment for their satisfaction. Needs can arise from tissue deficits, as in the case of hunger or thirst, or from the personality structure itself, as in a need for love, dignity, or self-actualization. Problems create needs, and needs give rise to problems. Both are defined for the individual by affective reactions, and, from a psychological point of view, they can be treated as similar phenomena.

Problems involve interactions with the environment in which accommodations must be made. As the individual interacts with the environment, emotions are aroused, which not only define (in part) the nature of the problem, but motivate and guide those behaviors representing the accommodations. For example, the environment may threaten an individual, thus creating a problem that is internally defined by fear. Fear also acts as a need, demanding some assimilative behavior for its removal. (Problems create needs.)

Needs* arise within the individual and, as in the case of hunger, are represented by affective reactions. Needs are satisfied by assimilating objects (called goals) from the environment. In the case of hunger, food is found external to the organism. Getting food from the environment represents a problem for the individual (in varying degrees). The more difficult it is for the individual to obtain food, the greater are the necessary accommodations. (Needs create problems.)

Needs and problems are simultaneously defined by the individual as both external, "out there," and internal, "in here." The "out there" is that aspect of the environment creating the problem or providing the objects of need satisfaction (goals). The "in here" represents the affect or the emotion defining the need or the problem. A person confronting something frightening will describe his problem in terms of the thing causing the fear and the fear itself: "That thing frightens me." Hunger is internal while the food is external.

---

* I am using the term *needs* to also include "wants," which operate in much the same way as needs. That which one wants requires assimilations from the environment and creates problems in the same way as do needs. One important issue in mental health involves the individual knowing the difference between what he needs and what he wants. When this knowledge is not present, wants operate exactly like needs, with all their intensity and preemptive power.

One difference between needs and wants requires explication. Much of what an individual wants involves changes in the structure of personality itself. A person wishes to be smarter, stronger, better looking, and so on. While many of the things people want must be assimilated from the external environment, others require accommodating changes in the personality itself.

"I want to eat food" expresses the simultaneous external and internal aspect of the need.

Unmet needs or unsolved problems are defined by negative affective states such as fear, anger, hunger, shame, guilt, and the like. Contentment, happiness, joy, and other positive affective states usually define the successful solution to the problem, or satisfaction of the need, both in their internal and external aspects. Positive affective states can represent a problem when their continued existence is threatened. Once again, when we examine that which threatens our happiness we will generally find that the causes are both situational and internal, with the internal cause being represented by negative affective conditions.

Needs and problems involve those situations that cause negative affective states and threaten the removal of positive affective states. To understand a problem or a need, one must simultaneously understand the nature of the external situation and the internal affect that defines the problem or the need in personal, feeling terms. Solutions are represented both by positive affective states and by the removal of negative affective states. The individual is likely to experience as solutions changes in both the external situational condition causing the affect and the affective state itself.

The situations that create problems need not be present in the individual's here and now. Negative affective states can be created by memories of past experiences or by the anticipation of real or .imagined future ones. Moreover, the solution to a problem can come from the change in a present situation, the manipulation of memories, or by reordering the future in the individual's imagination. In any event, the change in affective state is *always related to an interpretation of some real or imagined situation—past, present, or future.*

COGNITIVE DEVELOPMENT AND THE NATURE OF PROBLEMS AND NEEDS

In the previous section, problems, needs, and their solutions were defined by the effect of external or internal situations in creating various affective states. However, in chapter 8, I suggested that the affective state aroused by a situation was dependent on the manner of the individual's appraisal or his evaluation of that situation. An individual who remains unaware of some danger will not feel fear and thus has no *psychological* problem requiring a solution. People who cannot learn of something in their environment that can satisfy some affective need will not have a solution to their problem. Awareness of the environment is critical to both the nature of the problems that an individual entertains and the solutions available to him. One can say that people become aware of their needs and problems through primary appraisals; they solve their problems and satisfy their needs through secondary appraisals.

What is also important in this context is that many problems or needs exist *because of* growing intellectual awareness, which in turn occurs *because of* need satisfaction and problem-solving. The problems of the infant involve biological hungers and discomfort. Sucking, swallowing, and other simple repetitive behaviors create pleasurable solutions. However, with the development of intellect, the individual becomes aware of death and the need to create meanings in his life. The affective problems of a forty-year-old contemplating the meaning of life exist only because he had developed the intellect to inquire after and care about the nature of existence. As primary appraisals become more sophisticated, so, too, become the problems. As suggested in the last chapter, certain emotions, such as guilt or pride, depend for their existence on cognitive development.

Abraham Maslow (1968) suggested that our needs (and in the present context, our problems) develop in a hierarchy. He presented their emergence in the following order:

1. Physiological Needs
2. Security Needs
3. Love and Belongingness Needs
4. Self-Esteem Needs (includes the need for dignity, the need to be valued, and the need to be needed)
5. Self-Actualization Needs (includes the need for purpose, meaning and the fuller development of the human potential).

This list is by no means complete. Any emotional reaction of which human beings are capable can represent a need. Any emotion-need can demand behavioral assimilation for its satisfaction. Each emotion may combine with a virtually infinite number of cognitions creating an infinite number of differing need states. Any object or situation in the world can be a goal that satisfies a need or creates a problem for an individual. Our actual motivational hierarchy is therefore indescribable in any real sense.

Needs arise secondarily or antecedent to other needs. Human beings have a need to communicate, for example, that is made possible and is required by the need to love another person. Some general needs that I feel must be added to Maslow's list (or drawn from it) are the needs to be "good," to be valued, or to be needed. Related to these are the need to be admired, respected, or, perhaps, most important, the "need to be somebody." Throughout life the need to count for something is very powerful. Later, the need to be good (which in childhood assures the child of continued parental love) becomes the need to be virtuous and moral (a necessity in surviving socially, in continuing the life of the group, and in maintaining meaning and values in life).

Each set of "higher" needs emerges only when the "lower" needs are satisfied. I would suggest that the higher needs emerged because the lower needs were satisfied, and where in the process of satisfaction, the individual developed increased cognitive awareness. As was seen above, satisfaction of needs involves the creation of problems. The satisfaction of needs and the solving of problems leads to assimilation and accommodation, which represent adaptation. Growth (both cognitive and affective) takes place with successful adaptation because an individual demonstrates the capability to satisfy needs successfully (assimilation) and to solve attendant problems (accommodation).

Each emerging set of needs is represented by more complex cognitive-affective structures, which are generated by successful adaptations. Each emerging set of needs must be satisfied if an individual is to be fully human. Each individual struggles to satisfy emerging needs in one way or another. Each new need creates awareness of a new set of problems more complex than those that preceded it. The new problems must be solved, and the new needs satisfied, in addition to those already being solved and satisfied. Each gain in human personality allows for the assimilation of new situations, but at the cost of increasingly complex accommodations. Life is thus a series of assimilations, accommodations, needs, and problems.

Each gain in cognitive-affective complexity is measured by changes in the primary and secondary appraisals of the individual. Here, needs come into existence as an individual becomes increasingly aware of his environment. New demands for self-control and skills in problem-solving are reflected in the changes in secondary appraisals. Just as development can be seen as a series of assimilations and accommodations, needs and problems, it is also a series of changing primary and secondary appraisals.

To make the present discussion even more complicated, one can add that each cognitive-affective need expresses itself in a given situation that reflects a society, a culture, a time, and a place. In chapter 8, I suggested that each emotion, when understood in an individual-situational context, may have been different for each individual in each situation. The same principle exists with regard needs. For example, the survival needs of primitive man were expressed in his hunting behavior. He had a need to hunt and also the problems related to hunting. Modern man expresses his survival needs economically with regard to a complex marketplace. The need to make money and to buy and sell commodities and other products may have their origin in survival needs, but they are understood on a much different level indeed. Modern man's survival problems are much different than the primitive hunter.

With increased cognitive-affective growth, human beings create situations of increasing complexity that in turn demand growth or a-daptation of still further complexity. I will not argue as to which comes first, changes in culture or changes in the individual. It is enough to note that as each one changes, so does (or more accurately, each demands changes in) the other. Modern man has created a complex culture that in turn creates needs and problems of a complex nature. Modern culture demands complex accommodation if a-daptation is to be successful. Contemporary culture is thus a reflection of the increasingly complex imagination of modern people who have achieved very sophisticated cognitive-affective developments.

The goals sought by modern man are often products of his own developing imagination, and they reflect his complex man-made situations. Primitive humans did not conceive of the automobile so they did not want one. They did not build the kind of society in which an automobile was needed. The needs and problems of modern man, while reducible to the same categories of his primitive ancestor, are very different if viewed without that reduction taking place.

As an individual continues to solve problems and to satisfy needs, he assimilates and accommodates (adapts). Growth takes place in the cognitive structures that define the personality that emerges from these successful adaptations (and hereditary nudges). Sensorimotor intelligence gives way to preoperational and then to operational cognitive functioning. Concrete operations are superseded by formal operations. The changes in needs and problems being described in these pages are due to, and reflective of, the change from primitive to more advanced cognitive structures.

The more developed the operations, the more an individual becomes aware of his own cognitive structure. As the cognitive structure develops, needs arise from within the structure itself. Problems increasingly have as their goal changes in the cognitive structure. In chapter 11, I will discuss issues of will and self that result from the growing awareness by the individual of his own cognitive structure. It must suffice to note here that with increased complexity of cognitive-affective development, many means and ends involve the personality of the individual.

With growth, still other changes take place in relation to needs and problems, assimilations and accommodations. As the individual increases in cognitive-affective complexity, he develops needs that cannot be satisfied by immediately available objects: seeking fame and fortune or becoming educated or skilled, represent goals that can be years away. The problems in achieving them can be of enormous complexity. As the child develops an awareness of the range of dangers confronting him, the need for survival surpasses the need for pleasure; later his needs for purpose and meaning may surpass survival. Complex problems and needs require an increased capacity to delay gratification and to deal with the pain of deprivation.

When the objects of need satisfaction are distant and dear, the individual must be able to bear the discomfort of delayed gratification. Many needs must remain unmet. Conflict and frustration, stress and pressure must be confronted. With increased growth, the individual must also bear greater burdens of responsibility and loneliness. What skills must develop if an individual is to deal with physical and emotional pain? He must develop skills permitting justification of pain. *Justifications are achieved when an individual sees his pain as a means to some desired end.*

I will not at this time develop the argument that all human growth can be conceptualized as shifting means-ends relationships. The infant, dominated by primary-circular reactions, has means and ends fused. For example, Warren sucks his thumb for the pleasure he obtains. Sucking is its own reward. With the emergence of secondary-circular reactions, Warren engages in behavior that makes interesting things happen. Means and ends thus become separated. As the child grows, increasingly complex means are used to achieve an ever-widening number of ends. He learns to delay gratification as one of the means to his desired ends. Goals (ends) grow increasingly distant in the future and self-control improves, and with it goals still more distant in the future can be pursued.

As problems give rise to needs, and needs to problems, means become ends and ends become means. Exercising a skill for pleasure becomes a means of achieving a new pleasure. For example, a teen-ager enjoys practicing shifting the gears of his new car. Shifting gears is an end in and of itself. However, soon enough, shifting becomes a means of driving the car to new places. The end has become a means in a never-ending, ever-widening cyclical process. Throughout this process, and because of it, the youngster becomes more aware of the need to deal with the pain of deprivation and with failed problem solving. Growth demands obedience to pain and to the struggles it represents.

I have described the developing personality in terms of cognitive-affective functioning; the solving of problems and the satisfaction of needs; assimilations and accommodations; primary and secondary appraisals; and shifting means-ends relationships. Another constant in describing personality involves circular reactions. Piaget described three levels of circular reaction during the sensorimotor stage: primary, secondary, and tertiary. Each stage is marked by a shift in the nature of the pleasure that rewards the reappearance of the behavior in question.

Primary circular reactions are maintained by bodily pleasures, secondary and tertiary circular reactions are maintained by the interesting things produced by the behavior. B. F. Skinner called these circular reactions operant conditioning and demonstrated that this type of learning occurs at all ages. The maintenance of the operant behavior is due to the reinforcer. Reinforcers may differ but all of them operate in common as they continue to maintain the appearance of various behaviors.

As an individual grows, there are circular reactions (operant behaviors) maintained by successful survival, love, pride, meaning, and any other goals sought by individuals. Circular reactions also exist because behavior is successful in avoiding, terminating, or reducing negative affects (negative reinforcements). Circular reactions may be positive or negative. Later I will suggest that healthy development is marked by positive circular reactions while fixation and neurosis are marked by negative circular reactions (called vicious cycles, neurotic paradoxes, etc.).

I must now introduce a special type of need and problem that I will discuss in the section on defenses. Each individual must learn to deal with unresolvable problems, and needs that cannot be satisfied. *In short, he/she must contend with pain that is unjustifiable,* pain that is not a means to some end. This pain is caused by the fact that each human being lives in a world in which each living thing is the prey of some other. We are all victims of disease, accident, crime, and untimely death. Life is inherently unfair. Unjustifiable pain can be created by an individual's own actions as, for example, when he hurts others in an act of self-interest and cannot be forgiven by others or himself. Guilt and shame are often the most difficult needs to reduce or to terminate.

It must be clear that successful growth and adaptation does not in any way ensure happiness. Often our reward for continued growth is more struggle and more pain, more delay of gratification, more need for self-control, more responsibility, and more loneliness. The lives of the most fortunate (we all must deal with bad luck) are still lived in a world filled with incredible dangers, injustices, and horrors. One of the rewards of increased cognitive awareness is a fuller understanding of all the injustices, horrors, and dangers in the world. With increased awareness, each individual sees more clearly the damage done to others in pursuing his own needs. How individuals deal with unjustifiable pain represents a critical variable in whether they continue to grow and develop. What help they get in this endeavor is equally critical. I shall come back to this point momentarily.

ASPECTS OF DEVELOPMENT

Central to our theory are the reasons given to explain why some individuals develop meaningful, scientific skills in solving life's problems and others do not. If the existence of problems, needs, and their respective solutions and satisfactions, which are related to positive and negative affective experience, depend, in part, upon intellectual skill, then we can examine those factors that enhance and permit, retard and interfere with cognitive development. We can draw on all sources of material, including psychoanalysis, developmental theory, learning theory, humanistic psychology, and others.

Piaget (1952) posits that the child's earliest pleasures that could reward learning are the physiological ones that accompany the reflexes. The sucking schema is reinforced by the nonnutritive pleasure associated with sucking. We can hypothesize that schemas such as "looking" or "grasping" are reinforced by emotions such as interest, which are aroused when the child observes or touches the world around him. Interest and excitement seem easily aroused by almost anything in the infant's world. As long as the child continues to be interested in his environment, learning will occur.

As baby repeats his actions (circular reactions) he creates consequences that occur in predictable patterns. Child psychologists have long recognized the importance of predictability in the child's environment if he is to feel safe, learn the rules governing the interactions of objects and people, and begin to "trust" (Erikson, 1968; Lynd, 1968) the environment and himself in it. As the child begins to trust, the groups of objects and situations that arouse his interest continue to widen. With growing self-awareness, the infant/child begins to understand what success, competence, and pride feel like. (This topic will be discussed in greater depth in chapter 11.) These cognitive-affective structures add to the child's desire to explore and to develop physical and psychological skills.

Among the objects in the child's world are his parents and other people. Dynamic psychology has revealed that the child discovers that his parents are capable of arousing the most intense pleasures. Their smiles and praise reward learning more effectively than any other reinforcers. Strokes, hugs, and kisses are also powerful reinforcers that determine the shape and direction of the youngster's learning and point in the direction to further interests. Ultimately it is mother's pleasure that becomes the greatest source of pleasure to the growing child. The power of the parents to control the direction and the rate of early learning is apparently unparalleled in the human life span (or in the life of any other creature).

When parents are delighted with, and involved in, their child's learning, they not only reward such learning but provide a constantly modulated environment of increasing complexity. They help the child accommodate to the demands of his environment, and provide objects to be assimilated in need satisfaction. Linguistic studies

(Bruner, 1978; Moskowitz, 1978; Schaffer, Collis, and Parsons, 1977) of mother-child interaction reveals that the involved mother automatically and nonconsciously adjusts the complexity of the language she uses with her child as the youngster's linguistic skills develop. These parents not only provide a positive emotional climate in which to learn, but they implicitly change the rate and flow of information and environmental complexity that reaches their child.

Perhaps basic to our discussion is the child's affective need to please his parents. I will discuss in chapter 12, under the heading "psychotic landscape," how intense is the child's fear of being unloved by his parents. Clinical psychologists are always confronting abused children who blame themselves for their parent's cruelties, rather than admitting that they are abused, because of a fear of losing parental love. The child's intense need to feel loved and to please his parents also has much to do with the direction and speed of the child's patterns of learning.

Involved parents seem to demand and reward the learning of their child, whose desire to please the parents interacts with parental demand as the child attempts to reach goals considered important. Significant variables in determining a child's achievement and interests include not only the presence of positive expectations (Rosenthal and Jacobsen, 1968) but how realistic such goals are. The healthy parent sets goals that not only force the child to accommodate but are within reach of the child's assimilative behavioral patterns.

Another important issue related to the child's learning has to do with parental discipline: the manner in which rebukes and rewards are given, the range of behavior permitted the child, and the congruence between the parent's behaviors and those demanded of the child. We shall discuss each of these topics in turn.

Some children are rewarded and punished, while others are punished under the guise of discipline. Rewards teach a child what to do by positively directing behavior. Punishments suppress behavior, although at times such suppression is necessary. The key question, however, is "How can we help children maintain interest in the world around them?" Certainly young children must be protected from examining fire escapes, busy streets, bottles of poison, or any situation that can damage them. Discipline based solely on punishment can interfere with interest by not permitting the child to differentiate accurately situations that are harmful and wrong from those that are not. It is only by rewarding and punishing that a healthy differentiation can occur. Children must have limits set on problems they should try to solve and on objects to be assimilated.

An important topic related to discipline concerns the range or breadth of the child's acceptable repertoire of behavior. As children grow in skill, they seek to apply and test these skills in an increasingly wider range of situations. As mentioned above, some of these situations can be deadly or dangerous. Other situations may involve the destruction of property. Clearly, discipline is needed if the child is to remain safe and at the same time learn to respect property and become a decent member of his family and the community. However, the definition of what is dangerous or destructive can differ markedly from parent to parent. It is after all the parent's judgment that often defines what is dangerous or destructive.

Some parents set no limits at all. Their children are permitted to live in a kind of anarchy of choice. Most children are incapable of growing comfortably in such surroundings. Not only do ignored children get lost but they fall from windows, set their homes on fire, eat poison, write on walls, stop up toilets, and make their homes look like disaster zones. One can argue that any child who survives such a childhood, and the feeling of being unloved and uncared for that can accompany such extreme permissiveness, will have experienced and learned from an enormous range of assimilated situations.

Other parents see their child's world as a dangerous place, or they view their child as basically evil and destructive. Consequently, they set very narrow limits on what is tolerable behavior. The parent who will not let a child take increasing risks and make mistakes in his life prevents healthy growth. Whether by overprotection or overdiscipline, the child's range of acceptable behavior becomes limited and the range of situations in which he can remain interested constricts. The parent accommodates for the child. But children must explore their world, climb on it, socialize in it, touch it, taste and run around in it, if interest is to remain high. Being an effective parent in a dangerous world is, I am convinced, the highest of art forms.

Finally, we come to that well-known disciplinary phrase "Do as I say and not as I do." Children are motivated to please their parents. To do so is seen by the child as becoming like their parents. The child's logic runs as follows: "If my parents are perfect so is their behavior. I will be perfect just like them and they will love me for it." Parents who are fearful of the world, who lack interest in it, who never explore or take risks, often tell their children to learn, explore, and risk. Parents who hit their children may produce young adults who grow up to view hitting as the correct way to discipline and to solve problems. Most often such parents are disappointed to see their children become mirror images of themselves.

I believe that children adopt not only parental behavior patterns but also the goals those behaviors are intended to achieve. Social learning theorists suggest that vicarious learning, imitation, and modelling are the vehicles by which we become like our parents and adopt their interests and goals. I believe that children do learn to channel their interests in this way but they *identify* with their parents as well. Identification is a central concept of psychoanalytic theory, one that is important to the growth and maintenance of, or loss and constriction of, a child's interest.

Piaget believed that mental operations (thoughts) were internalized actions. Just how this internalization takes place is as yet unclear. Can we also internalize the actions of others? I believe so, and I define identification as "the internalization of the actions of significant others." For the purpose of healthy interest, internalization must be of consistent, available, firm, figures who practice what they preach, and whose lives display realistic goals and intense positive interests.

An important role of parents is to help children deal with unjustifiable pain. Children have accidents, become ill, and are at the mercy of all the injustices and difficulties of life. In addition to protecting children (helping them accommodate) and teaching them to increase their skills, parents (and other adults) must comfort children when unjustifiable pain is created. Some of the most important aspects of any individual's life are the social supports and comforts that make life bearable. There are hundreds of ways in which parents comfort their children: hugging and kissing, hearing confessions, and providing absolution for incurred guilts and shames.

One important way in which parents protect their children involves screening them from information that can be overwhelmingly frightening. For example, living in a nuclear age is terrifying enough for adults, but the idea of the world coming to an end in a fireball can be catastrophic to a child. Moreover, the youngster's realization that mommy and daddy can do nothing to help him is perhaps the scariest thing of all. Psychologists debate whether or not certain "truths" should be kept from children. I believe that when a child's mind is attempting to cope with reading and writing, dealing with other childen, teachers, and so on, it is best that the child not also attempt to find ways to forestall the end of the world. A number of psychologists have suggested that children today are "growing up too fast" and are being robbed of their childhood. I concur with this conclusion. The developmental cognitive skills of childhood are best managed when the child deals with issues of childhood and not with adult sex, pornography, war, over-population, or adult helplessness. The child can neither meaningfully assimilate nor accommodate catastrophic issues. Children who are immersed in unresolvable fear are more likely to become fixated and, as a result, turn to magical solutions or acting out as means of seeking resolution.

Involved parents seem also to demand more learning from their child by simultaneously rewarding such efforts to learn. The setting of appropriate expectations by parents (and teachers) has been demonstrated by R. Rosenthal and L. Jacobson (1968).

There are many variables that could be discussed in the context of keeping the child involved and interacting positively with the world. An obvious one would be the importance of permitting children to explore and make mistakes without rebuke or humiliation.

In general, the child's interest seems to flag the least when he is dealing with a rich, varied, stimulating, and safe environment that rewards his learning with praise and love.* The child seems to con-

---

* I am not advocating a childhood that is painless. I hope it is clear from the preceding pages that overindulgence is as dangerous to a child's growth as excessive deprivation. Some pain is necessary if the child is to learn to deal with it. Unless the child learns to fear for his survival, those skills, the development of which is motivated by fear and which insure survival, will not develop. The issue, however, is gauging the optimal level or amount of fear or pain in the life of each child that is conducive to insuring healthy development.

There seems to be, for each child, an appropriate rate of growth and increased adaptational skills that requires of the environment a maximal support of the child's efforts. Too much help involves overindulgence, which creates an environment that suggests to the child that growth is easy, that few painful accommodations need be made, and that the objects of need satisfaction are easily assimilable. Too little help creates a view that the world is hostile, that accommodations are too painful to be achieved, and that the objects of need satisfaction are beyond reach. Deprivation and overindulgence both lead to fixations of the child's development.

tinue assimilating and dealing with the discomforts and pain of accommodation so long as his environment supports and rewards such efforts.

With increased awareness the rewards provided by parents, teachers, and significant others can be augmented by self-reinforcements as the individual develops a more sophisticated knowledge of means-ends relationships. Once the individual becomes self-motivated by seeking future goals, the reinforcements provided by others become less important (see the "future principle" in chapter 11). Self-reinforcement of learning increases with the development of "meta-cognition" in which the child becomes aware of learning and engages in it for its own sake. The thrust of modern cognitive psychology is to aid the growing child in learning to learn. The individual becomes increasingly self-reinforcing under the sway of the competence motive (White, 1959) and the achievement motive (McClelland, 1953).

Not all individuals become self-motivated under the sway of positive long-range goals. Not all people develop the cognitive skills necessary to create and conceptualize life goals or to learn how to learn. The normal development described above, which requires a stable, rich, loving environment, seems to be available only to a minority of human beings. Many experience a development in which learning ceases, leaving the individual in possession of inferior cognitive skills and goals.

Psychoanalysis teaches us that people do not always behave predictably or lovingly to their childrn. A vast literature including the works of John Bowlby (1969, 1980), René Spitz (1965), Margaret Mahler (1968), Edith Jacobsen (1969), Harry Stack Sullivan (1952), Karen Horney (1950), Henry Guntrip (1969), D. W. Winnicott (1965), as well as a more empirical literature including that of Jerome Kagan (1978), Jerome Bruner (1966), and others, describes how mother might cause anxiety in the child through deprivation or separation. We learn how shame and guilt can cripple the child's efforts to learn about and manage his world. This literature reveals, in effect, how interest in the world can be shattered by negative emotion or affective pain.

The skills learned to reduce or remove interpersonally created affective pain or problems are different from those learned because of interest or other positive reinforcements. Pleasure makes an individual seek after the world, pain makes him escape from it. Sullivan

(1953) graphically describes the infant's retreat into sleep and apathy when confronted with terror-causing situations. Erikson (1968) describes the problems involved in developing autonomy and initiative when steeped in shame and guilt. How often do professionals see youngsters whose sense of autonomy is created by angry, negativistic modes of behavior rather than positive learning about the world in which they live? In the next section, we will see how defenses utilized by the individual to deal with negative affective experience might permanently cripple cognitive development.

We know that all parents do not educate their youngsters equally. Some parents simply do not know how to interact with their child in an appropriate, rewarding manner. There are those who interact with "pseudo-mutuality" or who understimulate their youngsters. The child who is left unattended in an empty crib, and later in an apartment (or house), has little with which to accommodate. Some children's efforts at learning are met with hostility, contempt, hatred, or even overt abuse. Learning may easily be fixated in such situations.

Some parents overstimulate a child with inconsistent demands or "double-bind" information. Standards may be set for the child that he can in no way live up to, thus producing constant stress, anxiety, and, ultimately, rebellion. The parent may be overprotective and so effectively communicate such anxiety about the dangers of the world that the child becomes crippled by phobic responses. The child's efforts at "separation-individuation" (Mahler, 1968) may be implicitly or explicitly short-circuited.

There is by now an extensive literature on the "culture of poverty" and its effect on learning. There are many works describing how inconsistent, anxious, neurotic people short circuit their children's learning. We can add descriptions of how authoritarian parents, teachers, governments, and clergy will forbid any learning and curiosity that might lead to an individual's questioning of authority, morality, and leadership. Perhaps no one has described the process of cognitive control better than George Orwell (1949) in *1984*. The church's excommunication of Galileo and the Scopes Monkey Trial are mirrored by recent headlines of school districts banning books.

Some parents (and teachers) provide appropriate help for the child in making necessary accommodations and obtaining need-satisfying goals. They neither do too little (deprivation) nor too much (overindulgence) for their youngsters. They provide a sheltering home life (or school) and comfort the child when pain is not a means to an end. However, some parents (and teachers) do quite the opposite. They not only make accommodations more difficult for the child, and remove objects of satisfaction, but also make the child a victim of unjustifiable pain. They not only fail to comfort the child, but create the child's need for comfort. Under such conditions growth becomes very difficult for the child.

The manner in which adults individually, institutionally, and culturally interfere with the learning process are endless and need only be hinted at here. Fixation occurs when a child lives in an empty or hostile environment. I have not dealt with the effect of hunger in both the physical and psychological development of the child. More of the world is hungry and impoverished than well-fed and well-off. The developmental obstacles of starvation and malnutrition are so obvious as to need no elaboration. Parents and teachers who behave in neurotic and authoritarian ways can interfere with cognitive growth. At this junction, however, I will turn to a dynamic reason for cognitive fixation, related to the above but inherent in the cognitive processes of the individual.

Imagination

One final topic needs introduction at this juncture, namely, the role played by imagination in human development. This important topic would require a book and not just the few paragraphs I can manage here. The human imagination plays a critical role in growth and adjustment as well as fixation of development and failed adaptation. Human imagination affects every aspect of individual and social existence in their many manifestations, which include fantasy, the arts, science, and religion.

Imagination begins during the preoperational phase with the "as if" games children enjoy playing. These games are later internalized and become the basis of the human fantasy life. The talented often re-externalize their imaginative production as music, paintings, novels, plays, poetry, and a host of other artistic productions. Some pursue the imaginative production found in science and theory building; others create religions, ideologies, and dogma's from their imaginations. All of these productions play a role in adaptation and growth.

Imagination enhances adaptation by providing the individual

with an arena for problem solving and need gratification. In games, plays, novels, and fantasy, he can watch himself and others find new means to ends. People are capable of mentally creating new combinations of behavior necessary to the solution of problems. In imagination, people invent new objects of satisfaction for existing needs. Children experiment with adult forms of behavior in their games; adults experiment in fantasy. Good art reflects aspects of life not easily available for general experiences, identifications, and edification.

Fantasy also proves a respite for the problems of living. The individual escapes from the cares of the world for a time, in music, literature, art, and in his own daydreams and play. In fantasy he is able to assimilate any and all of the goals he seeks for any and all of his needs. In his dreams and in play he can be any character and make any accommodation no matter how difficult. The arts, literature, music, and poetry provide him with the nurturing and comfort that his life and the people in it cannot or will not offer. In fantasy the individual escapes from the unjustifiable pain of sickness, accident, impending death, injustice, and all that is unfair. The imagination and its products provide him with the pleasure that makes life endurable.

But in order to be healthy and to promote growth, the imaginative products must be experienced by the individual on a temporary "as if" basis. He must know that he is fantasizing or watching a movie or a play that is make-believe. The individual must be able to continue to deal with real problems and to satisfy real needs with real objects of satisfaction. If not, he creates an *illusion* of successful adaptation. While initially comforting, illusion causes growth to stop. Assimilations are not really made; accommodations do not take place. I now turn to the role of defense in human growth and personality.

Imaginative productions reflect the developmental level of the cognitive-affective structures that give rise to them. Such products reflect either preoperational or operational logic. They reflect the affective needs as well as the tone of the producer. Works of art can be interpreted only by an individual whose cognitive-affective structure is complex enough to do so. Preoperationally defined imaginations lack logic and represent an internal situation in which reality and fantasy are more easily fused. Preoperational thought makes the line between "as if" and the real much finer and more difficult to find.

Fixation and Defense

Not all individuals develop the higher-order needs, cognitive-affective problems, and awareness. Some individuals are fixated and remain rooted in a world where people are not important or where physiological needs remain dominant. They may interpret their world preoperationally and thus find themselves chronically fearful, guilt ridden, shamed, or insecure. Still others seek love and belongingness at any cost and have no awareness of dignity and esteem as they do so. As Maslow suggests, few of us develop all of our social, moral, and intellectual potential. It is time now to turn to some issues related to normal and abnormal development.

The failure of normal thought development can be traced to missed or missing opportunities to learn and to a variety of situations that interfer with or impede learning. However, fixations of development can also be traced to the individual's utilization of cognitive or *ego* defenses. Fixation caused by environmental deprivation or interference may be referred to as *simple fixation;* that resulting from defense can be called *dynamic fixation.* How and when do such dynamic fixations come into being?

Defenses are employed when an individual cannot adapt or perceive affective (or physical) pain as a means to an end. Defenses are employed when individuals cannot meet their needs or solve their problems and cannot justify the failure. Defenses come into being to satisfy needs, to overcome problems, and to justify pain. They are acts of the imagination in which the individual confuses imagination with reality. Defenses create the illusion that failure has been avoided and that success in problem-solving and need-satisfaction has been achieved. The primary appraisal of the individual is thus distorted. Defenses permit the justification of any pain and, in fact, turn pain into pleasure.

Defenses satisfy needs by denying their very existence or by imagining an environment that is nurturing. In the latter instance, the nature of the need may be transformed. Problems are solved in a similar fashion. The source of the problem is either denied, reinterpreted, or imaginary accommodations are made to deal with it. The affective result of the problem, the pain, can be reinterpreted. As a result of defense, the problem is resolved, the need satisfied, and the affective representation to both is changed. Anxiety, fear, guilt, and shame are reduced, terminated, or avoided. Defenses change both the internal and the external aspects of a problem or a need.

There are many conditions in which painful affect is intolerable or the situation creating such affect is not within manageable limits. Hunger, the fear of death, social inequality and injustice, parental or teacher abuse, and much more, do exist. Even in those conditions where the negative affect is created by misinterpretation, there may be no way to correct the improper evaluation. In one case, the daughter of an acquaintance scalded herself with boiling water and had to be hospitalized. Throughout the hospitalization the child piteously begged to be taken home because "I'll be good and won't do it anymore." All explanations indicating that she had not been bad were to no avail. Life is full of situations in which individuals find it difficult to cope, subsequently endure negative affect, and ultimately resort to the use of defenses. These defenses not only reduce negative affects that define the failure of adaptation, but also provide the positive affective responses associated with successful adaptation. Defenses create imaginary adaptations.

Earlier, the point was made that human beings seek pleasurable affect just as they avoid negative emotion. The same reinterpretation that removes pain can be extended to produce pleasure. Karen Horney's (1950) insights are unsurpassed in this context, as she describes the means by which individuals invest their weaknesses, real and imagined, with neurotic pride. Once individuals are proud of a vulnerability, they not only no longer suffer but are glad that the newly interpreted "strength" exists.

Horney points out that such individuals begin to think of themselves as perfect (accommodations). The image of perfection is the type of defense that a preoperational child would have in his view of the adult. Utilizing preoperational thinking, the individual denies his weaknesses (or his imagined ones) and turns them into strengths. Isolation is reinterpreted as independence, passivity and compliance as goodness, and dependency becomes devotion and love. The loss of self-esteem, the fear of rejection, and feelings of worthlessness are replaced by pride, virtue, and a sense of moral superiority. Loss has been turned into gain, deprivation into satisfaction, and the insoluble into the soluble.

Finally, defenses create justifications that make pain tolerable. When an individual cannot see pain as a means to an end, the legitimate justification for that pain is lost. Defenses magically create justifications: necessity is turned into virtue, suffering is reinterpreted as pleasure, failure as triumph, and deprivation as satisfaction. Suffering *becomes* the only way to live as the individual becomes convinced that it *is* the only way to live.

Why do defenses create fixation? It has been my clinical experience that defenses based on fantasy *most often involve preoperational modes of thinking,* modes of thinking that lack the logic found in scientific, formal operations. While scientific thinking precludes wish-fulfillments, preoperational thought is magical; it allows one to develop the type of fantasy and "logic" that permits defensive distortions. Preoperational thinking permits the magical assimilations and accommodations that are natural to the young child but can be used by any individual of any age. *Dynamic fixation occurs if the defense is successful in "solving" problems, "satisfying" needs, or justifying pain. Success reinforces not only the content of the defense but the preoperational mode of thought that creates it.*

A defense can be created using any type of thinking but most often it involves preoperational mechanisms. However, once an individual uses egocentric, concrete, and animistic modes of interpretation successfully to reduce a negative affective state, then future interpretation (primary appraisal) of the same or similar situations will demand the same type of thinking. The continued use of primitive thought fails to permit changes in thought patterns. The individual, believing in the reality of the magical solution, is no longer in touch with the actual situational threats or the weaknesses of self that create the painful affects in the first place. Imagined adaptation is not real adaptation.

If a defense leads to a fixation in growth, then the consequences of the defense can be seen from the frame of reference of any or all of the aspects of growth that were discussed earlier. Defenses affect primary and secondary appraisals. They affect adaptation and the assimilations and accommodations that comprise adaptation. Need arousal, need satisfaction, and problem solving are also affected. The fantasy life and imagination are affected, as well as the manner in which an individual justifies physical and affective pain. In the following pages the reader can find examples of all of the above, even though the presentation does not systematically and explicitly deal with each aspect of development.

Some Aspects of Defense

Defenses usually must achieve two goals. First, they must deny some aspect of painful reality. Second, they must replace missing information with elaborations that will bring pleasure. There are defenses such as denial, repression, or selective inattention, that "rid" us of noxious stimuli. Other defenses, such as reaction formation, rationalization, and projection, elaborate or create a new reality after the old one has been obliterated from consciousness. Defenses thus involve primary and secondary appraisal systems.

Both denial and selective inattention create immediate problems, especially for older children and adults. Once an individual denies the existence of something, he avoids important information that he may need to behave appropriately when interacting with someone. Moreover, denying a dangerous shame- or guilt-provoking situation may reduce the negative affect but will still not provide the positive satisfaction of security, love, and other needs. When he must replace information that is upsetting with that which is comforting, he must employ his creativity in utilizing elaborative defenses.

Elaborative defenses justify distortions and bring much needed satisfaction. Horney's (1950) genius is demonstrated by her description of the positive elaborations of defense. She feels that individuals cannot live with the basic anxiety created when they "feel alone and helpless in a potentially hostile world." Moving "away from people, toward people and against people" denies the problem or vulnerability. However, the individual utilizes various cognitive mechanisms to demonstrate the superiority of his weaknesses or interpersonal shortcomings.

Defensive justifications lead not only to pride but to moral superiority as well. Jerome Kagan (1984) points out that, most often, people see as morally correct those behaviors that allow them to endure what they have no choice but to endure. Not only do defenses allow people to satisfy the need for "goodness" but they justify suffering as a means to that end. The puritans taught their children that God would punish them for sexual feelings and other "bad" thoughts. Successful denial of sexuality became the mark of a morally superior individual. Similarly, children who are physically beaten as punishment will often point with pride to how good they are as a result of having been beaten. The righteous poor may claim that God loves them *because* they are poor, and that the rich shall be denied heaven. Drug addicts and alcoholics frequently look down upon the "squares" who don't indulge.

Defenses often lead to solutions that stress pride, virtue, and moral superiority. Kagan (1984) points out that not only do the defenses justify suffering and deprivation, but they simultaneously satisfy the need for "goodness" and moral pride. Immanent justice suggests that children who suffer physical or psychological pain will see such pain as punishment. The child interprets the punishment as evidence that he is bad. The moral superiority and pride so often seen in defensive solutions represent an attempt to recoup the lost moral virtue and self-esteem that is irrationally lost in the first place.

In *1984,* Orwell seems to understand how raw power can lead to unbearable fear if applied correctly to human beings. Once fear sets in, almost any mode of behavior that reduces the fear, even morally indefensible behavior, will become morally correct. In history there is an exceedingly long list of barbaric civilizations that saw themselves as morally superior because of their barbarism. The brutal career of Nazism began in part as a defense against the pain produced by the social, political, economic, and religious breakdown of Germany after World War II. But once Nazism flourished it was perceived by its adherents as a morally superior order.

Individuals defend against pain by interpreting it as a means to an end. Often the "end" the individual chooses is virtue or moral superiority. "Because I suffer I am a better person." Two birds have been killed (so to speak) with one stone. Not only is the pain justified but a need to be good or virtuous has been satisfied. Acts of self-interest are justified in the same way. In the case of self-interest, the real nature of the act (the true end) is masked by a newly created fictitious end. In other cases, the means are reinterpreted, thus changing its true nature.

When parental child beating takes place, the parent is often angry and loses control, doesn't like the child, or is displacing anger away from someone toward whom it is dangerous to express. The parent beats the child and tells the youngster that the beating is for his (the child's) good. The real need and the means for such parental expression are reinterpreted to be components of an act of discipline. A politician may run for public office to satisfy personal needs for wealth, power, or anything but his stated (and personally believed) justification: public service. As in the case of the justification of pain, the defensive substitution of one means for another usually results in an increase of self-esteem for the creator of the defense.

Perhaps the greatest coup of imagination exists when the victim of an act of injustice is convinced by the perpetrator of the latter's justification for his act! The parent who beats the child states, "I did this for your good—you needed (and wanted) the beating." The child tells others how he was beaten for his own good—in fact, he is good *because* he was beaten. The politician tells his public that his actions are in the name of national defense. No matter how much money, freedom, or life is lost, his actions are really for them. And the public justifies its suffering by each member being convinced of how lucky and virtuous he is for "sacrificing" his money, his freedom, and the lives of his children. Such is the power of the imagination. If the claim is made that defensive justifications are the single most conspicuous aspect of most human interactions, would a charge of cynicism be justified?

If there is a flaw in human beings, it may well be their inability to endure pain, which precipitates the creation of imaginative solutions for its relief. Historically those solutions may be represented by benign creations or the sinister acts of hate-filled madmen. When we see a whole society invest pride and moral superiority in subjugating or destroying another race or religion, then there is no horror imaginable that humanity cannot use to create pride, moral superiority, or rectitude.

One fascinating discovery about defenses is that no weakness exists that cannot be turned into a strength simply by redefining its meaning. Moreover, self-esteem can be increased and the self built up by breaking down someone else. There is no strength that does not become a weakness or negative quality through redefinition. The following are samples of conversations that could easily take place demonstrating how easy it is to reinterpret strength and weakness:

a) I am flexible.
   No. You are irresponsible.

b) You are rigid.
   No. I am principled.

c) I love hard work and achievement.
   No. You are an obsessive compulsive personality.

d) I am assertive, aggressive, and I take every
   opportunity for advancement.
   No. You are a psychopath with no conscience.

e) I am good to my fellow man.
   No. You are a sucker.

f) I am gentle and kind.
   No. You are weak.

With little effort the reader can generate a long list of opposites that
are redefinitions of each other.

One of the most universal of human behaviors that serves as a
defense is labelling or stigmatizing of others. For example, calling
someone "crazy"—or if one is more sophisticated, "psychotic"—
immediately discredits anything that the person might say. Thus,
for an individual at odds with someone who reduces his self-esteem,
calling the other psychotic immediately reduces the validity of statements that hurt or cause problems. "Heretic," "Commie," and the
widest variety of racial and religious slurs can be utilized for defensive purposes.

Interpersonal defenses make the individual, and the person he
chooses to be, perfect. However, people just as easily dehumanize
others with these defense ploys, thus reducing them to other than human status. Once an individual dehumanizes others, he is no longer
sensitive to the emotions and the needs of those dehumanized.
"Niggers," "Spics," "Guineas," and "Kikes," are only some of the
terms that dehumanize ethnic and religious groups. Some years ago,
the "hippies" (college students) were at odds with the "pigs" (policemen) and "hard hats" (blue collar workers). The human capacity
cognitively to deprive others of their humanity and then act as if
they were less than human is universal and seemingly unending.

All religious and scientific theories can be used for defensive
purposes. Most religions have been created in part for defensive
purposes in the first place. Ernst Becker (1977) has described how
religion may be a defense against death and guilt. Those not imaginative enough to create their own defensive elaborations will find
no end to the ready-made fantasy supplied by parents, families,
friends, schools, churches, and the state. Chauvinism has long been
used to deny a plethora of painful emotional experiences.

Our discussion of defense is by no means complete. The human capacity to deny, to pretend to solve problems, and to meet needs is infinite. However, it is important to remember that whenever an individual is confronted with a need that cannot be satisfied, he is confronted with a problem that must be solved. If the problem cannot be solved in reality, then the wonderful human capacity for intelligent, cognitive creativity will surface in an effort to change the meaning of the situation that created the problem, and in so doing, a solution will soon be found. Not only will the individual feel that his deprivations do not exist, but he will at the same time create the illusion that he has achieved full satisfaction of his need.

IMAGINATION, REALITY, AND DEFENSE

It was suggested above that children and adults take steps to defend themselves against the unendurable pain brought on by unresolvable problems and unmet needs. Preoperational thinking is utilized as the basis of defense because such thinking is infused with magical and primitive thought mechanisms that lack the logic to prevent wish fulfillments from becoming reality. This process can be checked by the formal operations of scientific thinking, which prevent denial and distortions of reality.

If defenses are made up of preoperational thinking, can such thought also be responsible for an individual's initial desire to utilize defenses? The answer to this question is a qualified yes. It has been my clinical experience that when people use defenses *it is for real pain caused by real situations*. We live in a world in which each of us can fall victim to an unimaginable list of horrors, diseases, or situations in which we cannot meet our basic needs. Most of the patients I have treated were actually rejected, misunderstood, abused, and neglected. Their defenses were originally put in place to solve real problems. However, sometimes children and adults experience pain because of misinterpretations and faulty conclusions brought about by the use of preoperational thinking.

Children are constantly misinterpreting the reasons for events, as a result of the egocentrism, purposivism, animism, and magical omnipotence associated with preoperational thinking. For example, when parents fight, children will often assume that these arguments are because of or about them and, in so doing, the children assume a burden of guilt. The death of a parent can have the same effect. A child's inaccurate perceptions produce an intense negative emotion that gets reduced by a preoperational defense. Thus, in a real sense, preoperational thinking both causes and "cures" the guilt and anxiety.

Let us hypothesize that a child is physically or mentally abused. Preoperational thinking creates a phenomenon called "immanent justice," which is made up of two reciprocal statements: "If I am bad I must and will be punished" and "If I am punished I must have been bad." The abused child is incapable of saying, "My parent is drunk or disturbed and out of control." Instead, he will say, "Look how bad I am that this is happening to me and look how I upset my parents." The ensuing guilt, shame, and anxiety will lead to preoperationally based defenses.

As we will see below, children are not the only persons who misinterpret reality and experience guilt reactions. Once the thinking of any individual becomes fixated due to the use of defenses, subsequent defense will be needed because of unavoidable misinterpretations that follow. A vicious cycle sets in as defense mechanisms produce unnecessary fear, guilt, and anxiety, which subsequently produce a new round of primitive, magical defenses. As he justifies the magical defense with moral superiority and neurotic pride, the preoperational thinker gets locked in place leading to a new round of misinterpretation, defense, and superiority. And the cycle continues.

Another example of using defenses to respond to preoperational thinking is in order. The child of four or five years of age is known to develop night terrors. Little Melanie projects into the darkness of her room all manner of magical creatures from her own imagination. She thinks animistically and her thoughts are real. It is hard to distinguish between the real and the imaginary. Melanie shakes in her bed as "it" moves about in her closet or under her bed. How does Melanie deal with magical, preoperationally created terrors? With magical preoperational defenses, of course. She adjusts her blanket and pillow in a special way. She prays to a higher order of magical being—one based on goodness—to banish the forces of evil that are attacking her. Melanie spends hours creating magical evil and magical good. She creates the problem and the solution.

Primitive man plants his crops. The winds and rains come and destroy his corn, wheat, and rice. How easy it is for him to see the wind and rain as alive and having a purpose in destroying his crops. "The gods are angry (animism) and punish me because I am bad (immanent justice). I will pray to the gods and next year give them an offering of food (magical solution)." Melanie and the primitive man have invented religions in which their fears are explained and controlled.

The next step is for primitive man to feel proud and morally superior for his endurance and his success in getting the gods on his side. Ritual and social order begin to take shape according to the magical solutions offered to the magical problem. The consequences of this will be discussed in the next chapter.

Alcohol and Drugs

It is not the province of this book to discuss the effects of alcohol and other psychotropic drugs in any extended way; but no discussion of defense mechanisms can be complete without touching on this topic, especially since psychotropic drugs alter not only mood states but thought processes as well. The defensive consequences of smoking marijuana, for instance, are quite different from those associated with using alcohol, even though both may be sought primarily for their tranquilizing value.

The traditional view of alcohol and other drugs is that they deal with some negative affective experience. However, ingesting drugs also alters cognitive aspects of personality and this, too, is reinforced. Alcohol is a fast-acting tranquilizer that will reduce a teenager's anxiety; it creates paralysis in the judgment or in the interpretive capacity that led to his anxiety. By changing the thoughts and perceptions that inhibit him, the teenager is able to behave in a friendlier, more outgoing way that might lead to more successful social interaction. The powerful reinforcement of alcohol can be seen both from its negative and positive reinforcing aspects.

It can be noted that, initially, a youngster might involve himself in drugs not because he is seeking their reinforcing aspects but because taking the substance is a socially reinforced *rite-de-passage*. Once taken, the drug has its own reinforcement value, but it was social rejection and prestige that served as the primary reinforcers for ingesting the drug in the first place.

Each popular drug can be reinforcing because of social pressures and/or the substance's psycho-physical effects. Cocaine is currently quite chic and the pressures among the middle class and the wealthy to use and share cocaine can be very strong. However, the drug can deal most effectively with even moderate to severe depression and would probably be most reinforcing to those individuals suffering from that disorder.

Marijuana is a drug initially used by many young people because of social pressure and adolescent rebellion, and the drug is interesting precisely because much of its reinforcement value comes from its basic alteration of cognitive aspects of personality. Unlike alcohol, which is a strong tranquilizer, marijuana gratifies because of its ability to create interesting perceptual and cognitive phenomena. Many young people (and others not so young) become quite anxious and paranoid when smoking pot, yet they find it sufficiently rewarding to continue its use in spite of these drawbacks.

I take the theoretical position that marijuana's symptoms recreate preoperational and sensori-motor patterns of primary appraisal and thought that are interesting and gratifying to the user. Its use leads to an increase in perceptual experience and to a decrease in conceptual experience: colors get brighter, sounds become louder and more prominent, and food tastes better as one concentrates more intensely on specific sensations. One focuses more on sensory events, which leads many pot smokers to hail marijuana as an aphrodisiac. Not only does the individual become more aware of sensory events but he tends to center on specific aspects of the sensory field. He may focus on one note in a musical phrase or one instrument in a band to the exclusion of all else, producing interesting musical experiences.

While under the influence of marijuana, time perception collapses to the here and now (one reason for the sensory focusing described above). It becomes difficult to remember what is being said. Conversations become similar to the "collective monologue" of two-year-olds. The whole narrowing of conceptual thought makes it difficult to deal effectively with any verbal, abstract information. Thinking becomes extremely concrete. At the same time, there is a tremendous increase in egocentric experience, which may cause anxiety and ideas of reference (the belief that all events are occurring with reference to the experiencing individual) so often seen in marijuana usage.

All drugs tend to increase egocentrism in that they focus the individual's attention on himself and make it extremely difficult to collect realistic information about the world. We will return later to a discussion of the effect of drugs when we explore the consequences of using defenses. However, it can be stated here that one of the most difficult tasks anyone can undertake is to try to get a chronic drug user to see anyone else's point of view.

The Situation and Defense

In the last chapter it was pointed out that individuals behave appropriately to the situation in which they find themselves. If an individual employs a defense, it is likely to be utilized because some aspect of a situation demanded its usage. Once individuals use a defense in some situation, they change the meaning of that situation and are likely to continue using the defense and its concomitant mode of thinking whenever that situation arises. Of course generalizations do take place and when they do the individuals in question may continue behaving defensively toward a variety of situations that resemble the original. It is entirely possible, however, that some people behave nondefensively in all situations other than those producing the defensive behavior.

Let us imagine that Mark, a child of five, is seriously shamed by his mother because she caught him engaging in sexual behavior. The youngster might well defend himself by *denying* sexual feeling and elaborating on the need for perfect purity and honesty wherever his mother is present. The situation could be generalized so that all sexually arousing situations involving women come to arouse shame and the need for sexual purity. Mark stops maturing sexually with regard to women as his thinking about sex and his interpretations remain at the level they were when he was caught and shamed. Mark has become fixated due to the use of the defense.

However, the same little boy might never experience that kind of embarrassment with men. His growth within same-sex relationships continues to develop, mature, and become more adult as time goes by. He might even be able to discuss sex with other men, provided of course that there are no women present in the situation. An observer may wonder why Mark can be comfortable with men and yet be so immature with women. His immaturity may be much greater in social situations than during business hours.

Our hypothetical Mark is typical of most people. Only the psychotic is consistently immature in most areas of life, but even here the ability to interpret maturely might be present in many situations. Certainly those we call neurotic only manifest such behavior in some situations (which, as was pointed out in chapter 7, makes it a mistake to call anyone *neurotic*). Stanley Greenspan (1979) points to the scientist who uses formal operational thought during his working hours but behaves like a truculent child when returning home to his wife, reacting to the lateness of his supper with an egocentric, enraged interpretation. The same individual can interpret some situations with formal operations, others with concrete operations, and still others preoperationally, all in the same day. Most individuals will interpret situations with different degrees of maturity depending upon which situations arouse defenses. All individuals are capable of thinking more regressively due to stress or situational pressure; but unless a defense is utilized, their thinking will return to a mature form once the situational threat is relieved. If the individual cannot escape the situation or deal with the stress, his defense might be employed thereby creating a fixation in that situation.

Those whom we considered neurotic are so called because there are consistent situations in which they behave immaturely. Persons who behave neurotically are rarely aware that their behavior is due to preoperational, egocentric thoughts in the situations that led to their immaturity. However, neurotics are able to utilize their formal operation and evaluate their behavior once they are no longer involved in the situation that led to their preoperational thought. *Insight* is the ability to reflect on one's behavior and is dependent upon formal operations. Situations that are approached with fixated thinking rarely permit insight. Insight occurs before or after the regressed thinking takes place.

All individuals enter situations that will arouse intense emotions and lead to immature thought. Our mode of experience varies from moment to moment due to the level of affect and maturity in our thinking. Our behavior in each situation therefore depends on how we interpret its reality.

One final note. In most cases fixations are created when we think about people, not things. People are unpredictable and are able to create the most intense negative emotions. Most of us deal with the impersonal world in a far more clear and mature way than when confronted with other people in our lives. In general, the more important an individual is to us the less clear we are in our thinking and the more we are likely to use egocentric, preoperational thinking in interpreting their behavior and in planning our responses to them. It is a rare individual indeed who can think with equal maturity about the relative nature of the physical universe and the relative nature of differing human points of view.

10

Modes of Experience
and Their Consequences

THE COGNITIVE-AFFECTIVE-DEVELOPMENTAL-INTERPERSONAL (CADI) MODE OF EXPERIENCE

I can now introduce the concept of the CADI mode of experience. At any given moment our behavior is determined by the relationship of cognition to affect with regard to a specific situation. The situation is referred to as "I" because most important situations are interpersonal. The affect that is aroused by the situation and guides the individual's behavior is determined by the developmental level of the person's cognitions that are involved in both the primary and the secondary appraisals of that situation. In turn, the individual's cognitive level is determined by his past experiences as well as the intensity and the nature of the affect at that moment and place in time. We cannot understand an individual's behavior unless we ascertain his comprehension of and emotional feeling for that which is going on around him.

At each moment in time, all individuals experience themselves and their world in terms of a specific CADI mode of experience. Their behavior is determined by the goals they seek or by the people who live in that particular situation as defined by the CADI mode of experience, which differs from person to person and within each person over time. Increases or decreases in affect, developmental

193

cognitive growth, and changes in life situations, are all factors that alter the CADI mode of experience.

In most healthy human beings, the quality of thinking that forms the base of the CADI mode of experience changes with maturity. The potential to develop a mode of experience in which one can interpret one's world by meaningfully utilizing formal operations seems to exist in each of us (unless we become neurologically damaged). Most of us, however, become fixated at modes of experience much less mature than the CADI based on formal operations. Lack of environmental stimulation; deprivation of needs; pressures from the environment that undermine the capacity to learn, understand, and question; and intolerable emotional pain leading to defense, all create fixations in thought development, thereby placing us in many situations with primitive modes of experience and interpretation.

The difference between the psychologically healthy and the psychologically unhealthy depends upon the CADI mode of experience of an individual. No matter how mature our thinking or how excellent our self-control, all of us at times will utilize primitive CADI modes of experience. However, some individuals remain fixated in their thinking across so many situations and for so long a time that their behavior is never appropriate or effective in satisfying their life problems. Such individuals can never see themselves or others with any clarity. Primary appraisals are rendered permanantly inaccurate. If the fixations are severe enough in number and in age level, all learning may be impaired, including what one learns about the impersonal physical world.

The world is becoming more complex and demands more from us intellectually; so, too, more opportunity is provided for intellectual growth. Yet such demands and opportunities are not equal for all individuals. Equality is not to be found in the emotional climates within each child's home, culture, and society. The variations in maturity of different CADI mode of experiences are astounding as we move from individual to individual both within and between cultures.

THE CONSEQUENCES OF FIXATION

Traditional psychoanalytic theory viewed fixation in terms of an event (trauma) leading to the immobilization of sexual energy at pregenital levels. Therapeutic psychoanalysis created a situation in which the individual could become aware of the impulses that had become forbidden as well as the reasons for his feeling of danger in relationship to the impulse. Once the patient understood that the dangers created by the situation existed because of infantile mis-interpretations and/or threats by parents who were feared, the repression and defenses against the impulse were lifted. Once the defenses were removed the patient's *libido* could progress to more mature forms of expression.

Many contemporary therapists recognize that the traditional psychoanalytic viewpoint is too simplistic. Even when an individual understands the reasons for his original fears and begins to face them, much of his behavior remains problematic. What traditional psychoanalysis often did not take into account were the intrapsychic and interpersonal consequences that occurred because of fixation. A fixation occurring at age two will produce very different behavior in an individual at age forty than if the fixation had not occurred. During the remaining thirty-eight years, problems arising from the original fixation would have led to innumerable new fixations, to the failure of developing skills, and to the creation of problems wholly autonomous from the original problem. Insight into the original problem does little to change the weight of thirty eight years that followed the original trauma.

Let us say that Michael is chronically shamed by a parent. (In the present view, single traumas are rare; rather, we deal with the effects of patterns of interaction over long periods of time.) The child's shame means loss of parental love and loss of esteem in the eyes of significant others. After repeated interactions, Michael begins to feel that there is something wrong with his essential being and that he will never be loved or accepted. One of the first serious consequences of chronic negative emotion is that the child develops what Victor Raimy (1975) refers to as "misunderstandings of the self."

The child sees himself as bad, unworthy, and unlovable. This is an intolerable state in which Michael cannot justify or rid himself of the painful affect. At this point a defense is utilized to solve the intolerable problem. The child denies his worthlessness and, identi-fying with *his perception* of parental goodness, resolves to be just what mother and father want him to be. Children, seeing their par-ents as perfect in their roles, assume that they, too, must be perfect.

Their identification and modelling behavior becomes a caricature of real adult behavior.

There are of course variations to the above scenario. A parent may be quite immature and thus demonstrate behavior that is a caricature of maturity. He may demand of the child perfection and goodness that are totally beyond anyone, especially the parents themselves. As a result of the same fixation processes we have described as present in childhood, the parents believe in their childish self images of perfection. In the present view, however, the child who feels unworthy is quite capable of making his own distortions without the ideas being taught to him.

How does a child see the adult? First, adults are viewed as perfect, and, therefore, the child must himself be perfect. Such perfection not only denies feelings of unworthiness but undermines any further threats of shame. A perfect person can do no wrong and therefore should not have need to feel shame. Second, the child can concentrate on behaviors that will build perfection. He must be perfectly independent or perfectly good or perfectly free or, as in so many cases we see today, *perfectly happy*. If Horney was alive today, I feel she might well add this latter style of behavior or "appeal" to her list.

Little Michael has now resolved his problem but at an enormous cost. The thinking that permitted him to distort self must remain, along with the content of the fantasy and the particular behaviors that maintain his esteem. He now has need of a primitive CADI mode of experience that makes up his defensive structure. As he grows he moves from one situation to another in which his self-esteem can suffer. He will therefore utilize this primitive defensive CADI mode of experience over and over, reinforcing it time and again.

The more egocentric the individual's thinking becomes as he moves from situation to situation, the less well he can evaluate information about himself. His interpretations (primary evaluations) tend to be egocentric, and since he already believes he is inadequate or unworthy, he continually makes incorrect interpretations. As a result of his negative interpretation, he experiences more shame and more anxiety, requiring new reinterpretations of situations, more self-aggrandizement, and denials of problems. The very nature of the defense leads the individual to create the negative emotions from which he sought to to defend himself. Thus, an endless, self-reinforcing, negative feedback loop called a vicious cycle is in operation.

Donald Meichenbaum (1974) describes how emotionally overwhelmed a patient becomes because of some threat in the environment or some inner physical event. He is describing a process that takes place because the individual is thinking in primitive terms. Were an individual to confront a gunman who threatens to kill him, the fear aroused would be univerally understood. Similarly, an individual can be frightened as he walks on a safe street because his interpretation of the street's safety has utilized the mode of interpretation of a young child. Primitive thinking leads to more overwhelming and disorganizing emotion and, in turn, this keeps one's thinking on a primitive level.

Individuals who are overwhelmed with emotion and who think concretely do not set future goals easily. It is only future goals (we will discuss this at greater length below) that give us the ability to endure suffering, for the latter is tolerable if seen as a means to an end. Individuals who deal with uncomfortable situations by using primitive CADI modes of experience will not recognize the purpose of suffering or of being uncomfortable. The behavior of such individuals is often guided by the pleasure principle, which creates a circular pattern by further reinforcing the primitive CADI defense. A good deal of destructive behavior is due to individuals who see only the short-term gain and thereby fail to bear discomfort in order to achieve a superior long-term goal.

The more egocentric and defensive one's orientation the less information one will seek. One of the most serious results of having to maintain an illusion about oneself or others is that one cannot learn about oneself or others for fear of coming across negative information. No news becomes good news. However, the less one learns about oneself, the more one needs defenses, which obstruct knowledge, to replace that which one is missing.

There is yet another self-reinforcing feedback loop in operation. The more a person uses defenses, the more his thinking will retain the type of logic utilized in primitive patterns. Thus the person will remain concrete and tend to be unable to utilize deduction as a mode of planning future behavior. The individual's time concepts, involving himself and others, are likely to be inadequate, thus leading to further fixation of the self-image. The individual behaves in patterns that are youthful and no longer appropriate to his age. Moreover, he lives in the here and now to an excessive degree.

The thinking contained within a primitive CADI mode tends to be syncretic or overgeneralized. Hyperbole is often used to describe how the individual feels. The last situation encountered was the "very best" or the "very worst." One day everything is wonderful and will always be so, the next day life is awful and can never change. One reason depressed people are often suicidal is that they cannot imagine a time when they were not depressed or would no longer be depressed. The primitive modes lead an individual to see others as "wonderful" or "terrible" in a bewildering succession of metamorphoses.

Preoperational thinking does not permit seriation or gradation in values to be perceived by the individual. The preoperational CADI mode involves judgments that are of the all-or-nothing type. You and I are either all "good" or all "bad." Once categorized we cannot belong to any other category and thus a stigma exists. From the moment a primitive thinker says he likes you, you are the "best"; but make a mistake, and you are the "worst." Since preoperational thinking does not allow for any perception of time other than the here and now, you are either "always the best" or "always the worst." One who uses a primitive CADI mode can tell you, on the very same day, "You are always the nicest to me" and "You are never nice to me but always cruel."

There are hundreds of examples of the lack of seriation and overgeneralization in human behavior. Even psychologists fall victim to preoperational thinking when they use trait names to describe individuals. By saying someone is "psychotic" or "intelligent" or "neurotic" they create an all-or-none description. When an individual uses a preoperationally based CADI mode of self evaluation, they are either perfect or terrible. Hence, many patients can recognize no personal strengths in some areas, but simultaneously see no weaknesses in others. The reader can generate his own list of preoperational polar opposites that at any given moment can be the basis for evaluation of self or other, e.g., ecstatic (never just happy) versus miserable (never just blue); brilliant versus totally stupid; gorgeous versus hideously ugly.

The preoperational thinker is either optimistic, viewing each day as the beginning of a new adventure, or grossly pessimistic, feeling that pain will last forever. When we think preoperationally we center on the here and now. Primitive people have no real past except for that which is remembered and embellished by human imagination. History is remembered as a series of idealized myths.

The future is perceived vaguely or not at all. When things go well the person with a primitive mind enjoys the here and now to an enormous degree; when things do not go well the same person suffers unimaginably.

When experiencing people through a primitive CADI mode, someone new is seen as a new beginning and the person is idealized as perfect and all good. The new relationship begins euphorically as childish hope projects a vague but blissful future. Once a primitive CADI person experiences his first disappointment in the other, the latter is transferred from the nominal preconcept "good" to that of "bad." Gloom and pain rule as efforts are made to extricate the self from the now ruined relationship and to seek another perfect, idealizable individual who can be perfectly loved.

Not only does the individual utilizing preoperational modes of experience evaluate himself and others as either the "best" or the "worst" but the basis of these evaluations are primitive as well. As a result of centering, an individual who makes a lot of money, plays baseball well, or has any talent or skill becomes the "best." Once an individual is the best, the primitive evaluator cannot accept information contrary to the initial evaluation. Such is also the case if the initial evaluation had been negative; no positive information will change the primitive evaluator's mind.

The primitive evaluator is surprised if evidence does exist demonstrating that a person labeled the "best" is not always perfect. Gradations of morality cannot exist. A successful politician is discovered to have affairs, a baseball player takes drugs, a movie star is not a good mother. The primitive evaluator cannot believe that someone so successful, so easily idealized, and so perfect can have such flaws. Outrage follows the disclosure of imperfection, and if the imperfections cannot be explained away or denied, then the perfect, idealized person is now vilified and recast as perfectly awful—the "worst."

Perhaps the most difficult, primitively conceived demand of self and others is the need for motivational and emotional purity. Contradictory emotions or motives cannot be accepted. One can never love and hate someone at the same time. If one finds oneself feeling contradictory emotions or motives, then one motive or emotion must be denied: "I shouldn't feel that, so I don't." Without denial, a re-evaluation of worth is made: "I know I have been doing good things for *J*, but since I feel resentment I am really a bad person and not the good one I thought."

Another consequence of primitive evaluations of others involves comparing the worth of different people. An individual who makes more money than the evaluator is a better person then the evaluator. If the evaluator makes more money than another, then he is worth more than the poorer person. Smarter, more athletic, prettier, and similar adjectives are all turned into evaluations of a person's total worth, followed by the creation of hierarchies of worth between individuals. The wealthier, prettier, more athletic person becomes the "best"; the one who is inferior becomes the "worst." Those with imperfections of character, that is, possessing emotional or motivational impurities, certainly join the "worst" in comparative evaluations.

Dogmatic stereotypes are also examples of overgeneralization and lack of seriation provided by primitive CADI modes of experience. "All you people" is based on a structure of thinking that refuses to admit gradation of experienced individual differences in people, situations, or special cases from prematurely drawn generalizations or rules. The primitive modes of experience allow one to center on only the aspect of a situation before it is overgeneralized. Thus, one individual may focus on his shortcomings or on sad events, while another may be preoccupied with goodness or niceness. It is often hard to get the so-called neurotic to shift attention (decenter) from one topic to another.

Perhaps the most serious consequence of the use of defense is the unavoidable constriction in consciousness. When individuals deny and distort their perception of themselves, the environment, or other people, they reduce or terminate the uncomfortable feelings that such awareness had aroused. Their consciousness is organized, however, by aroused emotions. Interest, fear, love, and hate direct the attention and organize the conscious experiences of those people and objects that they expect will once again arouse various emotions.

If one cannot deal with fear, guilt, or shame, then defenses will begin to operate in any situation in which expectations predict the re-arousal of such emotion. Earlier, it was suggested that individuals seem to scan or monitor their environment without conscious awareness and that emotions can be aroused by these unconscious probings. Defenses, too, are aroused and mobilized by the same unconscious perceptions, affording the individual freedom from painful affects. The individual becomes more committed to not knowing than knowing.

The more areas of self and environment that are defended against, the less the individual "knows" about these sources of information. Individuals who seek to avoid all negative feeling can know very little about their environment. I submit that many of my students and my adolescent patients are incredibly ignorant about history, social and political information, or any of the situations that might arouse negative affects. Poor education explains some of these gaps in knowledge, but defense is needed to explain much of this ignorance.

Moreover, many well-defended young people have turned to culturally trivial interests to replace the missing information in their lives. Rock-and-roll, television, and the movies provide the meat of their consciousness, and then only the most shallow and trivial aspects of each of these areas. Feelings are aroused only in "safe" situations, such as the movies, where reality is known not to exist. Many of these young people are cognitively and emotionally "dead" in social and academic situations. As time passes, they need more and more shock in their movies and in their music to provide any feelings at all. They seek horror and sex films of the grossest dimensions in order to feel alive.

The pathological constrictions provided by defense are in both the intellectual and the emotional spheres. Each area owes its normal development to the other. I belabor this point because there are still so many educators who stress intellectual development without dealing with the youngster's emotional life, and many clinicians who deal with affect while ignoring the role of intellect in the arousal and control of emotions and drives. It has been said that we live in a "trivialized" culture. I agree, but I stress that such trivialization means both the constriction and the underdevelopment of intellect as well as the deadening of emotional life.

By turning away from the world, we must ultimately concentrate on ourselves. The primitive CADI mode invariably leaves one narcissistic, a condition in which one's awareness is focused on the self. I believe that while children are egocentric they are not narcissistic. It is the "neurotic" older child, the adolescent, and the adult who are both egocentric and narcissistic.

The more concrete and egocentric an individual's thinking becomes the more certain he is that his viewpoint is the correct one. Egocentrism is defined as the inability to take another person's point of view (Flavell, 1968). If we add to the egocentrism the growing feeling of being perfect, we can see that individuals who are operating with a primitive CADI mode of experience behave with indifference, arrogance, or inappropriate reactions to the needs of the others.

The individual who remains primitive because of defense is indifferent to others but not to himself. His feelings remain the standards for the behavior of everyone else. No matter what happens to anyone else, the defense-wielding person sees himself as the victim. Once self pity begins to reinforce the use of the defense, we can add one more powerful reason for the individual to remain fixated. Few problems are harder to deal with therapeutically than an individual who feels special and perfect because of all the bad things that he believes have happened to him.

I have described another aspect of the paradox of using defenses. An individual who was made to experience needless shame by an immature parent, developed a perfect self-image, thus fixating his thinking. As a result of being egocentric, he engaged in behavior that was increasingly inappropriate and selfish. The reaction he got from people induced shame and guilt that he actually deserved. His real behavior led to an interpersonal mess in which he was rejected and condemned by others.

Insight or reflective awareness is dependent upon formal operations. An individual whose thinking is fixated along primitive lines lacks insight whenever he is utilizing his defenses. He is always being hurt by others and is in need of his defenses. He is always being hurt because he is hurting others. The cycle is endless. Because the individual is always hurting, he very often has a scowl of anger or pain on his face. The reaction from strangers confuses him: "I didn't know that person and I didn't say anything, yet they didn't like me." Such words can be the result of primitive misinterpretation, but often they are valid percepts to interpersonal situations brought on by facial expressions and postural elements of which the individual has no insight or awareness.

Not only does the user of primitive CADI modes of experience alienate people in general, but often he chooses to be with people who themselves utilize primitive CADI modes of experience. The interaction of two individuals, each of whom fits the other's notion of perfection while initially reinforcing each other's distorted self-image, is well documented by clinicians. However, it does not take much time before each is attacking the other in order to be given the egocentric reinforcement each needs.

Two egocentric individuals see only their own point of view. The language they use with each other reflects the certainty that they are right. Each hurts the other with complete justification that his particular wounds are the only ones that count. Neither plays fair by sticking to issues and each person's arguments are *ad hominem.* The constricted time concept each has leads to accusations that begin with "you always" and "you never." (Preoperational thought is expressed as extremes and totalities.) The emotional hurt that each arouses in the other leads to an ever increasing need for the primitive use of CADI modes of experience with their images of self-perfection and egocentrism.

When egocentric individuals hurt one another, when they follow their self-interests to the exclusion of the interests of others, many justifications are required. Each blames the other for striking the first blow while denying his or her own responsibility in creating pain for their partner. One of the most common rationalizations involves stating "This hurts me more than you" or "This punishment is good for you—you need and deserve this pain." How many abused children hear that the abuse they live with is inflicted for their good and their self-interest? How many relationships or social agreements between people are based upon a shared defense? One individual inflicts pain or behaves according to self-interest and justifies his activities by convincing the other(s) that the actions are really in their interest. The pain the victim feels is justified by accepting the statements of the very person who creates the pain. One can see marriages, families, or even societies built around excuses for the self-interest of a few and the pain caused by that self-interest.

A male individual who fears the opposite sex may never speak to that gender as he grows older. Fears are reinforced with all manner of primitive, cognitive notions about the opposite sex. Let us say that in his late twenties a male cannot ignore his problem any longer and seeks professional help. The therapist will not only seek to help the patient understand the source of the fears and how his fears keep being reinforced by his defenses; the patient will have to be helped to learn the skills he has failed to learn in dealing with the opposite sex.

The failure to develop skills is one of the most serious consequences of utilizing defenses. By denying a problem one never learns how to deal with it. Learning occurs in stages, over many years. An individual of fifteen lacks the interpersonal skills of a twenty-five-year-old. Only by spending ten years learning how to deal with people will those skills emerge and develop. Skills exist because of the continual shift between assimilation and accommodation across a myriad of situations. Simply making an individual insightful as to why he thinks primitively does not permit him immediately to think in an advanced way. His increased social and intellectual skills will develop only with learning, practice, and patience.

Another consequence of defense also relates to the development of skills. Not only does using defenses in a given area lead to failure in developing skills, but the problems in those areas get worse for lack of attention. Some parents cannot deal with their child's problems for fear of confronting their own guilt and inadequacies. Perfect parents must have perfect children. The parents do not learn to develop the skills necessary to deal with their children, thus they cannot understand and discipline their youngsters. Neglect adds significantly to the child's problem. When they are finally forced to look at the difficulty, they not only lack the skills to deal with it but the problem has grown far out of proportion to what it was initially.

Throughout this chapter I have tended to focus on the interpretive styles produced by fixated CADI modes of thinking. Interpretations of reality involve the primary appraisals of the individual. However, an individual so experiencing reality will also behave according to less than mature secondary appraisals. While many of the examples provided in the chapter implicitly describe primitive secondary appraisals, it will be useful to explicate some specific qualities of behavior arising from such primitive thought. Secondary appraisals involve the manner in which an individual expresses emotion or other affective needs. They also involve the style of an individual's problem-solving.

The behavior of those operating with primitive secondary appraisals is marked by a poor level of self-control, planning, and judgment, but a high degree of impulsiveness. Secondary appraisals involve means-ends evaluations and the justifications that permit self-control. With primitive CADI modes, the individual often cannot see the reasons for delay of gratification and so gives in to needs and the dictates of the emotions as they arise (pleasure principle). He acts impulsively and plans activities inadequately. Often such behavior leads to poor problem-solving and inadequate need satisfaction. For example, a person may eat impulsively, too quickly, and consume the wrong foods because he cannot take the time to find the right foods and prepare them properly.

With primitive secondary appraisals an individual shows temper and other poorly controlled emotions. When angry he may yell, hit, or manifest other forms of assaultive behavior. Such an individual speaks without thinking and hurts the feelings of others without meaning to, often without being aware of it. The interpersonal relationships of such an individual suffer as he hurts, behaves impetuously, acts out, and speaks with poor judgment and a lack of self-control. Many more examples could be generated as the individual with immature secondary appraisals gets into difficulties in school, at work, in social situations, and within himself. Any such behaviors also set in motion negative circular reactions or vicious cycles and require more defenses, more fixation, and ultimately lead to more troublesome behavior.

Criticism is deadly to the individual who utilizes primitively structured defenses. Criticism implies imperfection, and that means painful emotions that suggest worthlessness. Accepting criticism involves seeing things as relatively good or bad. Criticism is responded to with anger, rage, and hurtful counter criticism. When one interacts with an individual who deals defensively, there will be arguments, charges, and counter charges. But more importantly, it becomes difficult to teach such an individual because self-correction is unacceptable.

The individual who uses defenses will, over time, become more and more alienated from his basic emotions as he becomes a caricature of a real person. For example, if he escapes from his "weaknesses" into a posture of power, his need for power becomes overwhelming. Life turns into what Horney (1950) called a "devil's pact." Power is ultimately seen as the basis of morality. Powerful people are good and the weak are evil. If the weak are "all bad," they are dehumanized and the power-hungry individual can do to them as he wishes. He assumes dictatorial powers over friends, family, or society itself. Criticism is stamped out, while critics are reviled, rebuked, or destroyed. The sources of all information are controlled and the information itself distorted to reflect the egocentric self-aggrandizement of the powerful.

Individuals can also see weakness and dependency as goodness. To be perfectly good is to seek out the powerful and to be controlled by them. By identifying with the idealized powerful one, the pre-operationally weak gain strength through magical fantasy. The "good" individual conforms to all demands made upon him and sees the goals of the powerful as morally correct and superior. Ignorance is revered as the powerful one wishes it. All criticism is quashed and sources of information turned over to the one who knows all. Much of human life and history has been shaped in this way.

There are numerous other consequences of defense that could be discussed here. We can summarize our discussion by suggesting that the more areas in which an individual uses defenses, and the longer the defenses are used, the more *real* problems are created: emotionally, intrapsychically, interpersonally. The more one defends, the greater the failure of basic learning and interpersonal skills. Many of the consequences are real and are created by the individual himself; they lead to still further defense and to a reinforcement of the primitive CADI. Before behavior can reflect maturity, an individual will not only have to learn about himself but develop skills that have failed to mature. The problems of a so-called neurotic—or worse, of a psychotic—are not just "in their heads." (The discussion of the consequences of primitive defenses in terms of guilt and morality can be found in chapter 12.)

The more an individual experiences various life situations through immature CADI modes, the more he sees those situations in childish terms. Egocentrism, animism, lack of logic, and a host of other preoperational mechanisms leave him to perceive a world that is unstable, difficult to manage, senseless, and overwhelming. I have discussed some of the inter- and intra-personal difficulties that result from these immature modes, but it is clear that the subject has scarcely been touched.

Every aspect of the immature individual's life can be affected by perceiving situations and people in black and white, all-or-nothing terms. Any situation can be made worse by poor judgment, denial, and by perceiving things in magical ways. In each situation the individual is capable of expecting too much because of his inability to seriate and accept half a loaf. His expectations are of the whole loaf or none at all.

Individuals feel compelled to control the whole situation and others in it or give up totally and control nothing at all. As they struggle for control of themselves and others, they resent and fear the very success they seek. Children cannot control their lives. The immature CADI mode makes the individual ambivalent: he tries to take over *and* give control to others at the same moment. He dreams great dreams while resenting and fearing those dreams. Such a person lacks the knowledge to realize his dreams and thus suffers endless disillusionment, anger, self pity, and bitterness. He condemns himself for the "worst" mistakes.

As his moods waver, as he moves from instant triumph to ignominious defeat, justifications abound as the immature individual struggles to maintain his pride and self worth. In success and failure he remains morally superior to others as he alternatively flatters and cajoles, condemns and puts down. And so he moves from situation to situation, person to person, convincing himself of his power and worth, while all the time growing more ignorant and fearful of the knowledge of self and others that can liberate him.

There are endless series of descriptions that could be made of the consequences of immature modes of experiencing. There are endless numbers of situations to be interpreted by an infinite number of cognitions interacting with any number of emotional states. All of the behaviors, motives, and goals of any human being are describable along a spectrum of immature to mature cognitive-affective modes of experience. I have provided some of these descriptions along with a conceptual tool that will permit the elaboration of many more.

11

Products of Developing
CADI Modes of Experience

In this chapter I shall discuss some consequences of developing cognition that are central to intelligence. "Ego," "self," and "will" are crucial concepts when describing the healthy or pathological personality. Self and will involve such concepts as "hope," "expectations," and "future orientation," which are equally important in determining how individuals function in relation to their world. Each of the above has been dealt with extensively elsewhere, but it is important to place them within the present theoretical context since these ideas involve CADI modes of experience.

SELF AND *EGO*

Self, will, and *ego* are all, in one way or another, the product of human intelligence and imagination. Without the qualities of human intelligence, including the linguistic apparatus necessary to give names to the concepts, each would cease to exist. A number of excellent discussions are available concerning the differences between "ego" and "self" (e.g., Chein, [1972]; Rosenberg [1979]). In the present theory, "ego" refers to a shorthand expression for all the psychological processes of an intellectual or cognitive nature that are involved in adaptation. Thinking, memory, language, reasoning, judgment, and so on are all "ego" processes. The present definition is similar to Isidor Chein's (1972).

Ego, however, is rarely used in the present theory, Roy Schafer (1973) points out that such terms are too easily reified and placed "within the mind" creating many linguistic and theoretical problems. This book is, in effect, a psychology of the *ego.* It attempts to describe processes of behavior in terms of the developmental changes in cognitive processes and in the interaction of such processes with the emotions and the environment. Throughout our discussion, however, I have chosen to use the term *person* or *individual* when describing an interaction with the environment. I have attempted to avoid using statements such as "the *ego* does this or that," in which the person is lost and with it a holistic view of people.

The present definition of "self" is similar to that provided by Morris Rosenberg (1979) who states, "The self concept is the totality of the individual's thoughts and feelings having reference to himself as an object" (p. 5). I would add "as the individual refers to himself as a *behaving* object." Rosenberg suggests that the self is *conceived* and, therefore, is an end product of the *ego,* or one's cognitive processes. With the emergence of more mature forms of thought organization, our intellectual processes become capable of developing conscious awareness of themselves. As our ability to abstract develops, we become one object of our own awareness. The self results from the conscious experience of one's body, possessions, *and of one's own* mental processes.

Psychologically, the most important aspect of self is awareness of how the *ego* operates. We become most proud of ourselves when we can see ourselves as intelligent; knowledgeable; possessing good perceptual abilities, memory, common sense; and other qualities. It pleases us to be graceful, quick, and to move well in sports, dance, and other activities. Our intelligence gives rise to our self but the self thrives on *ego* processes, such as intelligence, which bring it into existence. The self is subject and object. Thinking provides the existence of self; we experience ourselves as doing the thinking and as the object of our own thought.

The self results from intellectual processes but is not an epiphenomenon. As the self develops and becomes more articulated and abstract, it begins to act as the organizing force of consciousness itself. Thus, self is a product of consciousness that once formed acts to organize consciousness and to direct the very intellectual processes that bring it about. This is an example of the Gestalt principle of the whole being greater than and reorganizing the parts that comprise it. R. W. Sperry (1968) points out that consciousness results from a complex interaction of neural activity. Once consciousness emerges it acts to organize further neural activity; it is a transcendent or superordinate reality produced by nonconscious neural activity.

The self of the young child is quite different from the self of the adolescent, when formal operations come into existence. Initially, baby Warren has no awareness of self and so he tends to fuse means with ends. Self comes into existence as the child becomes aware of the consequences of its actions through the primary, secondary, and tertiary circular reactions. Warren observes the sensory consequences of his motor action and a rudimentary sense of self is born. He becomes aware that some objects (such as his thumb) feel sucked upon and others (such as a rattle) do not feel sucked upon. As movement becomes patterned, that which is body becomes delineated from that which is not body. The sense of self evolves and is thus improved. As Warren acts upon the world, he sees the degree to which he can influence events and thus increases his sense of self and its worth. Young children will give orders to adults to evaluate just how able they are to influence adult behavior. It would appear that for each child there is a specific degree to which they must feel in control of the environment. A sense of too little control can infuse the self with helplessness and rage; too much control instills an inflated sense of power and the emergence of tyrannical behavior.

Language, with its words to define *me, mine, I,* and so on, increases the awareness of self. Throughout childhood, Warren becomes aware of his effect on the environment and vice versa. With each leap toward operational thinking, the sense of self is retransformed. By the time concrete operations are reached, Warren can begin to classify himself and place himself within a variety of categories. His sense of "good me" and "bad me" shifts under the operations of seriation as he compares himself favorably or unfavorably to others across a wide variety of situations.

It is, however, only with formal operations that the youngster becomes conscious of himself as an abstract object defined by many activities and qualities. Part of the definition of the self that the child employs is based on the quality of thought processes that bring self-consciousness into existence. Thus, during the concrete stage, Warren can imagine that he is "a good athlete" or "a good student." During formal operations the child becomes aware of his own motivation and asks "Why did I say that?" or "How can I change this or that about myself?"

The younger child can be in awe and wonder of his world. The adolescent is conscious of awe and wonder. He can also be in awe of his own development. The adolescent becomes aware of flaws in the self, both real and imagined, and for the first time he begins consciously to correct (or defend against) aspects of the self. The youngster becomes aware of flaws in the world around him as well, after which he may begin to struggle with injustice and develop the ideals and passions that mark this age. Each adolescent ultimately decides how much or how little he or she will do to correct not only flaws in the world but those in the self.

If the child utilizes many defenses in the course of growing up, then the CADI mode, which includes self-awareness, may not progress to full articulation. Horney (1950) and Rogers (1961) both brilliantly describe the creation of self under the impact of negative emotions and defensive operations. Both suggest that the child must accept his "real self," which contains both positive *and* negative aspects, including affects, skills, appearance, and so forth. Anything we are or feel, physical and psychological qualities, can be the focus of awareness and hence of the real self.

Horney and Rogers describe the process by which a child is told (or discovers) that various drives, emotional reactions, physical qualities, or behavioral tendencies are bad, wrong, or otherwise do not live up to parental expectations. The negative qualities get denied and replaced with a self-image of perfection, or what Horney calls the "idealized self." Rogers describes a process by which the child does not include the offending qualities in the "phenomenal" or experienced self. In any event, what is described is a constriction of consciousness and a failure to develop a mature CADI mode of experience of self.

Harry Stack Sullivan (1953) described a similar process when he spoke of the individual liking the "good me," accepting and being unhappy about the "bad me," but rejecting the "not me." All self theorists agree that the more qualities of self that are not included in awareness, the more disturbed the personality. For the author, rejection of qualities of self implies a diminution of consciousness and of the process of being fixated in primitive CADI modes of experience. The individual who is afraid of himself cannot learn about himself, and this ultimately includes strengths as well as weaknesses. For an individual to be fully functioning he must be able to think meaningfully not only about the environment but also about his self. He must assimilate all of his qualities in order to make accommodating changes.

The self is a product of the imagination of others as well as ourselves. The source of many self attributes derives from the "reflected appraisal of others" (Sullivan, 1952). Mark is "just like father or mother," "has the qualities of personality of grandpa," "the stubborness and intelligence of Aunt Louise." He is "good" or "bad" and a hundred other statements that reflect real and imagined attributes. He is the vision and the dream (or nightmare) of parents, teachers, and society at large.

As he develops and moves closer to operational thinking, Mark's developing self-image, with its positive and negative qualities, also moves from the image created by others to the image he creates for himself. Consciously and unconsciously, he responds to the demands placed upon him to be good, strong, intelligent, and to try to bend himself to produce these qualities. He can produce them in actual behavior or in his fantasy. But the time comes, if his thinking develops, when he takes over the imaginative engineering of his self-image.

Adolescents will often go to extremes in creating a self-image that conforms to their needs to meet social and academic demands, the demands of rebellion, and the demands of personal uniqueness. Many needs and emotions get expressed in our self-image. Individuals tinker and adjust their self-image all of their lives and may go through periods in which they are, or think they are, wonderful or terrible. The fullness of the self-image, however, is related to the richness of the underlying cognitive-affective mode that creates that image.

Aristotle claimed that the unexamined life is not worth living. Perhaps the most important aspect of life to examine is one's self. Certainly it seems to be the most difficult. "Know thyself" is the ancient commandment that, according to this text, appears to be thwarted by the defenses that we seem to have such a proclivity to use. The more defenses we use, the more we hide our fears, guilts, and wants beneath moral superiority and all manner of neurotic pride—the more we live as if "do not know thyself" is, in fact, the commandment to follow.

SELF-DETERMINATION AND WILL

Edward Deci (1980) is one of the latest in a long list of psychologists who see self-determination or will as the bedrock of the healthy human personality. Others include Ronald White (1959), Silvano Arieti (1972) and Rollo May (1981). In the present context, self-determination is a consequence of a CADI mode of experience and not an inborn drive or a need, as suggested by Deci and White. Deci's (1980) definition of *will* can be the definition used herein: "the capacity of the human organism to choose how to satisfy its needs" (p. 26). A normative view of the individual must include a description of how human beings become capable of choice in pursuing their lives. Descriptions of pathology must include the failure of such a development.

Deci describes self-determination as a cognitive process motivated by "one's intrinsic need for competence and self-determination and, therefore, having the energy of intrinsic motivation available to it" (p. 28). Deci thus follows White's conception that we are born with a need for "effectance" or competency in regard to the environment. It seems to me that positing such an inborn motive begs two issues. The first is the law of parsimony. The second relates to those individuals who are weak in will or who are incompetent. Are they born without the inborn need for competence? Is there a process in their lives to suppress the motive? Or is the failure of will a failure in the development of human consciousness and thus involves a specific CADI mode of experience?

Self-determination, intentionality, or will exists in the human being in terms of the emergence of consciousness and various CADI modes of experience. The failure of self-determination or will is a failure of the development of various modes of experience rather than the suppression of an inborn drive. The healthy personality is marked by the courage to make meaningful choices, while all forms of pathology involve fixated CADI modes of experience that rob the individual of his ability to choose and intend.

Will or self-determination is not describable in the existential sense required by Jean-Paul Sartre (1957). Isidor Chein (1972) makes clear that we are bound by the laws of nature, which include the biological, the chemical, and the physical. However, physical and biological complexity gives rise to psychological factors not reducible to the physical or the biological, from which they are derived. Each human behavior takes place in a given situation and results from the individual's interpretation of that situation. The present situation may be similar to past situations but cannot be identical to them. Since interpreted meaning of a situation includes that which is unique to the present situation, part of the meaning an individual finds in each new situation is unique as well. That unique meaning cannot be determined by past experience or rules. Consciousness of the unique meaning found in each new situation allows the person some degree of freedom in choosing how to behave in that situation. Adaptation would be impossible without freedom to choose behaviors appropriate to new situations.

The rules of psychological organization are not understood but it seems clear that some of these rules are purely psychological in nature. As consciousness increases so does the human capacity to make various choices in various situations. Such choices are governed by the laws of nature that are psychological and not reducible to the antecedent conditions of chemistry, physics, or biology. The degrees of freedom people possess differ from individual to individual, but clearly they exist as key factors in human personality. In our theory, freedom is less than that given us by the existentialists but far greater than accorded to us in the robot status assigned by the behaviorists and other strident historical determinists.

How does the human capacity for will or choice develop? Can I create an explanation that avoids a "competency drive" or other intervening variable? I can if I define will as a function of human consciousness as do I. N. Mohanty (1974), Edmund Husserl (1962), Jean-Paul Sartre (1957) and Paul Ricoeur (1966), and go on to recognize that consciousness is organized around affect.

The early emergence of consciousness involves an awareness of things. Things arouse interest or fear; they are wanted and wished for as satisfying various problems or needs or are repelled and escaped from. The earliest form of will is the pursuing of "whim," as Piaget calls it. The baby is showing a primitive will when he reaches out for something interesting. He is conscious of the object and wants it because of his emotional relationship with that object.

Psychoanalysis has long defined the development of early will or intentionality in terms of negation and negativism. Arieti (1972) writes: "Will starts with a 'no', a 'no' that the little child is not able to say but is able to enact upon his own body. The child enacts a 'no' when he stops the urine from flowing in spite of the urge to urinate and the bowels from moving in spite of the urge to defecate. ... The individual has a choice. He may allow his organism to respond automatically in a primitive way or not" (p. 12). The development of negation is seen by the analyst as a function of the interference of the child's pleasure by adults who demand that he inhibit his impulses for social and reality reasons.

Identifying or internalizing those behaviors that demonstrate the will of the parents represent another important determinant of will. Opposing the will of the parent provides one opportunity to identify with that will. As described earlier, internalization of parental behaviors represents an important source of cognitive growth. The same identification provides a source of moral growth. The parents who stand firm in their resolve with their child and who demonstrate persistence and integrity in reaching their goals provide the source of internalizable material that enhances development of will.

The interaction with the social environment and physical maturation increases the scope of consciousness and brings new emotions into play. As the child's awareness of self develops, so does the awareness of the relationship of self and object. In opposing the will of the parent the child discovers a new pleasure. Accepting or negating leads to pleasurable consequences involved in exercising choice. The whim has produced a new organization of consciousness whose exercise is pleasurable and important. A new psychic organization comes into being that has become a superordinate regulator of lower functions. The increased consciousness of self enhances the capacity both to make and to control choices, and these are intrinsically rewarding on an emotional level.

According to Piaget (1981), "will is simply the affective analogue of intellectual decentration. *Will involves an affective change of perspective.* We end up with the final formulation: the will is a regulator to the second power, a regulation of regulation, just as from the cognitive point of view, the operation is an action of actions. The act of will corresponds, therefore, to the conservation of values, it consists of subordinating a given situation to a permanent scale of values" (p.64). Will is, therefore, a function of the consciousness that emerges with operational thought organized by various affects. It involves the growth of the consciousness of consciousness. Finally, it represents the intrinsic, emotional reward created by the emergence of higher-order consciousness.

A sense of competence grows with a child's increased awareness of his success. The pride taken by parents and others in little Warren's accomplishments begins to reinforce and to join with the child's pleasure in successful choices. As the awareness of self crystallizes, the child takes over the function of investing his success with pride. As more success is experienced, the child becomes aware of having a will, while the feeling of choosing and the carrying out activities become more important. At its culmination, self-determination is the result of the meaningful awareness of self and the possibilities of success in some environmental situation.

The more primitive the individual's perception of self is, the less he will develop a meaningful self that renders enjoyable and important the process of making choices. Such a person either follows "whims" or retains negation as his mode of choosing. Autonomy is defined by either saying a spontaneous yes, or, more usually, by reflexively saying no. The will is present but is constricted and primitive. The consciousness that permits self-awareness and a healthy pride in accomplishments fails to develop. Fromm (1943) describes this failure as "escape from freedom."

A final point: The self does not make choices. The individual or the person makes them based on the cognitive-emotional meaning of the situation in which he acts. "Self" is the awareness one might have of the fact that one is at that moment making a decision. A complex set of cognitive processes allows both the decision to be made and the individual to be aware of the decision-making process. The decision-making processes are *ego* processes, which, if complex enough, permit awareness of those processes to produce various emotional satisfactions.

It is my belief that self-determination increases in direct proportion to the awareness an organism has of its decision-making processes and the pleasure taken in exercising those processes. Many organisms make decisions but only humans are aware of and take pride in their choosings. It is in the act of choice that we are most human and our awareness of this fact makes freedom the precious thing that it is. Humanity needs the concept of "will" or "self-determination" to differentiate the fully developed human from all the lesser-developed organisms.

"Willpower" is often seen as a mysterious ingredient of char acter. If one can lose weight, give up smoking, or resist other temptations, then one has "willpower." If one gives in to temptation, then one lacks willpower. I submit that willpower exists when an individual finds a conscious reason to endure a deprivation. Generally, we find that if the endured pain can be perceived as a means to reach a more important goal (achieving a greater pleasure or avoiding a greater pain), then willpower comes into play. Therefore, "willpower" is a fiction that depends upon a state of consciousness that appreciates various means-ends relationships.

Failure to develop a healthy sense of will means a failure to develop a mature CADI mode of functioning. Some individuals never develop past the point of wanting to either please or displease their parents. Much adolescent struggle involves learning that life must be lived for itself and not for or against anyone else. When we are young we have an intense desire to please our parents. I believe that this universal and crucial affect exists to ensure that children will learn to be socialized and to develop the skills necessary for survival and success.

By age two a struggle begins in which children want not only to please their parents but also to separate from them. The process of separation-individuation is seen as a crucial one by theorists such as Margaret Mahler (1968). Parents must find some way to deal with their child's rebellion while at the same time being pleased by the child's growth. Discipline (see chapter 9) becomes an issue in this context. If the child feels he cannot please the parent, he may see negativism as his life goal and the solution of this problem. On the other hand, if parents pull the reign in too hard on the child's desire for autonomy, the youngster may make that struggle central to his development. The lack of will and of willful negativism result from the improper resolution of the struggle to separate and individuate.

FANTASY

One of the essential features of human personality is the ability to create fantasy. There are a number of excellent discussions of fantasy, but none is superior to Jerome Singer's (1966) landmark work. In the present context, I would like to discuss fantasy from its cognitive-affective-developmental aspects.

Imagination, as a function, begins, according to Piaget (1973), during the preoperational stage. The internalization of sensorimotor activity provides the basis for representational thought. The internal capacity to recreate external reality provides the basis for imagination in which the youngster begins to manipulate those symbols that represent external reality. Representational thought can be identified by and inferred from the presence of representational drawings, deferred imitation, and "as if" or imaginative play. The child's fantasies or daydreams remain partially external, and form the basis of such imaginative games as "cops and robbers," "house," or, in our times, "Star Wars."

Play and other fantasy productions of childhood are experienced quite intensely by the young child, who still has some difficulty in descriminating between external reality and imaginative production. Night dreams, in particular, may be remembered during the day as if they really happened. Selma Fraiberg (1968) called this period the "magic years" because of the child's difficulty in accepting fantasy *as* fantasy. Night terrors are common at this time. Magical omnipotence exists as the child believes his thoughts and wishes are real and can make things happen simply because of the presence of the wish.

Fraiberg and others have amply described the function of such externalized fantasy during this period. The child tries out new roles; works out inner conflicts; engages in wishfulfillment; gets even with powerful adults; corrects injustices; and deals with a variety of negative emotions including fear, jealousy, and others. The child enjoys play, which is self-reinforcing. In the process of sharing fantasies, the child also learns to communicate, to trust his emotions, and to work out social roles. For these reasons, psychologists have suggested that play and fantasy are functions too important for adults to interfere with.

During the stage of concrete operation, the child's play becomes "rule oriented" (Piaget, 1975; Flavell, 1968). Imaginative play becomes more internalized and less socially acceptable. Fantasy becomes more private and governed by censorship, unless it is common and publicly shared. The function of fantasy remains the same as before: wishfulfillment, the working out of problems and negative emotions, and so on. However, as children get older, much of their imaginative functioning extends well beyond the "here and now" fantasy. They create fantasies that anticipate the future; they daydream about the "not yet."

By adolescence, if formal operations emerge, children become aware of their fantasies and imaginative journeys into the future. Deductive thinking (or "hypothetico-deductive thinking," [Piaget]) is basically a function of the imagination. The adolescent, according to Flavell, begins to create "What if. . ." type questions, and answers them probabalistically. Gary Zukov (1979) makes clear that the new physics is in large measure an imaginative production.

Adults are capable of dreaming about the not-too-distant or the far-flung future. Planning one's life becomes an important activity, and imagining oneself in the future guides and organizes much present action. The awareness of oneself in the future lets one imagine one's death or the loss of loved ones and can arouse intense emotions.

All manner of positive and negative emotions can be aroused during fantasy—both fantasies of the present and of the future. For some the fantasy can become as real as reality itself, especially when rooted in strong emotion. Fantasized fears of the future can crush present activities as well as organize them. Fantasies of the present can lead to rage, hostility, sexual excitation, and a host of other intense emotional and physiological reactions.

We often see in clinical practice that fantasized situations created by an individual can be so real that he loses control over his fantasy and begins to employ psychological defenses. A fantasy can begin with mature thought processes only to regress, under the increased presence of emotion, to an experience in a primitive CADI mode.

The more primitive an individual's CADI mode of experience, the more likely he is to lose control of and become frightened by fantasy activity. The schizophrenic regularly becomes terrified of his own imagination. To control such terror, Recovery, Inc., a self-help group of hospitalized people, teaches its members to "anticipate with joy or don't anticipate at all." The aim of much cognitive therapy is directed toward helping people restructure their modes of anticipating future events in order to avoid "catastrophizing" them. Anticipation always involves some form of fantasy activity.

When individuals remain aware of the "as if" quality of imaginings, these productions remain an important source of pleasure. Human fantasies can become havens of escape as well as forums to practice skills and new mental combinations of activities. The imaginative functioning of the talented and gifted provide a panalopy of constructive productions, including art, music, and dance.

Theater and poetry enrich human life, giving it meaning and allowing individuals to better endure the pains that life inevitably has in store for them. Science, art, and religion exist alongside dogmatism, ideology, war, and rampant technology, representing the mature or immature, constructive or destructive aspects of the human imagination.

THE FUTURE PRINCIPLE

What remains of this chapter will deal with another consequence of developing CADI modes of experience in relation to time and the goals that individuals pursue. In order to develop the themes of this section, it is necessary to recapitulate some of the ideas already set forth concerning the development of cognition, while presenting the theory through a slightly different "lens."

Earlier, personality development was described in terms of needs and problems. This viewpoint was augmented with descriptions of the developing personality in terms of assimilation, accommodation, and shifting means-ends relationships. The "lens" to be utilized here describes personality in terms of changing "goals," those objects that satisfy needs or are assimilated as part of adaptation.

Freud described two modes of cognitive-affective functioning and experiencing (Brenner, 1955), each descriptive of a mode of thinking and the consequent manner of experiencing needs in relation to the objects and activities that satisfied those needs. The infant and the young child are dominated by the *primary process* mode of thinking and behave according to the *pleasure principle.* With increased *ego* development, thinking matures until it can be described as *secondary process,* which is thought-related to functioning that conforms to the *reality principle.*

If we view personality in light of cognitive theory (including the work of Piaget and Flavell), then a description in terms of the pleasure and reality principles and primary and secondary process thinking does not do justice to the full range of human experiential modalities. I suggest that the *ego* continues to mature beyond secondary process thought, eventually to be dominated by a "tertiary process of thinking." This mode of thought is correlated with a manner of functioning descriptive of the *future principle.* These three modes of functioning will be described, as well as some issues related to their development and interrelationships.

Brenner (1955) writes: "Expressed in simplest terms the pleasure principle states that the mind tends to operate in such a way as to achieve pleasure and to avoid its opposite" (p. 22). While our minds always seek pleasure and avoid pain, Brenner is referring to the mode of achieving such pleasure. During the operation of the pleasure principle there is a tendency "toward immediate gratification" of needs without regard for consequences. The infant cannot conceptualize reasons for delay, and, if the objects of satisfaction are not present, he is capable of creating their presence through hallucinatory phenomena.

In behaving according to the pleasure principle, the infant's thought is primary process. Ideas are organized around drives and emotional pleasure rather than conceptual logic. Ideas exist as images and movements rather than as concepts. Freud (1966) compared the infant's thought patterns to the nocturnal dreams of the adult, which also lack logic and reveal displacements and condensations of symbol and imagery. The dreaming adult "behaves" according to the rules of the pleasure principle.

If one views the primary process and the pleasure principle in Piagetian terms, then one is describing sensorimotor intelligence. Michael's behavior is dominated by "primary" and "secondary" circular reactions, that is, movements that produce bodily pleasure or interesting sensory phenomena. The objects sought by the infant during this phase are his mother; his thumb; and brightly-colored, interestingly-shaped objects that catch his attention. The rewards for acting on the object are contained within the action itself, suggesting few means-ends distinctions.

As time progresses, Michael becomes more aware of his object-world and his effects upon it. He learns that hallucinations are not as satisfying as real objects. He further discovers that many satisfying objects are made available to him by the will of another. The child must develop skills that permit him to gain the attention and to control the behavior of those who provide satisfaction to his needs. As his skills evolve, his awareness of means-ends relationships improves and becomes increasingly sophisticated.

Michael's expanding intellectual and motor abilities lead to an awareness that not everything he does pleases significant others. He can fall down, bump into objects, and cause pain and pleasure in an increasing variety of ways. He must possess the means not only to gain satisfaction from his parents, but also to avoid their displeasure. Michael learns of the emotional and physical pain that can accompany parental anger. He also discovers the dangers inherent in exercising new skills.

The development of the *ego,* which includes new skills as well as cognitions gained from increased interaction with the environment, helps lead to the development of secondary process thinking and to the reality principle. The reality principle includes "the ability of the ego to distinguish between the stimuli or perceptions which arise from the wishes and impulses of the id (affect) on the other" (Brenner, p. 64). Moreover, "with age there is a gradual increase in the individual capacity to postpone the attainment of pleasure and the avoidance of unpleasure" (p. 73). Plutchik (1980) describes some of the functions that might be ascribed to the reality principle and made possible by secondary process thinking.

> An organism must predict on the basis of limited information whether there is food, a mate or danger in its environment. Dependent on the prediction made, the organism makes a decision to attack, run, play or mate. From this point of view the complex process of sensory input, evaluation, symbolization, comparison with memory stores and the like—those processes we call cognitive are in the service of the emotions and biological needs. (p. 207)

The function of the *ego* is to permit survival of the organism as well as achieve satisfaction. The reality principle is achieved with the .secondary process thought that develops in the growing child.

Implicit in the above are two major differences between the reality principle and the pleasure principle. First, the reality principle permits (and exists because of) an attitudinal capacity to delay gratification in order to maximize pleasure and avoid pain, or loss of pleasure. Second, the nature of the goals of the child have also changed. The youngster has learned that there are more intense pleasures and pains involved in interacting with others than in satisfying himself. Being tickled by another is more pleasurable than tickling himself. Rejection or abandonment by the parent (or other important social figures) causes unendurable "basic anxiety" (Horney, 1950). The goal of the child is still pleasure and the avoidance of pain, but both the mode of achievement and the range of objects or goals of pleasure have changed. There has been both a qualitative and quantitative shift in his basic mode of experiencing the world.

Piaget's view of childhood development during the evolution of secondary process thinking and the reality principle finds Michael less egocentric and more aware of his external surroundings. His memory improves, as does his imagination, permitting delayed imitation, symbolization, and "as if" play. Concepts begin to form and the child develops internalized "operations." During childhood he will progress from "preconcepts" and "transductive logic" to true conceptualizations and inductive logic. Michael also has a clearer picture of means-ends relationships and the causal connections between the two. It is this awareness that permits the delay of gratification seen in the reality principle.

Cognitive psychology teaches us that human thinking does not stop developing with concrete operations and inductive logic, but many individuals develop what Piaget calls "formal operations." Formal operations permit propositional, "hypothetico-deductive" thought. The individual who achieves such thought can ask "What if. . . ?" and propose an endless series of logical conclusions to that question. Deductive reasoning appears in addition to the inductive reasoning. Formal operations permit insight into one's own thought processes. A person can think about thinking and wonder "Why did I do or think this or that?" I am suggesting that we call the thinking described in this paragraph "tertiary process" thought.

Tertiary process is correlated with behavior that functions according to the future principle. The goals of the individual become more abstract and idealized and the capacity to delay gratification moves from minutes or hours to years or even lifetimes. An individual might even be concerned with subsequent generations. Once the tertiary process is achieved, death intrudes into the consciousness of the individual in a new and meaningful way. Many of the goals involved in the future principle are "existential" in nature and most provide the individual with a sense and purpose of life. One finds the person aware of the finiteness of life, drawn toward the future, establishing abstract future goals, and being dominated by such goals.

Examining the shift from less mature to more mature modes of cognitive-affective functioning reveals various trends. The goals of the individual—both the intrinsically and extrinsically rewarding ones—begin as bodily processes, physical pleasures, and objects that satisfy basic drives. These goals change from more to less egocentric. They move from physical to interpersonal goals, from the concrete to the abstract, from the immediately available to the case of the future principle that is potentially never available. The infant with developing skills related to sucking and grasping objects such as the bottle and the breast, becomes the child with developng skills related to pleasing friends and parents, and finally arrives at the adult concerned for dealing with a political process in such a way as to ensure the life of unknown future generations. The individual must develop an increasing ability to delay gratification of needs.

Piaget described the process of means-ends changes as "assimilation and accommodation." In attempting to assimilate or utilize various objects, the developing individual must divert his attention to changing his existing skills or accommodating the demands of each new situation. The growth of physical skills and their internalization as mental operations produces new knowledge of and interest in new satisfying objects. The attempt to assimilate these new objects in turn creates the need for new accommodations. The development of thought or mental operations is both the cause and the consequence of ever shifting means-ends relationships.

The goals of the future principle are often *life goals* or, to use Adler's (1968) term, "fictional finalisms." As will be described below, such life goals are often abstract and achievable only in theory. Reaching for some goal that involves personal perfection is a fiction, as is achieving heaven and avoiding hell. Erikson (Browning, 1973) hypothesized that the mature individual, searching for a sense of the generative, was concerned with the next generation.

Life goals, like any set of goals, can be behavioral or they can involve objects. Seeking to develop one's skills to some theoretical perfection can occur in any area, whether it be professional, intellectual, physical, or spiritual. Writing a paper of tremendous insight or the "great American novel," composing a symphony or painting a work of art, or achieving perfect "enlightenment" are often the behavioral goals sought by individuals. Being a perfect parent or gaining adoration through the display of prowess are common goals involving the future principle. Goodness, truth, and mastery over life and death are often the unreachable life goals that dominate our behavior. Many of these goals involve attempts to create a perfect self-image.

Many objects may be sought as life goals. Individuals spend lifetimes seeking the "holy grail" in one of its many manifestations. They search for the "right" home, automobile, violin, antiques, works of art, and, in the case of so many people, the "right" amount of money. Often such expeditions involve a search for the "right" person, an individual who possesses the correct intelligence, sexiness, physical appearance, and prowess, among other attributes. People can, and will, seek an endless variety of objects or places that they believe will bring them emotional satisfaction. Some will spend their time seeking heaven on earth, others will just seek heaven.

The goals described above are different than the goals that emerge during the functioning of the pleasure or reality principles. The emergence of the future principle does not mean that the two earlier modes disappear; they are simply subordinated and organized according to the higher stage. In addition to biological pleasures and safety, the individual seeks goals that transcend those of the earlier stages. The ultimate goals of life continue to be pleasure and its retention as well as the avoidance, reduction, and termination of pain. The nature of pleasure and pain is defined in more broad and abstract terms and satisfied more intellectually than physically once the future principle establishes itself in the functioning of the individual.

The future principle is not always in evidence in many adults. It develops as a function of tertiary process thinking. It is dependent on a mature CADI mode of thought. An individual may remain fixated in his thinking because of defense mechanisms or an impoverished environment. He may fail to develop either the skills necessary to satisfy lower needs or to achieve the objects of satisfaction. The future principle may not only fail to develop but be unnecessary or superfluous. Individuals who are facing death, great danger, starvation, or other forms of immediate threat often must operate according to the reality principle. Where harsh conditions dominate a culture or an individual's whole life, the reality principle can be the dominant mode of behavior and secondary process thinking may predominate.

There are different styles of operating according to the future principle. Julian Rotter's (1966) concept of "locus of control" reveals that some individuals see future goals as a function of their own efforts (internal locus), while others see goals as beyond their abilities. The attainment of goals is dependent on the will of fate, the gods, or others who are powerful (external locus). Knowing when goals are attainable and when they are not, when effort should be expended to change things and patience developed to accept what life brings, are always important clinical considerations in dealing with a patient's use of time and the future.

Some individuals view the future calmly and worry only when danger is imminent. Some deny that the future can bring danger, and see their future world through rose-colored glasses. Still others, often seen clinically, "catastrophize" the future and continually worry about what might go wrong. Such individuals can become obsessive about all the imaginary and potentially real pitfalls in reaching their goals. There are those who so catastrophize the future, or worry about death, that they destroy any chance for happiness in the present. In general, it is pathological when an individual brings too much detail to his visions of the future.

Hope is a crucial aspect of the future principle and one much overlooked by modern psychology. Hope may be defined as an individual's belief in the probability of reaching future goals (Stotland, 1969). Psychology, the arts, poetry, and literature contain a wealth of material concerning the importance of hope in normal functioning. Similarly, hopelessness is seen as a devastating component in depression, suicide, and other pathological forms of behavior.

Faith is another crucial component in the future principle and perhaps even more ignored by psychology than is hope. If individuals are to continue pursuing life goals, they must continue to believe in their own abilities as well as the worthwhileness of the goals they pursue. Moreover, there must be a faith in the future. Many life crises begin when individuals lose faith in themselves, in their goals, or in the future in general. Many young people today seem to live in a morbid present, according to the pleasure principle, because they have been convinced that there is no future for them or for the human race. The constricted CADI mode of consciousness described in earlier chapters often does not encompass meaningful life goals.

Some individuals develop a future awareness but retreat from functioning according to a future principle. Our fear of the future can stem from either imagined constructions of future events or from a conviction that the future must repeat the past. George Kelly (1951) believes that future predictions are based on conclusions drawn about the past. We often see cases in which individuals conclude that all future relationships must be as painful as their parents' marriage or that their life must follow the course set by their elders.

When individuals fear the future they can live in the present according to the pleasure or reality principles. They might engage in a frantic pursuit of pleasure in the here and now, or they may concentrate on the minutia of their day-to-day existence. We can find many individuals who fulfill their responsibilities, deal with danger, and satisfy their needs appropriately but never dream or imagine their potential future goals.

The motivation to change one's present is often a function of one's awareness of future possibilities. Often a person's belief in a better future allows him to endure great pain in the present. At times, however, someone who has passively accepted a painful existence might suddenly find the present unendurable because he becomes aware of a potentially better future. We see patients in therapy who tolerate a mean present and reveal little motivation to change until the therapist reduces the patient's resistance to dreaming of and planning for a better future.

The development of life goals organizes day-to-day activities and gives them direction. A college student will randomly take course after course until he "finds a major" that defines a satisfying goal. Suddenly the student finds the selection of courses becoming easier and more logical. Studying becomes more meaningful once it has purpose, and even boring courses become endurable once they are defined as means to a desired end. The development of life goals creates intermediary goals that similarly organize and occupy us. Thus, for example, the desire to be a physician requires a college degree, medical school training, internships, and much more.

Individuals with an emotional commitment to a life goal and its intermediary steps are rarely bored or in need of "something to do." The bored individual is one who can meet all of his basic needs and for whom life and survival are not issues. Seen from this light, the achievement of a future principle takes on increased importance. When individuals state that their lives have no purpose, they mean there are no important goals to achieve. Life for such an individual has purpose only when basic biophysical needs are experienced. In the face of an existence without meaningful future goals, life becomes tedious, purposeless, and ultimately meaningless. Those who retire from work without meaningful leisure goals often show serious psychological and physical debilitation soon after they stop working.

Some individuals pursue goals that can never make them feel

fulfilled or make their lives meaningful. As mentioned earlier, money is a worthwhile goal if it is a means to some satisfying end. Some individuals will pursue money in and of itself, and their life goal will be to get rich. The manner in which these individuals pursue their goals may be inimitable to love relationships, social respect, and admiration. Such individuals can end up quite bitter and confused, never figuring out why happiness and meaning elude them even though the accumulation of riches was achieved.

Some individuals may achieve life goals too easily and then wonder about the purpose of their lives. Those who seek wealth may achieve it and find they have no reason to continue living or working unless they can turn their wealth into a means to some other end. Women in our culture are often taught that their only legitimate goal is to be a wife and a mother. By their mid-forties they suffer depression or emptiness as their children "leave the nest" and their husbands die or involve themselves in their careers. Research suggests that women with life careers are less prone to involutional depresssion and similar "mid-life crises."

Some people set goals that are too difficult to pursue, or too high to reach. They may remain anxious and frustrated all of their adult lives as attempt after attempt is made to reach some impossible height. Much adult depression and conflict involves the mid-life assessment of goals set when one was a young adult, eagerly pursued, and now as distant as ever. The re-evaluation and resetting of new goals in mid-life, for both males and females, can be one of the liberating and emotionally corrective processes that can take place.

Some individuals will convince themselves that they have reached goals of "perfection" when, in fact, they have not. Horney (1950) writes of the neurotics who believe they have achieved their "idealized self." As long as individuals know that their idealizations are abstract goals worth striving for, and can forgive themselves for not being as they wish they might be, their mental health can flourish. But the moment such people convince themselves of their own perfection, both they and those around them are in for much pain and emotional difficulty. The search for perfection can, therefore, be either an indication of mental health or an emotional disturbance.

Many life goals involve death and its avoidance or mastery. Many spiritual goals involve immortality. Ernst Becker (1973) has described how religion may involve the denial of death. Erich Fromm (1950) suggests that religion may either engender within the individual long-term "awe and wonder" at the mysteries of life and the nature of existence, or else it might become authoritarian. Authoritarian religion demands of its believers an obedience that can destroy the joy in life and lead to much interpersonal and cultural destruction. How much death and destruction has been wrought by humanity in pursuit of the "correct" afterlife or other spiritual future goals?

The twentieth century has not been an easy one for those whose life goals are spiritual. The belief in a god who gives life its meaning and purpose has suffered. Extolling the virtues of good citizenship has been made equal to chauvinism. It is increasingly difficult to find men to be "gods," who will interpret a plan that imposes upon life a set of goals that will bring purpose and meaning. With the gods gone, humanity must create secular, humanistic goals and generate faith in them to sustain itself. Those who join cults or partake in the forgetfulness and concreteness provided by drugs and alcohol are often those whose lives lack the direction, purpose, and meaning created by life goals.

DOGMA AND IDEOLOGY

Dogma is defined by the dictionary as "something held as an established opinion." *Ideology* is defined as "visionary theorizing." Both dogma and ideology are central creations of the human imagination; they contain solutions and answers about how human beings should live, how society should be formed, how cultures should function. Both are nonscientific and, therefore, easily invested with preoperational, defensive patterns of thinking. Dogmas are usually issued by churches, while politicians and other societal leaders employ ideology. Both are often used as impediments to further learning, self examination, and the development of formal operations.

There is nothing in either a given dogma or an ideology to stop learning and development. Churches have a responsibility to outline the tenets of moral behavior to believers and parishioners. The visionary theorizing of the philosopher who dreams of a utopia provides us with alternative views of ourselves and society and can set appropriate goals for change. The difficulties begin with both issues the moment the givers of dogmas and the ideologues approach their work with their own personal needs and defenses. Dogmatists and ideologues often have primitive CADI modes of experiencing the world. They then use the dogmas and ideologies in inappropriate ways to enhance personal power and to justify the satisfaction of personal needs.

Dogmatists and ideologues seem joyfully to sacrifice the lives and happiness of individuals on the altar of tenets and visions. Upon closer examination we find ideologues and dogmatists often dripping with self-congratulation, virtue, and moral superiority as they force others to live or die for the "good" of the individual so forced. Upon still further examination we find that those who force others to live with their visions have all manner of personal needs met as a result of their behavior. Self-interest reigns supreme as the ideologue is all but oblivious to how much others are sacrificing for his good.

Dogma sets forth demands on how people should live. Its pre-operational nature can be seen in the setting forth of standards for thought and emotions as well. It is one thing to tell people how they should live, it is quite another to tell them how they should think and feel. It is relatively easy for little Warren to follow the rules and in so doing not hit his sister, or possibly share his cookies with her. It is quite another for him to be told that he must love or like his sister and that he should not harbor any negative thoughts toward her.

An adult can much more easily choose not to commit adultery than to avoid sexual arousal when looking at an attractive person. When we are told our behaviors are immoral, while at the same time being taught how to behave properly, we have a chance of reaching our goals. But if we are taught to be perfect in thought and emotion, we are in trouble for sure. Not to feel and not to think is to deny one's humanity. The goal of not being human is crippling.

Contained within many religions are the dogmatic beliefs that thought and feeling are sinful. Such beliefs are, I suspect, based on the notion of magical omnipotence. Children who are told that god sees thoughts and will punish us for them, have great difficulty in overcoming the preoperational notion that real thoughts can be dangerous. The child of five is filled with fear of magical creatures from his own imagination. To be told by the adults in your life that such magical figures are real and can read your mind and punish you for what they see there, can produce such fixation of cognition and affect.

When examined, ideology also reveals preoperational excess. The liberal and conservative each reveal a commitment to extremes in their thinking. The conservative ideologue sees his country as having no faults, while the "enemy" has no virtue. Such villainy can neither be trusted nor compromised with. Liberals often criticize their own country while seeing the good in other societies. However, in the mind of the liberal ideologue all the ills in the world are due to society's evils, while the enemy is merely a misunderstood victim.

Ideologies often contain simplistic rationalizations for the possession of wealth and for the existence of poverty. Liberals often sing the virtue of the common man: he is all noble and not capable of any bad behavior (unless he is victimized). The rich, however, (and this from many wealthy liberals) are evil and abuse their less fortunate brothers. All that business people have on their minds is the enslavement of the poor. For the conservative, the rich are the morally superior, the chosen of god. After all, if they were not superior they would not be rich. The poor demonstrate their evil inadequacies; their cursed status in god's eyes renders them poverty-stricken.

Joseph Epstein (1985) points out that both conservatives and liberals drip with moral superiority as they espouse their viewpoints. Each comfortably dehumanizes the other as it takes the high ground of virtue for itself. There is much self congratulation, while in reality neither visionary puts into practice what he actually preaches. Liberals, he suggests, drip with moral rectitude, while conservatives evince smug superiority.

One could go on at great length detailing the preoperational mechanisms almost always found in the positions of the dogmatist and the ideologue, but such a description goes beyond the bounds of the current volume. However, there is much to be said for the view that human history has been written more by the dogmatist and the ideologue than by the scientist or the artist. The former have written history in blood, keeping humanity in darkness, all the while eating and sleeping very well.

IMAGINATION, RELIGION, AND SCIENCE

It must be clear by now that the human self-image, its sense of identity, its social institutions, and its sciences and religions are all the result of intelligence and imagination. The preceding sections represent only a few of the many imaginative productions that could have been discussed. The well-springs of human imagination are the emotive and affective needs. How well cognitive and social products solve individual needs and problems depends upon the maturity of the CADI modes used by both individuals and groups. Each cognitive product incorporates varying degrees of what we assume to be the real world. Each is also a product of varying degrees of defenses and imagination as well as reality-oriented cognition.

Psychologists at best are able to evaluate the cognitive-affective processes underlying each human cognitive-affective enterprise. The goal of any scientist is to understand the nature of the "real" world and to describe its functioning. Yet he can never be sure that human imagination will not play some role in the work of his science. He will never fully expunge defense from his imaginative functions, nor would it be useful to do so. To be alive is to require distortions of reality as well as reality itself. The very act of trying to understand and order the universe scientifically reflects the human inability to live in and accept the world as it is.

In chapter 1 it was suggested that science and religion are both imaginative products created by the same human needs. These two human endeavors differ only in the manner in which they bring order out of the apparent chaos of the universe. I do not mean to suggest that science is superior to religion as the basis of our lives or that one day it will replace religion. I believe that science represents the superior method of learning about ourselves and the world. It does not represent an alternative to the roles played by religion.

Religion has many functions: explaining and ritualizing death, and at the very least providing a sense of continuity with the future or a sense of immortality that makes mortality less terrifying. Religion creates a moral imperative, which acts as an incentive for following the social order. It seeks to redress the inherent injustice of living by promising an afterlife in which justice will be done. In addition, it gives explanations to the inexplicable and allows human beings to keep faith with themselves, with others, and with their goals. Religion gives life meaning and defined purpose. The scientist could not continue to function without a "religious faith" in the meaning of his scientific endeavors. The above is accomplished within religion by creating an alternative reality to that sought by science. It involves an act of imagination and is followed by acts of faith in that alternative reality. However, each act of imagination makes life palatable by denying and distorting the perception of scientifically defined reality. When an individual takes anything on faith he becomes dogmatic and experiences a constriction in consciousness. The struggle for the religious scientist, therefore, is to maintain a balance between the search for reality and the avoidance of the same reality.

Religion can be defined as any body of explanations accepted on faith rather than on scientific evidence. According to this definition, religions can be secular as well as supernatural. We might say that there is a religion of science created the moment an individual accepts on faith the methods, goals, and purposes of science. Scientists may differ as to how much they subscribe to the supernatural in their private lives, but they must keep faith with their roles as followers of scientific procedure if they are to pursue their goals. To this degree even scientists are dogmatic, and inescapably so.

If fantasy and faith must be accepted as necessities of purposeful life, then must one accept a limit on what one is capable of learning? If so, is there any hope for people to learn enough to solve the problems that threaten us? I believe the answer to both questions is in the affirmative. There are limits to what humans are probably able to learn, but these limits are as unknowable as is the amount we are capable of learning. We can solve our problems provided we are aware of how we distort, use faith, and attempt to keep defenses to a minimum.

While I believe humanity will always distort reality, existing beliefs can be questioned, and by examining them reduce their defensive qualities. We are capable of looking at beliefs, divesting them of pride and moral superiority, and looking at the silliness that inevitably creeps into them when they are held as dogmas. We can laugh at human distortions. And while we can never achieve absolute truth, we can expand ideas and reduce distortion to a minimum. Most of all, we can examine our belief systems for evidence of preoperational thinking and replace these with formal operations.

In the preceding I have described a quandary: We must learn

about ourselves and yet there seems to be limits on what we can learn. Science permits us the tools to learn and yet that same science, as a product of human imagination, involves defense, dogma, and faith. I know of no real resolution to the dilemma. Arthur Koestler (1978) felt that our world would soon come to an end through nuclear holocaust. War remains a fact of existence, and the nationalistic and religious ideologies that have justified wars and have made them "moral" are still with us. We now have the technology to destroy ourselves, and these technologies are also justified by our ideologies. Yet Koestler felt we have no choice but to believe that war will not come and continue "as if" our future is unlimited.

There is still time to prove Koestler's apocalyptic visions of the future incorrect. We are in a race between education and catastrophe. The fixated CADI modes of perception that now dominate human behavior are not innately or biologically determined; they are a consequence of hunger, illiteracy, dictatorships, and a host of factors that force children to grow up facing intolerable and hopeless situations. Situations can change to those that foster scientific thought, positive self-images, healthy will, and a fully developed future principle. Dogma, ideology, and reliance on authoritarian religions can be minimized; they take more from the individual than they give. In the next chapter, issues related to mental health, morality, and the healthy personality will be discussed—states of affairs that positive nurturing and education can produce.

12

Normal and Abnormal Behavior

One of the goals of this book has been to utilize the same set of principles in describing both normal and abnormal behavior. Since all human beings think and feel emotion—all live from moment to moment in some situation or another, and all interpret each situation with some CADI mode of experience—one should be able to describe virtually all behavior utilizing these central human characteristics. Notice that the assumption here is that descriptions, not necessarily explanations, can be made in terms of causation or etiology.

All forms of normal and abnormal behavior involve some type of CADI mode of experience. The etiology or development of pathological CADI modes can come from many sources. An individual might suffer from a neurological or biochemical anomaly of the central nervous system. These anomalies might be the result of genetically linked disease, accident, drug ingestion, or even environmental stresses. Individuals might become fixated in their development because of a neurological problem, but they will still have a describable CADI mode of experience that plays a profound role in their behavior.

Humans are living beings trying to solve various problems or satisfy needs in a succession of personal and interpersonal situations. People react in each situation according to their unique interpretations. What we describe as normal or pathological must, therefore, involve a CADI mode of experience in addition to whatever else is affecting or has affected behavior. My description of illness will not attempt a full explanation of pathology, only those aspects that involve a particular form of CADI mode.

One assumption concerning etiology of pathological behavior will be made, however. Once an individual becomes fixated in an interpretation of a situation, the dynamics described in chapter 10 will occur. Pathological behavior is shaped by primitive, overly emotional interpretations of the meaning of various situations. Whatever produced the original fixation—be it genetic, neurochemical, temperamental or social—also produces an autonomous set of problems stemming from the fixated thinking.

In the descriptions below, an attempt will be made to describe pathological behavior in terms of an individual interacting with an environmental situation. I will not describe the pathology in terms of qualities of the individual. Words like *schizophrenic, neurotic,* and *psychotic* will be used only as reference points required by the demands of common conventions. Individuals are not *borderline,* and they do not possess attributes called borderline. They behave in a borderline fashion if their interpretation of their world follows certain rules of logic and they experience various emotions in certain types of situations. Borderline is the result of a cognitive-affective mode of experiencing.

The above paragraph calls into question the whole issue of medical diagnosis as the basis for classifying of mental problems. It also questions the whole concept of mental illness. In the present framework, schizophrenia *may* involve some real illness, such as a neurochemical anomaly; however, the behavior itself does not constitute an illness. It would be impossible to separate those behaviors due directly to the neurochemical damage and those due to the consequences of the individual's primitive CADI mode of experience.

Unlike a medical illness involving a pathogen, the symptoms of a mental disorder cannot be seen as stemming from the illness in a direct one-to-one fashion. Moreover, in most forms of behavior pathology or abnormal behavior there is no underlying physical illness hypothesized. Even in schizophrenia, where my own biases suggest that some day an underlying neurochemical anomaly will be discovered, no disease has yet been found. I therefore have to agree with Theodore R. Sarbin and James C. Mancuso (1980) that schizophrenia (as well as all other diagnostic labels) is a moral judgment and not a medical diagnosis.

The issue of values and morality is one that must be wrestled with if one intends to reject the view that diagnostic labels are medically described diseases. It is my view that all definitions of pathology are based on someone's system of moral values. No matter how destructive a behavior might be to an individual or a society, to regard it as "sick," abnormal, or pathological is a value judgment. In another time and place, that same behavior might be viewed as constructive and appropriate. Rather than finding herself at the head of an army, Joan of Arc would today be found in a mental hospital and placed on phenothiazene. Twenty years ago, homosexuality and fellatio were perversions; today the former is an "alternative life style," while the latter is an essential of sexual foreplay. I can think of no behavior defined as pathological that someone else would not call "healthy."

Today's pathology can be tomorrow's health and vice versa. Much of the behavior that is currently considered healthy and admirable might well be classified pathological if we step outside the value system that defines health or pathology. If the human race survives, it may well look back upon many forms of contemporary religion and nationalism not as valued concepts, but as self-destructive delusions. In chapter 1, I examined the cognitive-affective phenomenon known as dogmatic religious experience; I suggested that much religious instruction leads to seriously fixated, immature CADI modes of experience.

A great deal of what passes for "typical normal behavior," if seen from the lens of the CADI mode of experience and the consequences that are produced therefrom, will qualify as pathological if we only recognize that normalcy is based upon the shared values of those individuals engaging in the behavior. Many marriages, much male-female interaction, and a good deal of family life stem from fixated modes of experience and are destructive to the individuals involved. Since our culture values the typical male-female relationship (in part because we know no other) we do not recognize how fixated these relationships may be.

We can ask whether or not the very world we now live in, with its nuclear armaments, nationalistic and religious bloodletting, poverty, starvation, overpopulation, and pollution, permits any of us to fully develop the most mature mode of thinking of which we might be capable. Jonathan Schell (1982) pictures our world as a ship loaded with explosives, while we, the passengers and crew, walk about playing shuffleboard and ignore the danger. Can such people be sane? We continue to funtion only because we pretend "as if" a war is not coming. Does this not describe conditions necessary to create universally primitive CADI modes of experience?

The reader can now ask whether or not the definition of pathology used in this context—namely, destructive fixations—is also based on a value judgment. Indeed it is. I repeat: All definitions of pathology are based on criteria established by someone's value judgment. History has shown us that there are no behaviors too odious or too destructive for some group to call nonpathological. Recall that the Nazi were quite proud of their attempts at racial purification.

Erich Fromm (1980) suggests that in every epoch there are conventional limitations as to what is acceptable or "normal" thought. Anyone suggesting ideas contrary to these conventions is likely to be called "crazy." The Inquisition in the Middle Ages called nonconventional ideas "heresy" (the religious and moral equivalent of "crazy"), and visited torture and destruction on the creators of these ideas. In our own time, Schell (1982) points out that those who wish for peace and an end to nuclear proliferation are the "crazy" ones, while those who practice "realpolitick" and build engines of destruction are "sane." One creates the criteria of "sane" and "crazy" based upon one's values; and if others agree with you, then sanity has been established!

Occasionally it is appropriate to label an individual pathological. Society, the individual himself, and the therapist might test their values and think through the criteria utilized in the diagnosis, thereafter deciding that indeed the individual has serious problems that are classifiable. When this is done, I believe the following caveats should be followed before we assume it is the individuals who are basically responsible for the primitive decisions they appear to make.

1) A label requires that we make an extensive study of an individual's thinking and emotional patterns in a wide variety of situations. Pathological diagnosis means that fixated behavior is found across a wide variety of situations.

2) A label requires that we simultaneously evaluate the demand

qualities of the situation with which the individual must interact.

3) We must be aware that the demands of situations are only in part due to the interpretive qualities of the individuals in those situations. It is all too easy for the diagnostician to see pathology as "weakness in *ego* structure" without ascertaining whether he or anyone else could solve the emotional problems stemming from certain situations. I will discuss below what I call "the psychotic landscape"—situations so demanding and so bizarre that no one could really adjust to or make sense of them. Heinz Hartmann (1958) often speaks of the "average expectable environment" necessary to the evaluation of strong or weak *egos*. Nowhere does he define such an environment, however.

I will now turn to some common forms of recognized pathology; and it must be reiterated that an examination of racism, for example, will reveal similar mechanisms of created CADI modes of experience to those found in many accepted diagnostic categories. In racial or religious prejudice, individuals center on one characteristic of an individual to the exclusion of all others. The object of racial or religious hatred is seen as "the worst" as gradations and seriations fail to appear in the evaluation. The dehumanization of the other builds up the racist self esteem while moral superiority masks and justifies the cruelty, the hatred, and the resulting guilt.

COMPULSIONS, OBESSIONS, AND ADDICTIONS

Common to many forms of "pathology" are compulsions and obsessions, the former being generally seen as behaviors that are uncontrolled by the individual performing them, and the latter as uncontrollable thoughts. The psychoanalytical theory of compulsions and obsessions involves the presence of an impulse and the defense against this impulse. The individual gains control over his impulses by "doing and undoing." In other cases, the compulsions and defenses are designed to occupy thinking and behaving, diverting attention from the real impulse pressing for expression.

If, however, we analyze compulsions and obsessions from the point of view of developmental psychology, we see that they are merely variants of universal behavior patterns. They are pathological, in part, because of the contexts in which they are expressed.

If we examine any compulsion or obsession, we see behaviors, overt or covert, that are repeated over and over again. An individual may be focally aware that he is performing these actions or he may be unaware of his performance, as in the case of "tics" and other similar behaviors.

When we discussed the cognitive development of the child during the sensorimotor stage, we saw that he learned or assimilated by use of circular reactions, or behaviors that are repeated although the goal of the behavior changes from stage to stage. The initial circular reactions are repeated because of the sensorimotor pleasure they produce. Later, circular reactions are reinforced by the "interesting things" they make happen. The circular reactions provide pleasure and practice as the child learns about his world and his effect on it. Moreover, the repetition of a behavior provides a form and structure through which to recognize a given situation.

As development continues, Piaget suggests, sensorimotor behavior becomes internalized and forms the basis of thought. We have no reason to believe that learning does not continue through internalized circular reactions. Learning theorists call such circular reactions "rehearsals," for whenever we must memorize some material or master a list, it stands to reason that we will repeat our efforts a number of times. Moreover, we may find that the very act of repeating a thought is calming or pleasurable, suggesting internalized circular reactions that are "sensorimotor" in nature.

It is my theoretical suggestion that compulsions and obsessions can be seen as circular reactions of various types that have specific aims as their reasons for existing. We see them as symptoms only when they are out of context with the situation in which a person is engaged or out of context in a developmental sequence. For example, a patient might grimace or rock, primitive motor circular reactions, appropriate to a baby but not an adult. Compulsions and obsessions, therefore, belong to a universal class of behaviors that in other circumstances are not called pathological, because of custom, value, and content.

S. J. Rachman and R. J. Hodgson (1980) have compiled an excellent description of compulsions and obsessions. A compulsion may involve "checking" or "cleaning," and this description fits well with the interpretation that compulsions are behaviors designed to satisfy various emotional reactions. Cleaning rituals are seen as magically neutralizing violent thoughts, while checking often appears to be taking steps to avoid criticism or guilt. What once might have been behavior in the service of a primitive CADI mode is retained when emotions lead to the recreation of that mode of function.

Developmentally, compulsions should be seen as more primitive than obsessions since the former are behavioral and the latter are internalized. An individual engaging in such seemingly uncontrolled activity must also be seen as trying to solve some problem related to a particular developmental task and a particular CADI mode of experience. Either the activity is pleasurable and removes pain or it is a means to some end. Often compulsive behavior is designed to achieve some material end that produces some solution (or imagined solution) to an emotional problem.

We can now see the relationship of compulsion to addiction. Behavior always has a goal or is a means to an end (except in primary circular reaction where the means and ends are the same). The goal of the compulsive behavior is often food, drugs, or whatever is designed to alleviate anxiety or to restore esteem (or, as in the case of gambling, possibly to produce wealth and power). All addictions and dependencies must involve compulsive behavior since the object of the addiction demands repetitious behavior. Often the procuring behavior becomes satisfying in and of itself as it becomes associated with the effects of the object procured.

Obsessions are mental behaviors or operations designed to solve a problem. Any individual with intellectual goals and pretensions understands the feeling of obsession. One cannot be dedicated to the solution of any intellectual problem without being obsessed with the problem. However, intellectual obsession is often tempered with other activities and involvements. It is also pleasurable. In the case of obsessions associated with primitive CADI modes, the individual often chooses something to think about other than his real concern. His obsession is never-ending: the problem he has chosen to think about has no solution because it is not really the source of his emotional pain.

The more primitive the pathology—that is, the more primitive the CADI mode of experience—the more infantile the compulsion and the content of any obsessions that might exist. Hospitalized patients often walk back and forth, grimace, shake some part of the body, and the like. These seem to be primary circular reactions, although some magical preoperational significance can also be attached to them. The borderline individuals will be obsessed with gaining the good opinion of their parent or other people. Often those who are overwhelmed with the fear of life will dwell endlessly on plans they will make, or courses they will take.

Compulsive complaining is common of even fairly well developed individuals who nonetheless develop an unsolvable problem in a given area and resort to magical, primitive, preoperational thinking to solve it. Excessive eating, drug taking, gambling, smoking, drinking, or whatever can all be seen as compulsions, usually with attendant obsessions, and all will eventually bring relief from some unsolvable problem.

Circular reactions are also relaxing, especially when they take the form of magical thinking. Prayer, which takes the form of repetition, gestures, and utterance, seems to be relaxing and gratifying, especially if the individual feels that such behavior will add to the solution. Herbert Benson (1975) describes the relaxation response precisely as such a compulsive or circular behavior and suggests that modern Americans turn to transcendental meditation and other forms of prayer because they have lost faith in the prayers of their own religion. He suggests that one reason people who pray may live longer is that such circular reactions bring a relaxation response.

DELUSIONS

Individuals with primitive CADI modes of experience might experience delusions or form systems of false beliefs. Both the purpose and the structure of the delusion can be seen as stemming from the properties of the primitive CADI mode of experience. (Of course, before a delusion is called a delusion we must be very careful that we are not simply describing good reality testing of a situation of which we are unfamiliar or cannot comprehend.) The purpose of the delusion involves its goal of solving the individual's problem by denying some aspect of the situation or re-explaining the situation in terms more salutory to the individual. The structure of the delusion refers to the mechanism of its operation in terms of its content and the form of logic and thought that supports its existence.

If we look at a common "paranoid" delusion we can examine both its purpose and its mechanism. An individual reports that there is a plot of scientists to take over the world. He has learned of the plot and is the only individual capable of foiling it. He has been confined to a mental hospital because the scientists have discovered that he is God and can stop them if he were free to do so. They regularly give him shock therapy, which is done with a machine invented by the plotters. The shock therapy immobilizes his godlike powers.

We can conjecture that our patient feels quite intolerably small and helpless. He has a poor self-image due to repeated real and imaginary rejections. He experiences guilt, shame, fear, and rage in his interactions with the significant people in his life. The delusion appears to him to solve his problems. (We have seen in chapter 10 that this solution causes more real problems than it solves; it demands that the delusion be kept in place and continually increased in strength and scope.)

The delusion makes him feel powerful. It also explains and permits him to predict the rejection he has felt. The delusion justifies his rage and explains away the shame and impotence of being hospitalized, while at the same time justifying his retreat from life to the safety of the hospital. The delusion, in short, helps him to avoid fear, shame, guilt, lonliness, and a sense of meaningless, while creating an illusion of control, pride, acceptance, meaning, and purpose.

Structurally, we can see in the delusion an enormous degree of egocentrism on the part of the patient. All of the world's scientific activities involve him. As God, he is a pivotal figure in the world, with his magically omnipotent power. His identification with God is achieved through the use of transductive logic, as are most delusions of grandeur. Piaget allows us to see that the logic of the delusion is identical to that of the young child who announces he is a fish because he swims. The motive behind the logic is not childlike but the logic itself is reflective of preoperational modes of thinking and experience.

The individual's fixation with plots and those who harass him also demonstrates the inability to *decenter* or to concentrate and attend to more than one issue. He remains preoccupied with his own weakness and the hurt he imagines others have done to him; there is little to be done to get him to think about the world around him. As with any primitive CADI mode, we find poor logic, centering, egocentrism, inability to differentiate between fantasy and reality, and a host of other formal, structured thought mechanisms.

FANTASY AND HALLUCINATIONS

As discussed earlier, fantasy and imagination are involved in a good many human activities. Freud suggested that in infancy the child would wish for his bottle and image it. The result was an hallucination. George Klein (1966) suggested that it takes a certain degree of development before an individual can experience the difference between an image of an object and the perception of that object. Hallucinations at any age can be viewed as fantasy material experienced as a real event. The ability of the hallucinating individual to discriminate between image and percept has been damaged. Hallucinations generally occur to an individual who is experiencing many life situations with exremely primitive CADI modes.

The preoperational child has learned the difference between percept and image but under certain conditions, he can "lose" the difference. Young children are capable of playing "as if" imaginative games with great intensity. The line between reality and fantasy can be a narrow one indeed. A three-year-old experiencing a nightmare can take much convincing before he believes he was not experiencing a real event. Even after the parent has succeeded, the child might remember the event as actually having happened when he awakens the next morning.

Many pathologies, especially the "borderline" ones, experience their fantasies as vivid and intense. They regularly create situations that play out their insecurities, their rage, and the rejections they have had and expect to have again, and then react to their fantasies as if they were very real situations. Individuals utilizing preoperational CADI modes of experience regularly lose control over their own made-up situations and feel rejected, hurt, vulnerable, ennobled, and the like. An individual may argue in fantasy with her mother, and lose the argument. She experiences the same intensity and irrationality as if the rejection were real.

The philosopher Allan Watts (1972) has suggested that it is our inability to distinguish between reality and symbology that lies at the root of many social ills. While collective delusions are rarely described in textbooks on abnormal psychology, such difficulties in testing reality have led to a human history drenched in blood. If we survive as a species it will be because we stop believing in our preoperational images of salvation and stop throwing away our lives for fantasies involving our images of god, nation, and the afterlife.

Fictional finalisms and images of the future and self are like those of the preoperational child when seen in "pathological" personalities. Karen Horney (1950) has described the images of self sought by the individual who looks to the future with a primitive CADI mode of experience. He seeks unrealistic levels of perfection in his behavior. The perfection is like the view a child holds of his parents: omniscient, omnipotent, and never committing any mistakes of any kind. The "pathological" individual tortures himself over his imagined failures.

The interpersonal perceptions of the individual with poorly developed cognitive-affective skills are as unrealistic as those he possesses of his own self-image. Again, it is Horney who has described the unrealistic demands that the neurotic makes on those around him. While the unrealistic interpersonal behavior of the pathological individual can be discussed under a number of headings, it fits this section on fantasy. The primitive CADI mode allows the individual to experience his egocentricity by permitting it to be assimilated into his wishes. Fantasy permits more assimilation than accommodation, and the primitive individual tends to react to people as if they were figments of his imagination rather than as individuals with qualities of their own.

THE PSYCHOTIC LANDSCAPE

Difficulty, like beauty, lies in the eye of the beholder. A situation that crushes one individual might merely challenge another. The more mature an individual's CADI mode, the less forbidding a situation might appear. Are there situations that create fixated pathology in any and all individuals? Perhaps not, but I believe there are classes of situations that come close to being universal in their ability to produce fixated, primitive CADI modes of experience. I call such situations the *psychotic landscape*.

It is suggested that fear of death is dealt with by nearly all individuals in a manner that denies its reality (Becker, 1973) or creates a "continuity with the future" (Lifton, 1979). Religion is universal, there being nearly two thousand organized sets of beliefs that in one way or another formulate ways for believers to transcend their mortal status. The psychological-fantasy management of death and dying is so universal and so ingrained in daily activity that it is often invisible.

There are other situations that also seem universally to create a need for denial and elaborated defenses beyond the well-documented fear of death and dying. Whenever an individual has lifelong beliefs threatened, defenses leap into existence. For example, a teenage girl of fifteen was told all her life that her father was dead. One day she opened the door to find a man who introduced himself as her father. Her immediate disbelief evaporated as the man produced convincing documentation as to his existence. Later that day, the child's mother, the source of the story of the father's death, confirmed his existence.

The fifteen-year-old was placed in a "psychotic landscape." Everything and everyone she believed to be true or real was called into question. Her very identity had been shaken. She became temporarily psychotic, creating delusional explanations about her father and mother. She also showed an inability to control her emotional responses in a wide variety of situations. She could neither assimilate nor accommodate to her new situation. It would be an interesting and massive study to chart the millions of such individuals confronted with similarly shattering pieces of information. Groups denied access to their traditions, beliefs, and values seem to disintegrate in the same way.

Another psychotic landscape seems to be created when individuals are confronted with proof that they are genuinely unloved by their parents, particularly their mothers. In my clinical experience, I have come across many individuals who are unloved by one or both parents. While such reality is devastating to children, I believe it remains only less so to adults of all ages. Any clinician who works with children knows the length to which a child will blame him/herself for the abusive action of parents. I have seen many adolescents and adults who have appeared to be less afraid of dying than admitting that they were unloved by their parents. Suicide is a more acceptable alternative to some than admission that one is or was unloved.

Much of the difficulties experienced by adopted children seems to stem from the same reality. I have worked with a number of disturbed adolescents who recognize they are genuinely loved by their adopted parents. They are still filled with compulsive fantasies that deal with the idea that their real parents gave them up for lack of love. It is my belief that the common adolescent search for real parents, initiated by adopted teenagers, is in part motivated by the need to prove that they are loved by their blood kin.

One final reality that produces a psychotic landscape is the discovery that people might be genuinely evil and destructive. I find that most human minds reject being faced with the reality that there is no act too hideous for some individuals to perform. And if one discovers that the offending criminal is unashamed, unrepentant, lacking guilt for his offense, and even enjoys and takes pride in such behavior, then most individuals really balk and defend against such reality.

Ever since Hitler, the intelligent and well educated have had to accept that there is no act too grotesque or too hideous for some to take pride in. The twentieth century has forced a view of humankind on us that includes the behavior of Stalin, Pol Pot of Indonesia, and Idi Amin of Uganda as well as Hitler and Mussolini. One can argue that the acceptance of true human evil creates a view of humankind that is filled with shame, self-revulsion, and loss of faith. There seem to be many suffering such an affliction. The opening of the death camps at the end of World War II is still for many an unassimilable reality.

The reality of atomic warfare is made possible by our knowledge of the men listed above. Many are no longer sanguine that the bomb could not be used because of its catastrophic consequences. We have been forced to believe, at least on an intellectual level, that there are those who would use the bomb even if it would wipe out all of humanity. One can describe the CADI mode of a religious fanatic who would use the bomb *because* it would end humanity.

Arthur Koestler (1978), Jonathan Schell (1982), Robert Lifton (1979) and others have amply described the universal denial of our twentieth-century reality. Even those of us who intellectually understand the psychotic landscape of our time, go about our daily living as if nothing were happening. We write books for future generations to read, raise our children, and look forward to the future. To accept—to fully accept—the above would mean the end of our ability to function.

Most individuals do not even intellectually understand the possible evil in some humans or the possibility of our ultimate destruction. They are "numbed" (Lifton 1978) to their lives or, as I have found, totally ignorant of their past, present, or future.

Elsewhere in this book, I have discussed the trivialized generation with which I deal as an educator and therapist. So many of the youngsters with whom I work do not study history, do not read the papers, or dream about their futures. Instead, they opt for insipid television shows, empty rock and roll music, and become angry at any adult who attempts to mirror their impotence, fear, constriction, and trivialization. It will take a future generation free of our real terrors (if one exists) to describe the massive pathologies of our time created by the aspects of the psychotic landscape under discussion.

There are still other ideas that create a psychotic landscape for many, if not all, individuals. The idea that life has no inherent purpose or meaning, except that which we human beings bring to it, is one such idea. Erich Fromm (1943) believed that the last time human beings were contented with their lot in life was in the Middle Ages when people believed that the Earth was the center of the universe, rich and poor served a divine purpose in their respective stations, royalty ruled by divine right, and all of life had an intrinsic reason for being.

Children seem to need the illusion that their parents are omnipotent and omniscient. (Parents often seem to need the same thought.) How else can they feel safe in a dangerous world? When children must worry about safety or death, how can they learn to read, write, or ride a bicycle? Young children reject the idea that their parents cannot perform great deeds or are helpless to make them better if they are ill. It has been my experience that children deal better with serious illness than they do with parental anxiety when they (the children) are ill.

My list of factors that create a psychotic landscape is not complete but it gives the flavor of what I seek to express. In the last chapter, I discussed the role of religion, dogma, and ideology in human existence and suggested that human beings may never feel completely comfortable with reality. In this section I am suggesting some of the reasons for people demonstrating pathology even when development occurs in relatively benign atmospheres.

TOWARD A DEFINITION OF NORMAL BEHAVIOR

Values, Morality, and Normative Humanity

In chapter 7 many current personality theories were criticized for having inadequate concepts of both the healthy individual and morality. It was also suggested that there was no way to separate the two concepts. The healthy individual recognizes that his/her best interests lie in dealing with other people fairly and with love. The mature person recognizes that survival, dignity, and ultimate self-actualization occurs only when people cooperate in meaningful ways.

This book has also explored the less-than-mature individual, one who interprets his world with immature, egocentric modes of experience and thereby interacts with others without regard for their feelings or needs. Short-term gain is perceived as the only possible gain, while long-term, higher-order satisfaction and growth become less likely or impossible. Self-interest is generally chosen over genuine caring, the former is then justified by interpreting it as morally superior. We call such individuals "neurotic," "psychotic," or "character disordered," but simultaneously we cannot avoid making a value judgment about the morality of these people.

In this final section I shall attempt to describe the healthy individual, and, in so doing, further the argument that mental health and morality are one and the same thing. The healthy person thinks meaningfully about those around him and concludes that he must behave in an ethical fashion. To be healthy is to recognize that certain things are to be valued over others and certain moral rules need to be followed.

In order to help develop the picture of the healthy or mature individual, we must first clarify some of the muddy waters surrounding the concepts of values, ethics, and morality. Before this is done I must restate an idea offered in chapter 7. Making value judgments is unavoidable when describing interpersonal relationships; however, avoiding condemnations is possible. As psychologists, we cannot help describing the healthy individual as more ethical and normal than the immature individual, but we need not condemn the less mature for their behavior, for in so doing, nothing is added to our understanding and our techniques. We can avoid condemnations only by being vigilant to the unavoidable reality that what we mean as "health" or "illness" is identical to "moral" and "immoral." We can avoid becoming a member of what Joseph Epstein (1986) calls the "Virtucrats."

One of the first difficulties encountered with a description of "values" is grammatical in nature. We often find ourselves saying that a person "has good values" or "has no values at all"; but values are not possessions, they are not nouns. The correct usage is that he "values this or that." *Value* is a verb in the sense "to value" or hold important. Generally we say an individual "has values" either if he values what we do or if we feel he values that which we feel is truly important and worth valuing. (Usually the two criteria are the same but need not be.)

When people think meaningfully about themselves and the world around them, they discover the important things to value. A mature CADI mode of experience leads to a valuing of love, life, learning, and dignity over materialism, authoritarianism, and the immediate gratification of one's own needs to the exclusion of co-operation. The neurotic values his/her survival over others, wants to be given to but never gives, and generally places excessive value on possessions. Pathology is not only a developmental failure of meaningful thinking but a failure in making good value judgments.

Morality is an even more muddled area than values. Grammatical usage is only one problem in relation to this topic. We do not *possess* morals any more than values are to be collected up and held in storage. Morals, like values, are not nouns or objects to be held or weighed; they are rules that govern human interactions. These rules can be fair or unfair, but once such rules become social conventions, they become the criteria of good, bad, right, and wrong.

A second problem in thinking clearly about morality comes from religion, particularly authoritarian religion. Religion, Harold Kushner (1981) suggests, exists basically to make life fair. One way religion achieves this is to get individuals to give up personal desires and self-interest to make group life possible. Only in group life can we survive and grow. Group life generally presupposes a conflict between the needs of the individual and the needs of the larger community. The developers of religion recognized (not consciously, perhaps) that an authority was needed to override the individual objections to sharing or modifying personal desires. God became the moral authority and the author of moral rules. But once we see morals as coming from God, we unfortunately remove them from psychological (and other forms of) scrutiny. It becomes difficult to question the products of the supernatural. Morals are developed by people. I will assume that all social rules, conventions, or morals have an earthly origin. Moreover, the originators of morality had particular CADI modes of interpreting reality when they created the moral rules, which makes any such rules flawed in various degrees (as are all human products). Let us examine the nature of these flaws.

Morality can arise from three "earthly" sources: our own discoveries, what others tell us, and defenses. Jerome Kagan (1984), in a superb discussion of morality, points out that children of two and three years of age show an excellent ability to see the effects of their behavior on other children. When one child strokes another, the first sees very different consequences than if he were to strike the other child. Our emotional reactions to stroking and striking are inevitable and wired into most of us through the process of evolution. (We must also assume that some people are born without a capacity for guilt or shame.) Even if no one ever told us that it is nicer to stroke than strike, we would discover this for ourselves.

Young children are also capable of judging their work and productions against those of other children and adults. They do not have to be told that some individuals do better than others. Criteria of excellence that form the basis of the standards for moral judgment are all about us from the time we are born. Kagan argues that even if all moral teachings were to disappear, children would grow up with a sense of morality, and their children would have similar standards.

A second source of morality is found in the beliefs of parents, teachers, clergy, and others who influence children. A child can only learn so much on his own. In chapter 9 we discussed some of the important roles played by adults in guiding the development of the child. Morality is no different. The child's intense desire to please his parents makes being good an important goal early in the life. (I will discuss below that we make ourselves seem moral and good even if we are bad—especially when we are bad.) The child is vulnerable to the moral development of the parent. We can ask if an immoral adult can teach a child to be moral. Or can adults use immoral means to make a child moral?

The third source of morality is defense. People want to be moral and good at all costs. Being good and worthy is basic to one's self-image. When people pursue self-interest to the exclusion of what they know to be correct behavior they experience guilt, shame, and loss of self-esteem. Often they compromise themselves in order to survive by doing what is necessary. As discussed at great length in chapter 9, defenses allow justification and rationalization of actions. Moreover, guilt and shame can be removed and replaced by pride. Ultimately, an individual salves himself the most when he sees himself as morally superior to others. The "magic" of defense permits weakness and immorality to be transferred into cherished virtues.

The discoveries of children are prey to mistakes. The adults who teach morals are similarly capable of making mistakes. If, in fact, much of moral development is defensive, then who can be trusted to distinguish the moral from the immoral? Often those who are the most rigid in denouncing others while proclaiming their own moral superiority, those who use the "shoulds" to tyrannize others, and those who seek power to control the morality of others, are the individuals whose morality is based primarily on defense. We can see that moral rules, if not of divine origin, are suspect indeed.

I now come to the third problem in understanding morality. Psychology has created special organs of moral sensitivity to understand the special nature of moral rules. Therefore, the individual has a *conscience* or a *superego*. Reification sets in, and suddenly moral behavior is based upon "overly harsh *superegos*" and the like. I suggest that one does not need concepts like *conscience, ego ideals,* or *superego* to discuss morality intelligently. Instead, morality involves an individual's ability to evaluate the rules governing interactions, rules invented by people living in a given social situation. It further involves an individual's willingness to follow those rules and to feel appropriate emotions when the rules are followed and when they are not. Social morals are often invented by people with various CADI modes of experience and are interpreted by these same individuals.

Once the divine origin of morality is rejected, we can see that some of the rules governing the behavior of people are good while some are bad. Good moral rules are like good values; they make individuals give up things. But as Philip Reiff (1966) suggests, these things are returned improved and enhanced. Some personal needs are given up, and, in return, the safety and pleasure of the group experience are achieved. Individuals learn that there can be no survival without group survival, no dignity without group dignity. People cannot love alone. Without justice life is intolerable.

Sometimes the people who generate the morals or laws of a society have mature CADI modes of interpretation and have a good understanding of the needs of both the group and the individuals who comprise it. In such circumstances the morals promulgated are just and achieve their purposes. However, sometimes the morals promulgated are not for the good of the group or for the average individual. Perhaps these inferior rules benefit only the promulgators.

A healthy moral sense involves the ability to differentiate between good rules, which, when followed, bring those who follow them greater emotional satisfaction, and bad rules, which benefit only a few. The individual with an immature CADI mode of interpretation cannot differentiate between good and bad rules. "Good" is what makes him/her feel good immediately. "Good," for the neurotic, is that which fits into an egocentric view of social organization. The rules promulgated by the neurotic take the form of "neurotic claims" (Horney, 1950) or demands that the behavior of others comply with the same rules.

The Healthy, Mature Individual

How can we describe the healthy or ethical person? Views of the healthy, mature person abound in the literature and reflect the values of the theorist doing the describing. Carl Rogers (1961) details the "fully functioning individual," while Abraham Maslow (1968) speaks of the "self-actualizing person." The present description will be kept brief to avoid redundancy, but it will focus on the cognitive-affective qualities of psychological health. The healthy, mature individual is one who sees the world through a particular CADI mode of experience in a variety of situations.

The mature CADI is based on operational thought patterns. This means that mature individuals can possess object constancy with people as well as with inanimate things. To conserve a person is to see him as possessing a constant identity whether he is happy or sad, angry or loving. It means seeing the self as constant across situations and accepting oneself in failure as well as success. Operational maturity means being able to seriate. "Good" and "bad" are rarely (though they can be) extremes, but come in all gradations. The self is rarely the "best" or "perfect"; and it is just as rare to find it the "worst" or "unforgivable." Perfection is an unreachable goal sought in a series of increments or steps.

Maturity allows for the conservation of time. History is appreciated and the future is wondered about. At the same time, the lack of absolutes permits one to realize that no one ever lives "happily ever after." Suffering is usually finite as well. Mature individuals can decenter their perceptions of people, focusing neither on good characteristics nor on poor ones, but instead see themselves and others as amalgams of behaviors whose worth varies from situation to situation.

Mature CADI allows an individual to discern those moral standards and sources of pride that are based on real strength and the
genuine good they bring to self and others. Such thinking helps
avoid neurotic pride and the kind of righteous moralizing that results in an individual seeking to justify some necessary suffering or
fear of some authority. The healthy person is moral and ethical
based upon behavior and not self proclamation.

Healthy individuals think meaningfully about themselves and
others. Formal operations are in evidence in human relationships *as
well as* in dealing with the object world. Such individuals behave
scientifically in seeking solutions to their needs and the problems
they encounter. These people hypothesize, theorize, test solutions in
reality, and modify their ideas as reality demands. They can generally live with doubt and uncertainty while avoiding dogmatic explanations about the issues and problems that concern them. Their
lack of dogmatism is not weakness, since they do live by principles
and ethically based values.

Mature individuals react fully to their emotions. They react appropriately to each situation with full but modulated emotional responses. Their cognitive skills permit accurate primary appraisals of
affect-arousing situations and mature, socially acceptable secondary
appraisals. Maturity permits one to both laugh and cry where appropriate. Such people are cognizant that they bring pain as well as
pleasure, that they hurt as well as help others. There is, therefore, an
acceptance of shame and guilt as appropriate, normal, and healthy
reactions to situations. Further, there is the understanding that guilt
is best assuaged through expiation and atonement.

Healthy people live ethically based lives because they understand that survival and meaning can best be achieved (if not
exclusively achieved) through mutual respect, cooperation, sharing,
and helping others to grow. Such people respect the rights of others
without denying the needs of the self. Maturity means accepting
laws that are just but also seeking to abolish laws that are unjust.
Health allows us to admire the accomplishments of the strong, the
able, and the talented without being contemptuous of the weak, the
poor, and the unhealthy. To be healthy is to love justice and to live
according to flexible morals that promote growth.

Mature individuals react with enthusiasm when it is appropriate
to do so. They feel and demonstrate passion about a variety of life's
situations. Passion is the natural outgrowth of an individual who

has developed with an intact interest in his/her world. Health involves an enthusiasm in reaching one's goals and a recognition that without passion life becomes empty, stagnant, and not really worth living at all. Work becomes life-enhancing only when individuals have interest, enthusiasm, and passion for their labor.

Those who think meaningfully do not seek pain but accept it when it comes, especially when it means growth. Trauma can crush, but when overcome it can be a real source of growth. Maturity means a CADI mode capable of understanding the means-end relationship of pain to growth. Victor Frankl (1962) has suggested that the manner in which we suffer is the mark of our potential nobility.

Healthy individuals recognize that their central psychological processes are cognitive. Learning about these processes and their growth becomes central to the pleasure of the mature individual. There is pleasure accommodating to those situations that demand a stretching of existing skills. While these skills may be primarily cognitive and thus reveal a growth in knowledge, as well as the means to ask questions and seek answers, there is an increased power in problem-solving. In the final analysis, metacognition (a style of learning to learn) develops along with an enjoyment of its use.

Certainly maturity does not mean that growth is primarily cognitive. The mature individual shows growth and increased pleasure in the development of motor functions, artistic expression, and a host of technical accomplishments. The journeyman carpenter, for example, who becomes an artisan satisfies criteria for maturity in that context. Passion, excitement, and interest can be maintained in a wide variety of tasks that render life meaningful, bring it a sense of purpose, and permit an infinite degree of growth.

Maturity means keeping an open mind to the ideas of others; in fact, it means seeking out and becoming excited by divergent opinions. At the same time, mature thinking involves the development of a "crapfinder" that allows the trivial, the fadish, and the superficially stylish to be distinguished from the meaningful and the useful. Maturity may not permit one to define quality, but it certainly allows one to recognize it when it is experienced.

The mature individual evaluates each person with whom s/he interacts according to operational criteria on a case by case basis. Steps are taken to avoid seeing life as a morality play in which idealized and villified individuals, perfectly good or perfectly evil, oppose one another. He avoids ideologies in which individuals are excused of their failings, *a priori,* by casting them as the victims of fate, the gods, the rich, the powerful, the government, or "society." Maturity means recognizing that while all individuals are victimized by others, (some more, some less) people are also capable of victimizing themselves.

Similarly, the mature individual avoids ideologies in which people are assumed, also on an *a priori* basis, of being able to rise above their condition if only they try a little harder. It is recognized that some individuals are victimized and crushed by adversity, others lack abilities and opportunities and cannot improve themselves no matter what their motivation. (Wishes are not real.) The mature individual recognizes that greater talent, skill, or knowledge does not in and of itself produce an individual of greater morality or essential worth. Science, as yet, has no way of discerning which human strengths or weaknesses are due to luck or effort, and it is unable to tell the difference between those who *cannot* overcome their weaknesses and those who *will not*. Maturity means taking pride in accomplishment but also being sympathetic and nurturing toward failure.

Mature cognition involves the growing awareness that the more one knows the more there is to know. The most advanced scientist is still ignorant when faced with the essential question of his/her field. To be fully cognizant of one's ignorance means accepting the pain of such ignorance but also recognizing that life is filled with unresolvable ambiguities and paradoxes. One's vantage point produces the truth of one's perceptions, and many situations can be viewed from an infinite number of vantage points. For example, maturity means living with the awareness that individuals are not responsible for what they have become, and yet they are totally responsible for what they do.

Mature individuals realize that nearly all life styles, personality types, and cultures have advantages and disadvantages. To be rich and famous allows great freedom but carries enormous responsibilities and penalties. Great power magnifies the neurosis in one's decision-making capabilities as well as revealing one's genius. Our culture blinds many to the joys of simple, anonymous living. People seem to value greatness over goodness. The tragedies caused by those leaders whose vision of greatness obscured both their personal needs for power as well as the basic needs of the individuals who follow them are endless in history and continue in our time. The

United States and the Soviet Union may well destroy the world as they compete for greatness.

When individuals give up visions of greatness and ideals such as nationalism and religion, which provide meaning by elevating their lives above the ordinary, they must find a new way of finding meaning. The Buddhists suggest that when people emerse them-selves in the details of their lives and live each minute fully by focusing on activities *for their own sake*, they overcome the ego-centric illusion of their separateness from the larger world. Maturity means living with appropriate life goals but fully experiencing the present moment. In this way the I-you distinction is broken down and life is experienced fully—perhaps the only genuinely meaning-ful way of living.

It seems to me that Freud's real genius is revealed when he suggests that life contains no meaning other than that which we give it. If the universe (through God or the gods) has not ordained a purpose for humanity, then any search for meaning in that direction is neurotic. The best an individual can do is to live each moment and struggle with a world that excites one to increase not only skills but knowledge and awareness as well. It seems, then, that enlight-enment is the ultimate meaning when it exists as its own end and not as a means to some other end.

Maturity and health means being able to laugh at the absurdi-ties of life as well as one's own behavior. So, too, can the healthy person empathize and sympathize with the pain of others without experiencing undue guilt or being overwhelmed by the unfairness of life. Maturity means trying to change unfairness without creating a fantasy that denies unfairness with a personalized vision of a para-dise that does not exist. However, maturity does mean enjoying fantasies that are gratifying and that help to solve problems.

Finally, maturity recognizes that death is everyone's end and that all happiness and triumph is temporary. It means giving up the preoperational search for perfect, infinite happiness and accepting pleasure as temporary and unique to the moment. In spite of this, or because of it, the healthy individual seeks to create and, by so doing, recognize that in the creative act entropy is best held at bay. Work and child-rearing take on their proper meaning when they are generative, and it is the person who thinks meaningfully who dis-covers this. There is no healthy denial of death (Becker, 1973) or continuity of life (Lifton, 1979) without creativity. Immortality is most closely approached with those creators that enrich the lives of others beyond the parameters of the life of the creator.

Individuals are most mature when they experience (or never lose) the baby's mode of living in the world. Babies delight in each moment as they learn: moving from primary to secondary to tertiary circular reactions, their cognitive awareness and physical skills increase yet they maintain their joy in learning. Babies live in each moment even as it is moving forward to the next, thus forward development never stagnates. They become bored with things learned and move on as the new becomes the old.

The fictional finalisms that human beings pursue can be evaluated in the same manner. Do future goals permit life in the present to be enjoyed for its own sake while being directed to increase knowledge and experience of the world and of the universe? To learn about the world means to increase both its pleasures and its terrors. People can experience good (quality) food, sex, friendships, travel, material possessions, books, music, ideas, conversation, relationships, and so on without ever becoming stagnant.

In earlier chapters I discussed those visions of greatness, ideology, and totalitarian absurdity that stagnate human joy in the moment. The mature individual can dream of greatness but does not do so at the cost of developing neurotic pride. Nationalism and religion do not sacrifice either the individual or the joy of living when the latter are in their mature forms. Parents will not sacrifice their children for the glory of the family or for some goal that they think will enhance the family at the expense of love, learning, and the joy of creativity.

THE DESIRE TO KNOW AND THE DESIRE NOT TO KNOW

Maturity involves the understanding that knowledge can bring despair as well as joy, burden and responsibility as well as freedom. When a person illuminates the world with his mind, he sees ugliness as well as beauty, horror as well as nobility. I believe that deep within each human being is a desire to learn about the self and the surrounding world. To learn is to add to human survivability. People are rewarded with all manner of positive affective experience as they learn and grow. Opposed to the desire to know is a powerful set of fears that motivate a desire not to know. I believe that at every moment in time each individual and every society is in conflict; that either the desire to know or the desire not to know is in the ascendency.

Toward the end of his life Freud grouped all human motivations into two categories, those of Eros, the life force, and Thanatos, the death urge. I believe I am doing the same thing, but, as in so many areas, my focus is not on *id* impulse but on cognitive-affective orientation.

We are born with a potential to develop intellectually and emotionally. I have argued throughout this work that the core of human personality is based on congitive-affective development. People do not become fully human unless they continue to actualize their cognitive-affective potential. Yet, I have spent quite some time describing and hypothesizing reasons to explain why fixation of human understanding is the rule rather than the exception. I have suggested that to develop the full range of human intellectual-affective powers is to confront and grow within the demands of reality. However, to illuminate fully our world and our role in it is, as Kierkegaard states, "to tremble with dread."

Erich Fromm suggests that a powerful motive exists in all people to escape from freedom and from the burdens of responsibility that it entails. The number of negative human emotions people seek to escape is quite large and includes fear, guilt, shame, anxiety, and a host of others. They seek to deny death, illness, and many other real fears. Escape is sought from self-induced affects and those brought about by other people. Feelings of shame and guilt are often very real and are based upon greed, lies, and every imaginable hurt that can be inflicted upon others. Often greed (for example) is itself a defense against a more basic fear; but once aroused and arranged in deepening layers, an ever expanding list of imaginative defenses are required.

Defenses require justification by pride and moral superiority. As people defend they must be perfect. How many aspects of our financial, educational, political, and religious institutions are based on defense and, therefore, committed to not knowing. The more our institutions reflect the commitment to avoid seeing into themselves and their vulnerabilities, the more self-protecting and self-serving they become. As this self-protection occurs, the institutions and those governing them seek to prevent each individual from gaining personal insight into themselves or the world in which they live. Ignorance comes full tilt in what is perhaps the most vicious circle of all: The individual builds a world to keep ignorant of himself, and the world creates individuals who are ignorant and committed to ignorance. Since intellectual awareness represents the surest path to freedom, defensive not-knowing must represent a path to security. Built into every preoperational defense is ignorance of that which upsets people. Humanity seeks to escape from the freedom, vulnerability, power, and responsibility that knowledge brings. The fear of knowing and its defense mechanisms can be institutionalized, justified, and turned into a source of pride and moral superiority. All around us religions teach pride in submission and acceptance of authority, leaders spring up in religion and politics, all claiming to have the answers for their flocks. With charm and persuasive ability, few of these leaders lack followers.

Once institutionalized the desire not to know is reinforced by the seekers of power, the sellers of drugs and fairy tales, and all those forces that come into existence as an extention of defenses against thoughts and feelings. Churches and states become authoritarian, books are burned, thoughts are called heretical, education is controlled, scientific activity is hobbled, and those creative few in the community who speak their minds are reviled and despised. In every school, one can find teachers who teach alongside those who try merely to control and indoctrinate. The more powerful the leader the greater the attempt to control information, education, and thought. In Orwell's *1984* it is the thought police who strike the most terror.

Some seek escape not in powerful leaders, empty slogans, dangerous causes, or mindless cults, but in individual withdrawal and pleasure-seeking. Many of the young turn away from a frightening world into television screens upon which flash pretty pictures: they listen endlessly to loud, vacuous music while stoned, or they otherwise lose themselves in trivia. In the novel *Mockingbird,* Walter Tevis (1980) describes a future in which the human race is dying as robots tend to basic needs and the population "enjoys" constant drug-induced happiness and quick sex. Tevis's book is as horrifying as Orwell's in that Tevis makes us see that worldwide psychic death can occur even without the oppressions of the police state.

The Old Testament book of Genesis begins with a description of God creating the universe and the creatures living within it. In these early pages, it is clear that God is primarily a creative intelligence, eventually creating humankind in his image. One would think, based on the Bible, that to be creative and to understand the universe would bring humanity closer to the Maker's original intention. We find that, psychologically, people are most human when they learn, create, and use their minds (both intellectually and emotionally) to pierce the mysteries that surround and fill them. Yet Genesis also describes the same Creator forbidding his human creations to eat of the fruit of the tree of knowledge. According to the underlying religion of Western society, original sin involves the growth of human knowledge and understanding. It is sinful to become fully human! Contained within the most basic of human documents is described the most basic of all human conflicts: the desire to know versus the desire not to know, growth versus fixation, independence and freedom versus safety and security.

If we look at the Bible as God's actual words, then a number of hypotheses leap to mind. Is God jealous of people becoming god-like? Or perhaps God didn't really make humanity in his image? Or were people created with an inherent flaw that makes them dangerous if they know too much? Perhaps God himself has a basic conflict about knowing and not knowing. One can also look at the Bible as a human work, reflecting the minds of ancient seers and revealing their conflicts about knowing. It is clear, however, that the basic conflict I am positing is at the heart of those religions that stimulate and then prevent full intellectual growth.

The twentieth century reflects the basic conflict and has heightened it. As humanity enters the final decades of this millenium, it has indeed assumed the power and responsibilities of the gods. Its knowledge of atomic weapons has unleashed the power of death over the whole world and all species of life. A biological revolution is being embarked upon in which the nucleus of cells will yield the secrets of life, aging, and death, as well as insights into the birth and death of the universe. Knowledge has liberated and terrorized: as large numbers of people surge forth to find new answers, many shrink from the knowledge as they seek new forms of authoritarian religion (including cults), drugs, and alcohol. Many flee into fantasies of sex and materialism or they turn to raw power in ever deepening cycles.

This century has brought forth an unparalleled increase in the lifespan and the quality of life for millions. People have more art, music, and dance available than ever before. Yet the twentieth century has produced some of the worst monsters and horrors in history: the holocaust, famine, disease, and incredible poverty. The physical world is probably far better understood than is the social world: atoms, molecules, and cells are better understood than the psyche and the soul. People have become scientific in some areas of life, solving age-old problems, but in many essential areas our level of knowledge is nothing short of primitive!

I have written this book in an attempt to focus attention on some of the factors that inhibit as well as foster the growth of human intelligence. I believe people are capable of fostering an expanding human intelligence, but full human actualization will not be accomplished without enormous effort. Prometheus was punished by the gods for giving humankind illuminating fire. As with the book of Genesis, humankind's most basic myths force the recognition that full and responsibly-used human knowledge will not be attained until ambivalence about knowing is overcome. The goals of psychology must be to continue to study the development of the human intellect and affect in order to find ways to help create a psychoanalysis and an educational system of truly human proportions.

Psychoanalysis (not the pallid versions often in evidence today) was a tool created by Freud to strip away defenses and learn about what humans really are. I have tried to show how many existing theories can add to an effective psychoanalysis. The analysis must start with psychology's own ambivalence concerning knowledge. It must look at how its pallid theories are defended with pathetic images filled with arrogance, pride, and moral superiority. Psychologists must understand fully how they aid or fight against social forces that seek to perpetuate ignorance and justify the greed, the power, and the mental enslavement that threatens to destroy humankind.

Bibliography

Ables, B. S. *Therapy for Couples.* San Francisco: Jossey-Bass, 1977.

Adler, Alfred. *Understanding Human Nature.* (Trans. by Walter Berger) London: George Allen and Unwin, 1968.

Allbee, G. W. "The Protestant Ethic, Sex and Psychotherapy." *American Psychologist* vol. 32 no. 2 (1977).

Allport, G. W. and H. S. Odbert. "Trait-names: A Psychological Study." *Psychological Monographs* 47 (1963):1, Whole of #11.

Ansbacher, H. L. and R. R. Ansbacher (eds.). *The Individual Psychology of Alfred Adler.* New York: Basic Books, 1956.

Arieti, Silvano. *The Will to Be Human.* New York: Quandrangle Books, 1972.

———. "Cognition in Psychoanalysis." *Journal of the American Academy of Psychoanalysis* vol. 8, no. 1 (1980):3–33.

Bandura, Albert. *Social Learning Theory.* Englewood Cliffs, N. J.: Prentice Hall, 1977.

Bateson, Gregory. "The Birth of a Matrix or Double Bind and Epistemology." In *Beyond the Double Bind,* Milton Berger (ed.) New York: Bruner Mazel, 1978.

Beavers, W. D. *Psychotherapy and Growth: A Family System*

Perspective. New York: Bruner Mazel, 1977.

Beck, Aaron. *Depression: Clinical, Experimental and Theoretical Aspects.* New York: Hoeber Medical Division, Harper and Row, 1967.

Becker, Ernst. *The Denial of Death.* New York: Free Press, 1973.

Bem, D. J. and A. Allen. "On predicting Some of the People Some of the Time: The Search for Cross-Sectional Consistencies in Behavior." *Psychological Review* 81 (1974):506–520.

Benson, Herbert. *The Relaxation Response.* New York: Morrow, 1975.

Bieber, Irving. *Cognitive Psychoanalysis.* New York: Aaronson, 1980.

Blanck, Rubin and Gertrude Blanck. *Ego Psychology: Theory and Practice.* New York: Columbia University Press, 1974.

Boring, C. G. *A History of Experimental Psychology,* 2nd ed. New York: The Century Company, 1957.

Bowlby, John. Attachment and Loss, Series: Vols. 1 and 2. New York: International Universities Press, 1955.

Brenner, Charles. *An Elementary Textbook of Psychoanalysis.* New York: International Universities Press, 1955.

Broadbent, D. F. *Perception and Communication.* New York: Pergammon Press, 1958.

Browning, Don S. *Generative Man: Psychoanalytic Perspectives.* Philadelphia: Westminster Press, 1973.

Bruner, Jerome. *Toward a Theory of Instruction.* Cambridge, Mass.: Harvard University Press, 1966.

———. "Learning the Mother Tongue" *Human Nature* (September 1978):43–49.

Chein, Isidor. *The Science of Psychology and the Image of Man.* New York: Basic Books, 1972.

Cohen, Morris Rapheal. *Reason and Nature.* Glencoe, Ill.: Free Press, 1953.

Cowan, B. A. *Piaget: With Feeling*. New York: Holt, Rinehart and Winston, 1978.

———. "Introduction" in *Intelligence and Affectivity* by Jean Piaget. Palo Alto, Calif.: Annual Reviews, 1981.

Cuddihy, J. M. *The Ordeal of Civility*. New York: Delta Books, 1974.

DeCaprio, H. *Personality Theories: Guides to Living*. Philadelphia: W. B. Saunders Company, 1974.

Deci, Edward C. *The Psychology of Self-Determination*. Lexington, Mass.: D. C. Heath and Company, 1980.

Digman, J. H. "Personality Factors, Semantic Factors and Factors Analysis." Paper presented at the Society of Multivariate Experimental Psychologists, Denver, Colo., 1977.

Dyer, Wayne. *Your Erroneous Zones*. New York: Funk and Wagnals, 1976.

Elkind, David. *Children and Adolescents: Interpretive Essays on Jean Piaget*. New York: Oxford University Press, 1977.

Ellis, Albert. *Humanistic Psychotherapy*. New York: McGraw Hill, 1974.

———. Taped untitled lecture given at Institute for Rational Emotive Therapy, 1975.

Epstein, Joseph. "True Virtue." *New York Times Magazine* (November 24, 1985):65–95.

Erikson, Erik H. *Identity, Youth and Crisis*. New York: W. W. Norton & Company, 1968.

Erenwald, Jan. *Psychotherapy: Myth and Method*. New York: Grune and Stratton, 1966.

Flavell, John. *The Developmental Psychology of Jean Piaget*. New York: Van Nostrand Reinhold, 1968.

Fraiberg, Selma. *The Magic Years*. New York: Scribners, 1968.

Frankl, Victor. *Man's Search for Meaning: An Introduction to Logotherapy.* Boston: Beacon Press, 1962.

———. *The Will to Meaning.* London: Plume Books, 1969.

Freud, Sigmund. *The Complete Introductory Lectures in Psychoanalysis.* (Trans. and edited by James Strachey) New York: W. W. Norton & Company, 1966.

———. *A General Introduction to Psychoanalysis.* (Trans. by J. Riviera) New York: Perma Books, 1957.

———. *The Ego and the Id.* (Trans. by J. Riviera) New York: W. W. Norton & Company, 1962.

———. *The Standard Edition of the Complete Psychological Works: Three Essays on the Theory of Sexuality.* Vol. 7, (Trans. by James Strachey) New York: W. W. Norton & Company, 1905, pp. 125–245.

———. "The Interpretation of Dreams." In A. A. Brill (ed.) *The Basic Writings of Sigmund Freud.* New York: Random House, 1938.

———. "Civilization and its Discontents." In R. M. Hutchins (ed.) *Great Books of the Western World.* Chicago: Encyclopedia Britannica, 1952.

Fromm, Erich. *Escape from Freedom.* New York: Holt, Rinehart & Winston, 1947.

———. *Psychoanalysis and Religion.* New Haven, Conn.: Yale University Press, 1950.

———. *The Art of Loving.* New York: Harper, 1956.

———. *The Greatness and Limitation of Freud's Thought.* New York: Harper and Row, 1980.

Golding, William. *The Lord of the Flies.* New York: Coward-McGann, 1962.

Greenspan, Stanley I. *Intelligence and Adaptation.* New York: International Universities Press, 1979.

Guntrip, Harry. *Schizoid Phenomena, Object Relations and the Self.* New York: International Universities Press, 1969.

Haley, Jay. *Problem Solving Therapy*. San Francisco: Jossey-Bass, 1976.

Hartmann, Heinz. "Ego Psychology and the Problem of Adaptation." (Trans. by D. Rapaport) *Journal of the American Psychoanalytic Association Monograph #1*. New York: International Universities Press, 1958.

Horney, Karen. *The Neurotic Personality of our Time*. New York: W. W. Norton & Company, 1937.

———. *Self Analysis*. New York: W. W. Norton & Company, 1942.

———. *Our Inner Conflicts*. New York: W. W. Norton & Company, 1945.

———. *Neurosis and Human Growth*. New York: W. W. Norton & Company, 1950.

Husserl, Edmund, *Ideas: General Introduction to Pure Phenomenology*. (Trans. by W. R. Boyce-Gibson) New York: Callier Bowles, 1962.

Inhelder, B. and J. Piaget. *The Growth of Logical Thinking from Childhood to Adolescence*. (Trans. by H. Parsons and S. Milgram) New York: Basic Books, 1958.

———. *The Early Growth of Logic in the Child*. (Trans. by E. A. Lunzen and D. Papert) New York: W. W. Norton & Company, 1959.

Izard, Carroll E. *Human Emotions*. New York: Plenum, 1977.

———. (ed.) *Emotions in Personality and Psychopathology*. New York: Plenum, 1979.

———. "Emotion-cognition Relations in Human Development." In C. E. Izard, J. Kalen and R. B. Zajonc (eds.) *Emotion, Cognition and Behavior*. New York: Cambridge University Press, 1984, pp. 17–37.

Jacobsen, Edith. *The Self and The Object World*. New York: International Universities Press, 1964.

Kagan, Jerome, R. Kearsley, and P. Selazo. *Infancy: Its Place in Human Development.* Cambridge, Mass.: Harvard University Press, 1978.

Kagan, Jerome. *The Nature of the Child.* New York: Basic Books, 1984.

Kelly, George. *The Psychology of Personal Constructs.* 2 vols. New York: W. W. Norton & Company, 1951.

Kernberg, Otto. "Borderline Personality Organization." *Journal of the American Psychoanalytic Association* 15 (1967).

Klein, George. Personal communication with author, 1966.

Klein, Melanie. *Contributions to Psychoanalysis.* London: Hogarth Press, 1948.

Koestler, Arthur. *Janus: A Summing Up.* New York: Random House, 1978.

Koch, Sigmund. "The Nature and Limits of Psychological Knowledge: Lessons of a Century qua 'Science'." *American Psychologist* vol. 36 no. 3 (1981):257–269.

Kushner, Harold. *When Bad Things Happen to Good People.* New York: Schocken Books, 1981.

Lasch, Christopher. *The Culture of Narcissism: American Life in an Age of Diminishing Expectations.* New York: W. W. Norton & Company, 1978.

Lazarus, R. S., A. P. Kanner and S. Folkman. "Emotions: A Cognitive-Phenomenological Analysis." In R. Plutchik and H. Kellerman (eds.) *Theories of Emotion.* New York: Academic Press, 1980, pp 189–217.

Lazarus, R. S. "Emotions and Adaptations: Conceptual and Empirical Relations." In W. J. Arnold (ed.) *Nebraska Symposium on Motivation.* Lincoln: University of Nebraska Press, 1968.

———. "Thoughts on the Relation Between Emotion and Cognition." *American Psychologist* 37 (1982):1019–1024.

———. "On the Primacy of Cognition." *American Psychologist* 39 (1984):124–129.

Leeper, R. W. "A Motivational Theory of Emotions to Replace 'Emotions as a Disorganizing Response'." *Psychological Review* 55 (1948):5-21.

Lewin, K. *The Conceptual Representation and the Measurement of Psychological Forces.* Durham, N. C.: Duke University Press, 1938.

Lifton, R. J. *The Broken Connection.* New York: Simon and Schuster, 1979.

London, Perry. *The Modes and Morals of Psychotherapy.* New York: Holt Rinehart and Winston, 1964.

Lorenz, Konrad. *On Aggression.* New York: Harcourt Brace, 1980.

Lund, Helen Merrill. *On Shame and Search for Identity.* New York: Harcourt, Brace and World, 1968.

Lustman, Seymour. "A Perspective on the Study of Man." In *The Psychoanalytic Study of the Child,* Vol. 27. K. Eissler, A. Freud, M. Kris, and A. Solnit, (eds.) New York: Quadrangle Press, 1972.

Mahler, Margaret S. *On Human Symbiosis and the Vicissitudes of Individuation.* New York: International Universities Press, 1968.

Marin, Peter. "Living in Moral Pain." *Psychology Today* (November 1981).

Maslow, Abraham. *Toward a Psychology of Being.* 2nd ed. Princeton, N. J.: D. Van Nostrand & Company, 1968.

Masterson, James. *Psychotherapy of the Borderline Adult.* New York: Bruner Mazel, 1976.

May, Rollo. *Man's Search for Himself.* New York: W. W. Norton & Company, 1953.

———. *Psychology and the Human Dilemma.* New York: D. Van Nostrand & Company, 1967.

———. *Freedom and Destiny.* New York: W. W. Norton & Company, 1981.

McClellend, D. C. *The Achievement Motive.* New York: Appleton-Century-Crofts, 1953.

Meehl, Paul. *Clinical versus Statistical Prediction*. Minneapolis Minn.: University of Minnesota Press, 1954.

Meichenbaum, Donald. *Cognitive Behavior Modification*. Morristown, N. J.: General Learning Press, 1974.

———. *Cognitive-Behavior Therapy: An Integrative Approach*. New York: Plenum Press, 1977.

Minuchin, S. *Families and Family Therapy*. Cambridge, Mass.: Harvard University Press, 1974.

Mischel, W. "Emotions and Adaptations Conceptual and Empirical Relations." In *Nebraska Symposium of Motivation*. W. J. Arnold (ed.) Lincoln: University of Nebraska Press, 1968.

———. "On the Interface of Cognition and Personality: Beyond the Personality Debate." *American Psychologist* 34 (1979):740-755.

Mohanty, I. N. *The Concept of Intentionality*. St. Louis, Mo.: Warren A. Green, Inc., 1974.

Moreau, J. "The Problem of Intentionality and Classical Thought." *International Philosophical Quarterly*. 1 (1961):211-234.

Morris, Charles G. *Psychology, An Introduction,* 4th ed. Englewood Cliffs, N. J.: Prentice-Hall, 1982.

Moskowitz, B. H. "The Acquisition of Language." *Scientific American*. 239 (1978):92–108.

Mowrer, O. Hobart. *The New Group Therapy*. Princeton, N. J.: D. Van Nostrand & Company, 1964.

Orwell, George, *1984*. New York: Harcourt Brace, 1949.

Peterfreund, Emanuel. "On Information and Systems Models for Psychoanalysis." *International Review of Psychoanalysis* 7 (1980):327–344.

Piaget, Jean. *The Psychology of Intelligence*. (Trans. by M. Piercy and D. E. Berlyne) London: Routledge and Kagan Paul, Ltd., 1950.

Piaget, Jean. *Biology and Knowledge.* Chicago: University of Chicago Press, 1957.

———. *The Origin of Intelligence in Children.* New York: International Universities Press, 1952.

———. *The Construction of Reality in the Child.* (Trans. by M. Cook) New York: Basic Books, 1954.

———. *The Child and Reality.* New York: Grossman Publishers, 1973.

———. *The Development of Thought.* New York: Viking Press, 1975.

———. *Intelligence and Affectivity.* Palo Alto, Calif.: Annual Review, Inc., 1981.

Plutchik, Robert. "Cognition in the Service of Emotion: An Evolutionary Perspective." In *Emotions* by D. Candland, J. R. Fell, E. Keen, A. Leshrer, R. Plutchik and R. H. Tarpiz. Monterrey, Calif.: Brooks Cole, 1977, pp. 189–213.

———. *Emotions: A Psychoevolutionary Synthesis.* New York: Harper and Row, 1980.

Popper, Sir Karl. *The Logic of Scientific Discovery.* New York: Science Editions, Inc., 1961.

Rachman, S. J. and R. J. Hodgson. *Obsessions and Complusions.* Englewood Cliffs, N. J.: Prentice-Hall, 1980.

Raimy, Victor. *Misunderstandings of the Self.* San Francisco: Jossey-Bass, 1975.

Rapaport, David. *Organization and Pathology of Thought.* New York: Columbia University Press, 1951.

Reiff, Philip. *The Triumph of the Therapeutic.* New York: Harper and Row, 1966.

Ricoeur, Paul. *Freedom and Nature: The Voluntary and the Involuntary.* (Trans. by K. V. Kohuk) Evanston, Ill.: Northwestern University Press, 1966.

Rogers, Carl. *On Becoming a Person: A Therapist's View of Psychotherapy.* Boston: Houghton Mifflin, 1961.

Rosenberg, Morris. *Conceiving the Self.* New York: Basic Books, 1979.

Rosenthal, R. and L. Jacobson. *Pygmalion in the Classroom: Teacher Expectation and Pupils' Intellectual Development.* New York: Holt, Rinehart and Winston, 1968.

Rotman, Brian. *Jean Piaget: Psychologist of the Real.* Ithaca, N. Y.: Cornell University Press, 1977.

Rotter, J. B. "Generalized Expectancies for Internal versus External Control of Reinforcement." *Psychological Monographs* 80 (1966): Whole of #609.

Russell, Bertrand. *Human Knowledge: Its Scope and Limits.* New York: Simon and Schuster, 1948.

Sarason, Seymour B. "An Asocial Psychology and a Misdirected Clinical Psychology." *American Psychologist* 36 (1981):827–837.

Sarbin, Theodore R. and James C. Mancuso. *Schizophrenia: Medical Diagnosis or Moral Verdict?* New York: Pergammon Press, 1980.

Sartre, Jean-Paul. *The Transcendence of the Ego: An Existentialist Theory of Consciousness.* (Trans. by F. William and R. Kirkpatrick) New York: Noonday, 1957.

Schacter, Stanley. and J, Singer. "Cognitive, Social and Physiological Determinates of Emotional State." *Psychological Review* #9 (1962):379–399.

Schafer, Roy. "Internalization: Process or Fantasy?" In R. Eissler et al. (eds.) *Psychoanalytic Study of the Child.* Vol. 27, New York: Quadrangle Books, 1973.

Schaffer, H. R., G. M. Collis, and G. Parsons. "Vocal Interchange and Visual Regard in Verbal and Pre-Verbal Children." In H. R. Schaffer (ed.) *Studies in Mother-Infant Interaction.* London: Academic Press, 1977.

Schell, Jonathan. "Reflections." *New Yorker* (February 1, 8, 15, 1982).

Seckel, Al. (ed.) *Bertrand Russell On God and Religion.* Buffalo, N. Y.: Prometheus Books, 1986.

Seligman, M. E. *Helplessness: On Depression, Development and Death.* San Francisco: W. H. Freeman, 1975.

Sheldon, W. H. *The Varieties of Temperament: A Psychology of Constitutional Differences.* New York: Harper, 1942.

Simon, Laurence. "The Therapist-Patent Relationship: A Holistic View" *American Journal of Psychoanalysis* 41 (1981):213-225.

Singer, Jerome. *Daydreaming.* New York: Random House, 1966.

Skinner, B. F. *Walden II.* New York: Macmillan, 1948.

———. *Science and Human Behavior.* New York: Macmillan, 1953.

———. *Beyond Freedom and Dignity.* New York: Alfred Knopf, 1971.

———. "What Is Wrong With Daily Life in the Western World?" *American Psychologist* vol. 41, no. 5 (1986):568-574.

Skynner, A. C. *Systems of Family and Marital Psychotherapy.* New York: Bruner Mazel, 1976.

Sperry, R. W. "Mental Unity Following Surgical Disconnection of the Cerebral Hemispheres." In *Harvey Lectures.* New York: Academic Press, 1968.

Spitz, R. S. *The First Year of Life.* New York: International Universities Press, 1965.

Stotland, Ezra. *The Psychology of Hope.* San Francisco: Jossey-Bass, 1969.

Sullivan, Harry Stack. *The Interpersonal Theory of Psychiatry.* New York: W. W. Norton & Company, 1953.

Szasz, Thomas. *The Myth of Mental Illness.* New York: Hoeber-Harper, 1967.

Tevis, Walter. *Mockingbird.* New York: Bantam Books, 1980.

Tillich, Paul. *The Courage To Be.* New Haven: Yale University Press, 1952.

Thomas, A., S. Chess and H. G. Birch. *Temperament and Behavior Disorders in Children.* New York: New York University Press, 1968.

Tomkins, Silvan. *Affect, Imagery and Consciousness,* Vols. I & II. New York: Springer, 1962, 1967.

Triemsman, A. "Contextual Cues in Selective Listening." *Quarterly Journal of Experimental Psychology* (1960):242–248.

Watson, J. B. *Behaviorism.* New York: Peoples Institute, 1920.

Watts, Alan. *The Book: On the Taboo Against Knowing Who You Are.* New York: Vintage Books, 1972.

Whittaker, C. " A Family Is a Four Dimensional Relationship." In *Family Therapy.* P. J. Gueren (ed.) New York: Gardner Press, 1976.

White, R. W. "Motivation Reconsidered: The Concept of Competence" *Psychological Review* 66 (1959).

Winnicott, D. W. *The Maturational Process and the Facilitating Environment.* New York: International Universities Press, 1965.

Wolfe, J. *The Practice of Behavior Therapy.* New York: Pergamon, 1982.

Wood, B. G. "The Religion of Psychoanalysis." *American Journal of Psychoanalysis* 35 (1975):151–175.

Zajonc, R. B. " Feeling and Thinking: Preferences Need No Inferences." *American Psychologist* 35 (1980):151–175.

Zukov, Gary. *The Dancing Wu-Li Masters.* New York: William Morrow and Company, 1979.

Zweig, Stefan. *The World of Yesterday: An Autobioqraphy.* Lincoln: University of Nebraska Press, 1964.

Index